VERGELTUNGSWAFFEN
THE THIRD REICH'S V-MISSILES
THEN AND NOW

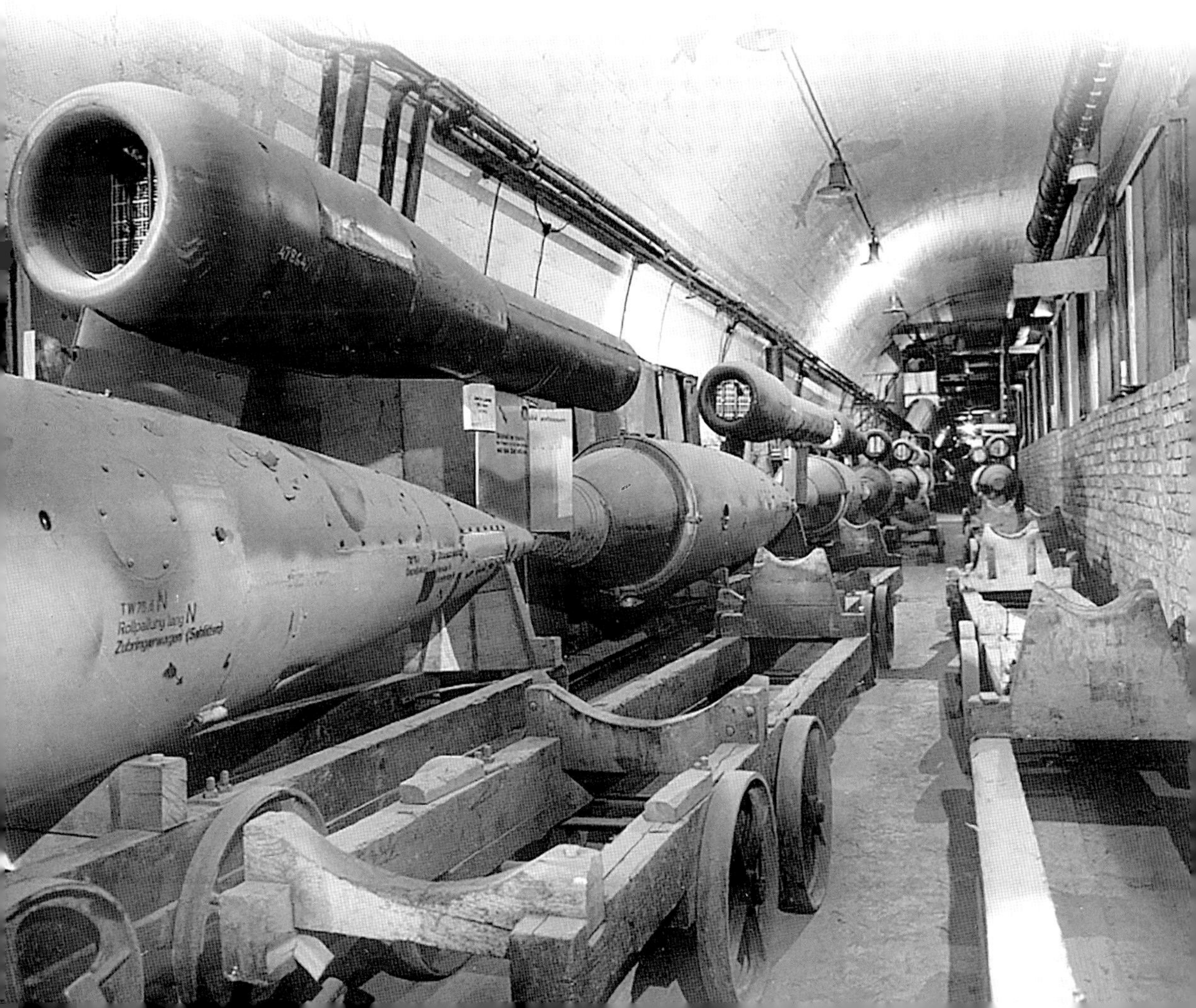

VERGELTUNGSWAFFEN
THE THIRD REICH'S V-MISSILES
THEN AND NOW

by Jean Paul Pallud

AFTER THE BATTLE

An Imprint of Pen & Sword Books Ltd

Vergeltungswaffen, The Third Reich's V-Missiles – Then and Now

Published by After the Battle
An imprint of Pen & Sword Books Ltd
47 Church Street, Barnsley,
South Yorkshire, S70 2AS
Tel. 01226 734222
Fax. 01226 734438
Email: enquiries@pen-and-sword.co.uk
Website: **www.afterthebattle.com**
www.pen-and-sword.co.uk

Printed and bound in India by Parksons Graphics Pvt. Ltd.

ISBN: 9781036101381

Commissioning Editor: Rob Green
Editor: Jean Paul Pallud
Design: Paul Wilkinson
Cover design: Jon Wilkinson

Credits:
Parts of this book were originally published in *After the Battle* magazine: 'The Secret Weapons: V3 and V4' in issue 114 (November 2001). The book also takes references from 'The V-weapons' edited by Winston Ramsey in issue 6 (November 1974), and 'The Peenemünde Rocket Centre' by Jan Heitmann in issue 74 (November 1991) and 'Nordhausen' by Karel Margry in issue 101 (August 1998). These stories have been adapted and enhanced to produce this book and 200 additional photos are included.

Acknowledgements:
The Editor would like to acknowledge V2ROCKET.COM, the A4/V2 resource site that shares the precious photos of Frank Micklethwaite and Charles Black, two British officers who participated to Operation 'Backfire', and the Wikimedia Commons contributors for the remarkable photos they make available to all. The Editor extends his appreciation to the KZ-Gedenkstätte Mittelbau-Dora, the Peenemünde Historical Technical Museum, the United States Holocaust Memorial, Alvin Gilens and Alain Feltes, to Manfred Bornemann, author of *Geheimprojekt Mittelbau, die Geschichte der deutschen V-Waffen-Werke*, and to Dr Dieter Hölsken, author of *V-missiles of the Third Reich*.

Photo Credit Abbreviations:
AMAH – Association Maisons-Alfort Mille ans d'Histoire; BA – Bundesarchiv; DM – Deutsche Museum; Georges Phillips – K. H. Schwerdtfeger Collection; LAC – Library and Archives Canada; LC – Library of Congress; NASM – National Air and Space Museum; NHHC – Naval History and Heritage Command; SSETO – Society for the Study of the ETO; USHMM – United States Holocaust Memorial Museum; USNA – US National Archives. Unless specified otherwise, all illustrations are from the *After the Battle* archive.

Front Cover: On September 8, Lehr- und Versuchsbatterie 444 launched two rockets against Paris. The first disappeared in flight but the second hit Maisons Alfort, south-east of Paris, a few minutes after 11 a.m. This picture was taken at Blizna where some 215 rockets were test launched between November 1943 and the end of June 1944.

Back Cover:
Top: At Maisons Alfort, on September 8, 1944, the first ballistic missile in history crashed near Rue des Sapins and Rue des Ormes (now Rue Arthur Dalidet). Several houses were destroyed, many others badly damaged. Six people were killed, and 36 injured. (AMAH)

Centre: On November 25, 1944, a V2 launched from Loosduinen in the Netherlands hit Warwick Court, a small alley off the coast of Holborn, at 11.16 a.m. Five residents were killed and 40 injured in the attack. Rescuers search the rubble and wreckage for survivors.

Bottom: On November 27, ten minutes after noon, a V2 rocket crashed at the intersection of Frankrijklei, Keyserlei and Teniersplaats. It was one of the worst V2 attacks, killing 126 people, including 26 allied soldiers, and injuring 300. (Another source, which includes in the count the wounded who died in hospital in the days that followed the bombing, puts the death toll at 157, including 29 allied soldiers.)

Background photo: A V1 flying bomb in flight. The pulse-jet engine of the missile pulsed 50 times per second with a terrible noise that gave rise to the name 'buzz bomb'. Witnesses described how the distant buzzing sound grew into a deafening rattle that either grew quieter as the missile moved away, or stopped abruptly. The eerie silence which followed the engine cut-off, a dozen seconds before the explosion, was the most difficult to bear.

CONTENTS

Propagandists of the Third Reich gave the name V3 to the multi-chamber HDP cannon. This photo was taken at the Hillersleben test range where test firing of the first 150mm HDP gun began in late 1943. This prototype gun was intended only to test internal ballistics and other basic technical issues, hence the almost horizontal barrel. The operational guns, to achieve their maximum range, were to be fired at an angle of 50 degrees. Four cross sections of the barrel are visible in this photo as well as the screwed breech blocks that closed the side chambers. (BA)

INTRODUCTION

THE DESIGN, PRODUCTION, AND COMBAT deployment of the Third Reich's V-weapons is a complex and multifaceted story. Remarkable technological achievements, a barbaric use of slave labour, propaganda promising to turn the tide of war and, finally, ineffective weapons...

The cutting-edge technologies developed by Nazi Germany allowed it to use the first cruise missile and ballistic missiles in history. This, alongside the introduction of the first jet fighter and the first developments of anti-aircraft rockets, paved the way for future advancements in weapons technology. The Americans and Soviets seized on these developments and the scientists and technicians who developed them, which led them to produce in the post war years the intercontinental ballistic missiles of the Cold War and the rockets of space conquest.

However, relying heavily on forced labour in their production, these remarkable technological advances were deeply linked to the horrors of Nazi Germany. The barbaric Mittelbau-Dora camp where thousands of inmates died, forever taints the image of what otherwise would be considered monumental technological achievements.

Unlike Great-Britain and the United States, Nazi Germany failed to standardise and centralise its war production, leading to delays and wasted resources. Hitler's dictatorship let rivalling interests struggle for favour in the regime. Competition and squabbles between the Wehrmacht and the Luftwaffe were rife, and the SS schemed behind the scenes to take control of the production and deployment of the V-weapons, which they would finally win out. All of this resulted in a never-ending struggle for priorities, with development and production being halted, only to restart, and design orders for odd devices that would yield little or no tactical and strategic benefit.

The V2 and other advanced weapons deployed by the Third Reich during the final phase of the war have given rise to oft-heard speculation: what would have happened if these weapons had been deployed earlier, in which case Nazi Germany might have won the war?

Actually, the V1 cruise missile and the V2 strategic ballistic missile arrived too early. Their attacks on London and Antwerp had no strategic result because the missiles lacked precise guidance systems. Greater accuracy was out of reach with the technical means available at the time, the age of computers and micro-electronics being still far in the future. The two weapons, the strategic ballistic missile and the cruise missile, required a great deal of refinement before they were deadly military weapons, with a nuclear warhead.

The true superweapon of World War II was the atomic bomb, and Nazi Germany made very limited progress in nuclear technology. The reasons for this failure have been debated, but it is reasonable to say that if German physicists had designed a bomb, the Allies' relentless air bombing campaign would have destroyed the uranium isotope separation plants, and the nuclear reactors producing plutonium, long before they produced the materials needed to build a bomb.

In fact, the V-weapons proved to be cost-ineffective weapons, except arguably the V1 flying bomb, and made no difference in an already losing war. The net result of the V-weapons, deployed or not, was that the Third Reich wasted a lot of resource and technical expertise in developing and producing trail-blazing designs that yielded little tactical and strategic advantage, and some exotic devices of no interest at all.

Jean Paul Pallud

The Rheinbote, a four-stage solid fuel rocket, may have been the V4. On December 24, 1944, Artillerie-Abteilung 709 fired 24 Rheinbote rockets against Antwerp from a wood near Nunspeet, and another batch of 20 rockets in mid-January. This photo was taken during test launches at Waldheim, now Drogoslaw in Poland, in November 1944.

GROUNDBREAKING TECHNOLOGIES

IN THE EARLY 1920s, a number of young Germans became enthusiastically interested in the development of rockets as space vehicles. Hermann Oberth, a medical student at Munich, published in 1923 a book entitled *Die Rakete zu den Planetenräumen* (The Rocket into Interplanetary Space) the first edition of which sold out rapidly. The book strongly supported the use of liquid rocket fuels, discussed the possible construction of liquid-fuel rockets, and considered the problems of orbiting the earth with such devices. The book led to the formation of the Verein für Raumschiffahrt (Society for Space Travel) in 1927 with the goal of building the rockets contemplated by Oberth. Its membership rose rapidly to around five hundred, enough to support a journal, *Die Rakete* (The Rocket). The society obtained permission to use an abandoned military facility in Reinickendorf, a suburb of Berlin, to test their rockets. Among the members of this society was the 19-year-old student Wernher von Braun who attended the Technische Hochschule at Berlin.

For its part, without any particular contact with the Verein für Raumschiffahrt, in 1929 the German Army established the Versuchsstelle Kummersdorf West, a site for developing and testing rockets at Kummersdorf, a village some 25 kilometres south of Berlin. The Army was looking for a cheap, light rocket and was interested in the newly-emerging liquid-propellant rocket as a potential weapon. Under the auspices of the Heereswaffenamt-Prüfwesen (Army Ordnance Department, Research and Development Section) experiments began under the direction of Hauptmann Walter Dornberger, who graduated in 1930 from the Technische Hochschule Berlin with a degree in mechanical engineering.

In the meantime, the economic depression had caused a sharp decline in the membership of the Verein für Raumschiffahrt, and by the fall of 1932 the society was seeking support from the Army. Dornberger went to Reinickendorf with Oberst Karl Becker, head of the Ballistics and Munitions Branch of the Heereswaffenamt, but they were disappointed by the small, elementary rockets they were shown.

Von Braun graduated in 1932 with a degree in mechanical engineering and in November the Army invited him to carry out the experimental work for his thesis on rocket combustion at Kummersdorf; he entered the Friedrich-Wilhelm University of Berlin and received a doctorate in physics in 1934.

Work at Reinickendorf ended in the winter of 1933-1934 and Dornberger recruited many members of the now defunct Verein für Raumschiffahrt.

The first new rocket developed by the Kummersdorf team was the liquid-propelled A1, an abbreviation for Aggregat 1. Powered by an alcohol-liquid oxygen engine developing 330 kilogrammes of thrust, the A1 was 1.4 metres long and 30 centimetres in diameter. After a few successful static tests, the A1 was redesigned in 1934 and named A2. Its dimensions and performance were nearly identical to the A1. In December 1934, on the North Sea island of Borkum, two A2 rockets, which were named 'Max' and 'Moritz' after two troublemaking characters of a well-known illustrated story, made successful flights to altitudes of about two kilometres. The demonstration convinced the military that the rocket could be a weapon, which gave new impetus to the rocket program.

In March 1936 Generaloberst Werner von Fritsch, the Commander-in-Chief of the Army, visited Kummersdorf and was shown the firing of rocket

Members of the Verein für Raumschiffahrt, around 1930. From left to right: Rudolf Nebel, Franz Ritter, unknown, Kurt Heinisch, unknown, Hermann Oberth, unknown, Klaus Riedel, Wernher von Braun, unknown. Klaus Riedel holds an early version of the 'Mirak' rocket. (LC)

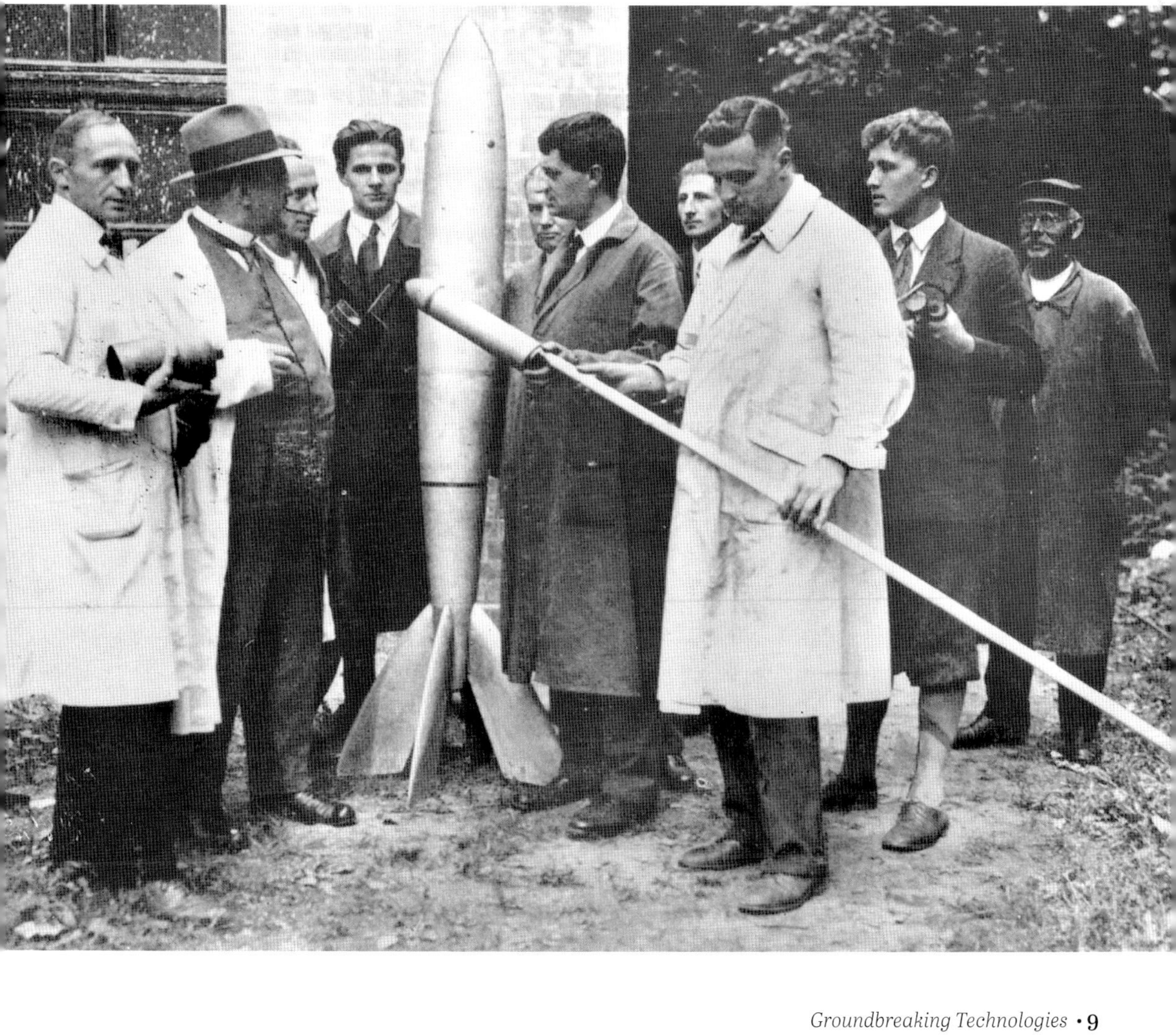

engines. Von Fritsch was enthusiastic and allowed Kummersdorf to apply for additional funding for the rocket program.

Dornberger, by then chief of the Abteilung 11, a branch of Development and Testing Group (Amtsgruppe für Entwicklung und Prüfung) of the Army Ordnance Department, began considering a test centre that would allow development and testing of the very large rockets then envisioned. The new proving ground would have to be located on the coast where rockets could be launched over the Baltic Sea, parallel to the coastline so that the trajectory could be easily observed by camera and by radio. Dornberger and von Braun met with Generalleutnant Albert Kesselring, Chief-of-Staff of the Luftwaffe, to discuss the project and the decision was made to set up a joint Army-Air Force research establishment.

The choice fell on Peenemünde, a small fishing village on the right bank of the river Peene where it flows into the Baltic. The name of the town in fact means 'the mouth of the Peene'. The area in which the proving ground was to be built was a nature reserve of dunes and marshland overgrown with oaks and pines behind a reedy foreland reaching far out into water.

This area had two major advantages: its remoteness which met the requirements of security and secrecy, and the fact that the eastern coast of the Usedom peninsula looked out over an uninterrupted expanse of German-controlled sea 180 kilometres in length.

The construction of the research establishment began in the summer of 1936. The army installations, called Heeresversuchsanstalt Peenemünde (Army Research Centre Peenemünde), was located generally along the eastern coast of the Usedom peninsula, from its northernmost tip to the village of Zinnowitz, 15 kilometres further to the south. Research and development laboratories, workshops, and the headquarters office blocks were constructed among the dense woods near to the north-eastern corner of the peninsula. Every effort was made to leave as many trees as possible to provide natural camouflage. This part of the new establishment became officially known as Entwicklungswerk - Werk Ost (Development Works) or Peenemünde East. To the north, on the boundary between the forest and the sandy foreshore, nine rocket test stands were built. Three stands for engine tests were constructed in the woods north-east of the village of Karlshagen.

In the north-west corner of the peninsula, the Luftwaffe occupied a much smaller area than the Army and built an airfield, known as Erprobungsstelle der Luftwaffe - Werk West (Luftwaffe Test Installation) or Peenemünde West, which became a centre for the test flying of secret types of aircraft.

In the south-west corner of the peninsula a large coal-fired, steam-turbine power station was built which provided 30,000 kilowatts of electricity. There was also a factory to produce the liquid oxygen which was used as rocket fuel. The small existing Peenemünde harbour was deepened and improved.

A new housing estate called Karlshagen Siedlung (Karlshagen Housing Estate) was built north of Karlshagen for the scientists, engineers and administrators and their families. The new compound was provided with

Four test launches of A3 rockets were carried out at Greifswalder Oie in December 1937. (DM)

shops, schools, and a sports field. It had all the characteristics of a model village, and it was soon home to more than 3,000 people. South of the housing estate there was a camp for foreign workers.

The different parts of the research centre were linked by a new road network and by a 75 kilometres long electric railway, which started at Zinnowitz, south of Karlshagen.

For reasons of secrecy and security, most of the original inhabitants were evacuated and soon there was almost nothing left of old Peenemünde with its thatched fishermen's houses. There was a security border that stretched from coast to coast across the peninsula and everyone who reached the border had to present a special pass to be allowed in.

There was a security boundary stretching from coast to coast across the peninsula and everyone who reached the boundary gate had to show a special pass to be allowed in.

The Army moved the first 90 employees from Kummersdorf to Peenemünde Werk Ost in May 1937, and the Luftwaffe began operations at Werk West in 1938. In October 1937, with the move to Heeresversuchsanstalt Peenemünde in full progress, the first rockets of the new A3 series were launched from Greifswalder Oie, a small island eight kilometres off the northern coast of Usedom. The A3 was 6.7 metres long and 67 centimetres in diameter, and it had a take-off weight of 740 kilogrammes. Its motor produced 1,500 kilogrammes of thrust for 45 seconds and it was provided with quite a sophisticated guidance and control system. However, four test launches of the new rocket in December 1937 failed. The engines performed well, but the new guidance system did not and the rockets lost stability after climbing a few hundred metres and crashed.

Using the large amount of data already accumulated, the rocket team produced the lay-out for a new rocket, the A5. It was to have the same propulsion system as the A3, a greatly improved structure and an improved guidance and control system. The A5 measured 5.8 metres long and 78 centimetres in diameter and had a take-off weight of 900 kilograms.

Its first four flights during the summer of 1938, without the guidance systems, proved the validity of the mechanical design. The new guidance

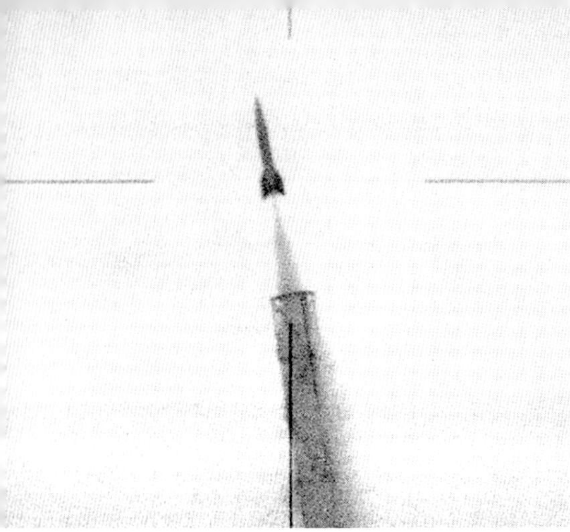

From the summer of 1938, A5 rockets were test launched from Greifswalder Oie. From the autumn of 1939, the new guidance system worked perfectly and for two years A5 rockets were successfully launched and recovered, reaching an altitude of 12 kilometres and a range of 18 kilometres. (DM)

system tested beginning in the fall of 1939 worked perfectly, as did the parachutes system, and the team successfully fired and recovered A5 rockets for the next two years.

As flights of the A5 continued, components were designed and developed for the much larger A4. In the autumn of 1939, the Army awarded the A4 project the highest priority. By then the Heeresversuchsanstalt Peenemünde was fully staffed and equipped when all remaining personnel were transferred from Kummersdorf. Now holding the rank of Oberst, Dornberger was in charge with research into both liquid-propellant and solid-propellant rockets, as well as all controlled guided missiles except those of the Luftwaffe. The Heeresversuchsanstalt was commanded by Oberst Leo Zanssen, with Wernher von Braun as civil technical director.

Reporting to von Braun were nine major departments: Technical Design Office; Aero-ballistics and Mathematics Laboratory; Wind Tunnel; Materials Laboratory; Guidance, Control and Telemetry Laboratory; Development and Fabrication Laboratory; Test Laboratory; Future Projects Office and Purchasing Office.

By early 1940, a whopping 550 million Reichsmarks had been spent on Peenemünde in its first two years. More than 18,000 scientists, engineers, technicians, and other personnel worked at Heeresversuchsanstalt Peenemünde and thousands more were under contract at research centres and universities across Germany. In March that year an A4 engine was successfully tested for the first time.

Rapid victories in Poland in 1939 and in the West in 1940 led to a reassessment of plans and priorities, and the requirement for a long-range rocket appeared unnecessary. Peenemünde was therefore removed from the priority list for men and supplies. However, after the Luftwaffe's failure in the Battle of Britain, and then the first setbacks in Russia in 1941, Peenemünde's priorities were raised again, enough to ensure continued development of the A4.

In early 1942, the first A4 rockets became available and the first test firing of the V-1 rocket took place from the VII test stand on March 18. The Reich Minister of Armaments and War Production, Albert Speer, was present to witness the event. The rocket failed. Rocket V-2 was launched on June 13 with Speer again attending in company with the armament chiefs of the three branches of the armed forces, Generaloberst Friedrich Fromm, Generalfeldmarschall Erhard Milch, and Admiral Karl Witzell. It was another failure. A gyro malfunctioned immediately, the rocket went out of control and crashed into the Baltic less than a kilometre away. Rocket V-3 was launched successfully on August 16, only to break up 45 seconds into the

This aerial photo of Peenemünde was taken on June 23, 1943 by Flight Sergeant Ernest Peek aboard a Mosquito of 540 Squadron. In the centre right are the Peenemünde Sud production plants with the IW repair and maintenance hall (top) and the F1 pre-production hall where the first assembly line tests were about to begin; top right, the southern end of Peenemünde East, the development works; at the bottom right is the northern end of the housing estate. At centre left is Prüfstand XI, which was to be the test stand for rockets produced in F1.

flight due to a structural failure and fell into the sea nine kilometres from the launching site.

The launch of the V-4 rocket on October 3 was the first successful test flight of the A4. The rocket rose perfectly into the sky, the engine was shut down by radio signal after 58 seconds as scheduled, after which the rocket continued

Another photo taken the same day by Flight Sergeant Peek shows rockets and two trailers at Prüfstand VII. This photo was a decisive piece of evidence at a special meeting of the Defence Committee of the War Cabinet on June 29, which decided that Peenemünde should be bombed as soon as possible.

a ballistic trajectory, reaching the maximum altitude of 84 kilometres, the first rocket to reach the edge of space. It fell into the Baltic Sea 190 kilometres downs-range, four kilometres from its intended point of impact.

The rocket had shown that it had a range almost double that of the famous 'Paris Cannon' of the First World War, and this with a warhead ten times larger. In December, Hitler signed a decree written by Speer authorising mass production of the A4 rocket.

In December 1942, Speer established the Sonderausschuss A4, the A4 Special Committee, in the Ministry of Armaments and War Production with

In 1942, the Heeresversuchsanstalt Peenemünde was the most advanced establishment of its type and its wind tunnel was the first in the world in which aerodynamic forces could be measured at supersonic speeds, from Mach 1.2 to Mach 4.4. The wind tunnel was undamaged during the Bomber Command attack in August 1943 and it was subsequently transferred to Kochel am See in Bavaria. The Americans carefully dismantled it in 1945 and shipped it to the United States where it was installed at the Naval Ordnance Laboratory in White Oak, Maryland. This is where this photo was taken: the measurement section appears in the background on the left, with the Schlieren optical system producing a shadow pattern of the airflow around the model. This pattern was focused to be observed on a screen or in a camera. (NHHC)

Built in the woods north-east of Karlshagen, Prüfstand I was designed to carry out static combustion tests of rocket engines. The facility consisted of a concrete substructure with an attached steel frame, all measuring 15 metres high. The substructure contained a workshop and measuring room, as well as tanks for storing compressed nitrogen. Railway cars carrying fuel could be moved in the substructure. (LC)

On April 21, 1940, the A4 rocket engine was successfully tested for the first time at Prüfstand 1. This series of historic photos arrived in the United States with German scientists in 1945 and ended up in the archives of the Marshall Space Flight Center. (LC)

Gerhard Degenkolb as director. Degenkolb made a name for himself in 1942 when, as head of the Rail Vehicles Committee, he managed to remarkably increase the production of locomotives.

In February, the chief of the 'Production Planning' committee at the Sonderausschuss A4, Director Detmar Stahlnecht, set up a production program involving two sites, the pilot production plant (Versuchsserienwerk) at Peenemünde and the Zeppelin factory at Friedrichshafen. The program planned for a production of ten units in May, increasing to 100 in October, and ultimately reaching 600 per month by September 1944. It was planned to produce a total of 5,150 A4 rockets at the two sites.

In April, Degenkolb included the Rax factory in Wiener Neustadt in the program and increased the A4 production target from 600 rockets per month at two sites to 900 per month at three sites.

The new plan called for Zeppelin and Rax-Werk to begin production in July 1943, and by October they would each produce 100 rockets per month. Total production should reach 900 rockets per month in January 1944, 300 per each of the three sites.

From January to April 1943, 11 A4s were test launched at Peenemünde to test the systems, half of them were partial successes, the rest were failures. These first rockets were assembled in a large workshop located in a woodland between Peenemünde East and the housing estate. A pilot production plant was built nearby and for mass production two large production halls known as Versuchsserienwerk or Peenemünde Sud were built, the largest, Fertigungshalle 1 (Mass Production Plant 1), measured 248 metres long and 120 metres wide.

We composed this photo by stitching together two photos taken in the measurement room of Prüfstand I during the testing of a rocket engine. On the left was Kurt Heinisch, a veteran of the Verein für Raumschiffahrt, and on the right, looking through the periscope, Werner von Braun. (LC)

Fuelling of the A4 Rocket V-3 being carried out at Prüfstand VII on August 16, 1942. The protective wall in the background, ten metres high, protected the site from the sea wind and prevented sand from being blown from the nearby beach. The launch was another failure, with the rocket's nose breaking 45 seconds into flight. The V-4 rocket was the first successful test flight of the A4 on October 3, 1942. It flew too steep due to a pitch program problem and reached an altitude of 85 to 90 kilometres, becoming the first rocket to reach the edge of space.

The A4 rocket's combustion chamber burns in two stages during launch. Step 1: Alcohol under gravity and oxygen under low pressure flow to the combustion chamber where the mix is ignited by means of a pyrotechnic igniter. Stage 1 gives a thrust of approximately 2.5 tonnes and lasts approximately 4 seconds. If the flame configuration at this stage is correct, stage 2 is commanded from the control room. The rocket's electrical connections (Stotz plugs) are then thrown off, relays in the control compartment operate valves in the fuel and steam unit system, causing production of superheated steam that drives the turbine and pumps. Alcohol and oxygen are thus injected into the combustion chamber, giving a thrust of 25 tonnes and the rocket takes off. We do not know which rocket was depicted in this photo taken in 1943. (NASM)

Although the A4 was the most spectacular missile developed at Peenemünde, it is not the only secret weapon being worked on at the site. On the other side of the peninsula, at Peenemünde West, from mid-1942, teams of civilian and Luftwaffe technicians carried out tests with the Fi 103 flying bomb.

The history of the Fi 103 dates to the early 1930s, when the Reichsluftfahrtministerium (Ministry of Aviation) revived its interest in remotely piloted aircraft at a relatively cheap cost. Work progressed to the point where a working example had been developed by November 1939.

In April 1942, Robert Lusser of the Gerhard Fieseler Werk made a preliminary design for a pilotless flying bomb powered by a pulse jet engine and directed towards the target by a pre-set guidance system. The Argus pulse jet engine was flight tested from April 1941, first mounted under a Gotha Go 145 biplane, and by 1942 it had proven its reliability.

The project of a flying bomb designed to deliver a 500-kilogram warhead to a range of 300 kilometres was submitted to the Luftwaffe on June 5, 1942. Lacking a heavy bomber suitable for bombing England, the Luftwaffe was

Despite its secrecy, the Heeresversuchsanstalt Peenemünde attracted a continuous flow of personalities from Berlin. In March 1941, Dr. Fritz Todt, Reich Minister of Armaments and Munitions, visited Peenemunde with a large delegation comprising General Emil Leeb, head of the Army Ordnance Department and General Friedrich Olbricht, Chief of Army General Office (on the left at first rank, with the Knight's Cross). Von Braun, in civilian clothes in other photos in this series, showed them around the site.

very interested in this expendable unmanned aircraft which simple design was ideally suited to low-cost mass production. The Fi 103 project was approved on June 19 and given top priority. The flying bomb received the military cover name Flakzielgerat 76 (FZG 76) and the code name 'Kirschkern'.

Development of the Fi 103 was then transferred to the Erprobungsstelle Karlshagen (test facility) in Peenemünde West.

Fieseler delivered the first complete airframe in August and the first glide test flight took place on October 28, with an airframe without a pulse jet being dropped from a four-motored Focke-Wulf Fw 200. The aerodynamic behaviour of the airplane proved to be excellent. The first powered flight took place on December 10, when the V-7 prototype was launched by an Fw 200.

In the autumn of 1942, a launch ramp was built on the northern corner of the Peenemunde West airfield. Its rocket powered sledge was capable of propelling the Fi 103 missile to a speed of 350 km/h and sending it flying over the Baltic Sea, with a flight path parallel to the Pomeranian coast. The first ground launch took place on December 24, but the V-12 prototype failed to reach nominal speed and fell into the sea after a minute of flight.

Ramp launches continued through the spring of 1943 and by the end of July, 68 Fi 103 prototypes had been launched, but only 28 of these test flights had been successful. One of them, however, covered a distance of 220 kilometres.

Set up in February 1943, the Kommission für Fernschiessen (Commission for Long-Range Weapons) met in Peenemünde in May to review developments of the A4 and Fi 103. Present were Speer, Generaloberst Fromm, Generalfeldmarschall Milch, Admiral Karl Dönitz, and Karl-Otto Saur, State Secretary in the Ministry of Armaments and War Production. On the 26th, they viewed two successful A4 launches (rocket V-26 launched around noon and rocket V-25 later in the afternoon), followed by two launches of Fi 103 flying bomb, both failing and plunging into the sea. The commission decided nevertheless to recommend that both weapons be mass-produced. As Dornberger observed, 'the disadvantages of the one would be compensated by the other's advantages': the Fi 103 missile was relatively inexpensive and quick to produce, and likely to be ready for action soon, which was not the case with the A4; the Fi 103 flew at low speed on a constant course and altitude, making it vulnerable to enemy defences, but no effective defences existed to stop the A4 supersonic rocket.

In February 1943, the destruction of the 6. Armee at Stalingrad dealt a devastating blow to German morale. The final defeat of the Axis forces in North Africa in May confirmed that the moment was a turning point. Realising the need to bolster the war effort by boosting research and development, the Germans began recalling scientists, engineers, and technicians from the front line. The recall included 4,000 rocketeers from the Peenemünde teams. Dieter Huzel later recalled how 'Overnight, Ph.D.s were liberated from KP duty, masters of science were recalled from orderly service, mathematicians were hauled out of bakeries, and precision mechanics ceased to be truck drivers.'

On July 7, Dornberger and von Braun were received by Hitler at the FHQu 'Wolfschantze' in East Prussia. Also present were Speer, Generalfeldmarschall Wilhelm Keitel, Chief-of-Staff of the Armed Forces, and Generaloberst Alfred Jodl, Chief of the Operations Staff. Von Braun narrated a film showing the successful launch of prototype V-4 in October 1942, and scale models of the Channel coast firing bunkers were shown, as well as plans of supporting vehicles for mobile launch batteries. Hitler was thoroughly impressed and Dornberger later reported his comment: 'Why was it I could not believe in the success of your work? If we had had these rockets in 1939, we should never have had this war.' Hitler gave top priority to the A4 program, ordering a monthly production of 2,000 rockets. This was a completely unrealistic figure, but a new 'Degenkolb Programme' was issued later in July, which called for a production of 1,200 rockets per month from November, 1,500 in January 1944 and 1,800 in April. To fulfil this plan, a fourth factory was to participate in the program, the Demag Fahrzeugwerk in Falkensee, west of Berlin.

OPERATION 'HYDRA'

Allied intelligence services had been watching Peenemünde for months without any clear idea as to what was going on there. In April 1943, Prime Minister Churchill appointed Duncan Sandys to lead an inquiry to study the information and report on counter-measures. The investigations confirmed the existence of rocket activities at Peenemünde and Sandys reported to the Chiefs-of-Staff that the Germans were developing rockets and were probably well advanced. On July 15, the Chiefs-of-Staff and Churchill decided to launch an attack of the heaviest possible scale on Peenemünde as soon as the moon and weather permitted.

Three separate areas were designated to be attacked: the Development Works at Peenemünde East, the Pilot Production Works at Peenemünde

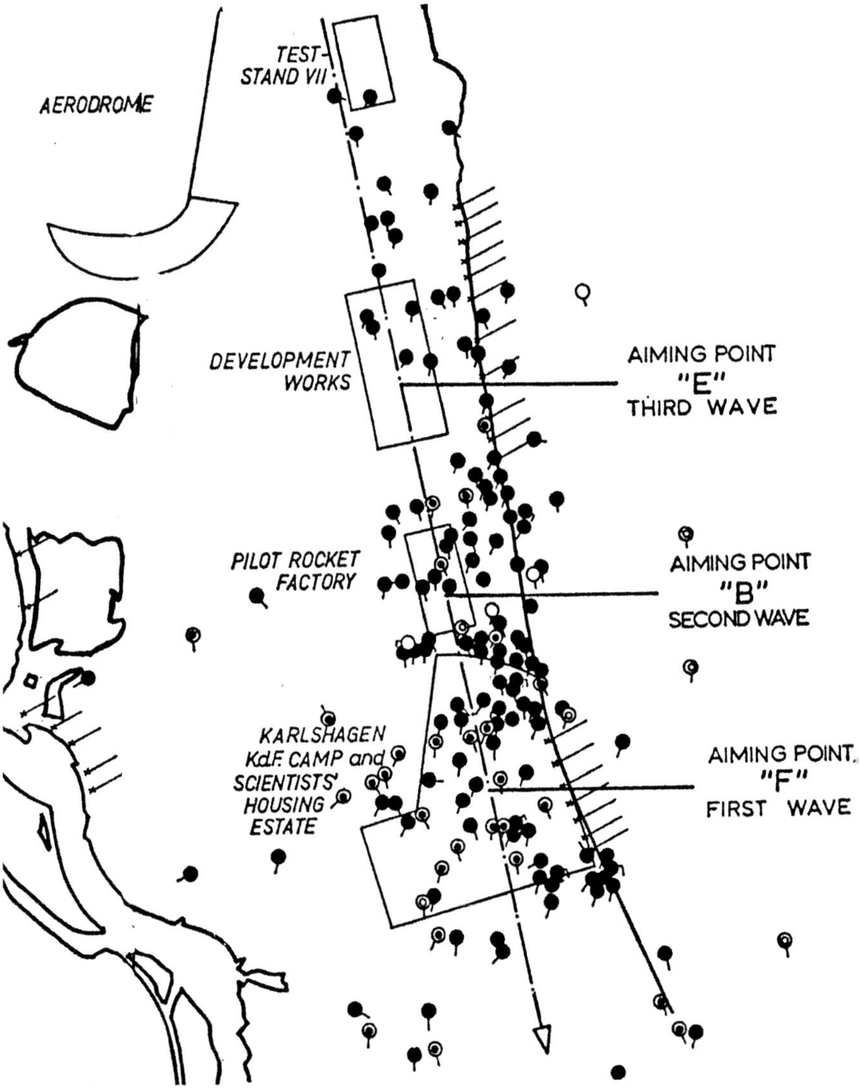

Three aiming points were designed for Operation 'Hydra', one for each of the three waves of bombers: the scientists' housing estate (aiming point F), the Production Works at Peenemünde Sud (aiming point B) and the Development Works at Peenemünde East (aiming point E). An innovation for the operation was the designation of a 'Master Bomber': circling over the target, he was to call in new pathfinder markers and direct the crews as to which markers to bomb. Group Captain John Searby of 83 Squadron carried out this task on the night of 17/18 August.

Taken from a Halifax of 102 Squadron on the night of August 17-18, this photo shows pathfinder markers above the Production Works at Peenemünde South. The south corner of the F1 building appears at the top right.

South, and the housing estate in an attempt to kill as many scientific and technical personnel working on the project as possible.

Omitted were the power station and liquid oxygen plants, the rocket test stands and the Trassenheide foreign workers camp. The Luftwaffe airfield and the facilities at Peenemünde West were ignored because the Allied intelligence was not yet aware of any link between Peenemünde and the Fi 103.

The night of August 17 to 18, 1943 was chosen for the raid which was codenamed Operation 'Hydra'. To keep Luftwaffe night fighters away from Peenemünde, eight Mosquito pathfinders were sent to Berlin to simulate the opening of a major raid by dropping typical pathfinder markings of target.

At 00.17 a.m., the first markers were dropped on Peenemünde and the first wave of 227 Stirling and Halifax bombers began their attack, aimed at the scientists' housing estate. However, due to difficulties encountered by the pathfinders, many of the bombs fell further south on the foreign workers' camp at Trassenheide, killing at least 500 of them. At 00.25 a.m., the second wave of 113 Lancasters attacked the Pilot Production Works at Peenemünde

Most of the bombs dropped by the 227 Stirling and Halifax bombers of the first wave fell south of the target, the German scientists' housing estate, and hit the foreign workers' camp at Trassenheide, killing at least 500 of them.

South. Eight minutes later, the 180 Lancaster and Halifax bombers of the third wave bombed the Experimental/Development Works at Peenemünde East. Rerouted upon the discovery that the Berlin raid was fake, Luftwaffe night fighters appeared over Peenemünde just before the third wave arrived.

A total of 1,600 tons of high explosives and 250 tons of incendiary bombs were dropped, but 80 percent of all bombs fell in open countryside and half of the remainder hit non-industrial or non-military areas. The liquid oxygen plant was unharmed, the supersonic wind tunnel was intact, damage to the vital telemetry and guidance control building was light, and Test Stand VII had been only lightly damaged by the few scattered bombs that had landed nearby.

The loss of housing was quickly overcome by billeting those bombed-out people in the surrounding area. Dornberger later said that work in Peenemünde had resumed after a delay of only four to six weeks.

Of 12,000 people living in Peenemünde, 8,000 of whom were involved in the rocket program, 732 were killed. Only 120 were Germans, the rest being foreign workers and prisoners of war, whose Trassenheide camp had been hit hard. Among the prominent scientists, only Dr. Walter Thiel, chief engineer of the A4 rocket engines, and Dr. Erich Walther, chief engineer of the rocket factory, were killed.

On August 21, Peenemünde buried its dead. Between Trassenheide and Karlshagen a clearing had been made in the woods and mass graves prepared, although some of the prominent dead had individual graves.

V1, THE FIRST CRUISE MISSILE

HAVING TOLD THE HISTORY of the early research and development of large rockets and cruise missiles, in the early 1930s, we now turn to the study of the development and operational deployment of each of the four Vergeltungs-Waffen or 'Revenge' weapons, although they were not immediately known by that name.

The development of the FZG 76 flying bomb – the future V1 – was approved in June 1942, with top priority, and in May 1943, the Commission for Long-Range Weapons recommended that the weapon be mass-produced, as well as the A4 rocket.

The FZG 76 flying bomb was powered by an Argus AS 109-014 pulse jet

From December 1942, and throughout spring of 1943, test launches of the FZG 76 took place at the Erprobungsstelle Karlshagen (test facility) at Peenemünde West. In July 1943, the Lehr- und Versuchskommando Wachtel was established at Zempin, just south-east of Peenemünde, to train operational troops in the live firing of the flying bombs

engine developing 366 kilograms of thrust. Ram air opened a loose flap valve grid and entered the engine intake, while nine nozzles atomised fuel into this airstream; the fuel then ignited, and the explosion closed the flap valve; exhaust gases escaped through the chamber's venturi, which accelerated the gases, creating thrust; whereupon the ram air opened the intake and the cycle repeated. The operation took place at a rate of 42 cycles per second, which gave the engine a characteristic throbbing noise, and the V1 was to become infamous as the 'buzz-bomb'. Compressed air contained at 6.2 megapascals in two spherical tanks forced fuel from the tank through the fuel atomisers (there was no fuel pump).

An autopilot developed by Askania Werk regulated altitude and speed

However, due to production difficulties, the FZG 76s were not delivered as planned and the training program was seriously hampered and the first flying bomb was launched late in October. These images are from a Luftwaffe training film showing the launch procedure. The Dampferzeuger (steam generator) having been connected, the pulse jet engine was started. The catapult was then triggered, hydrogen peroxide (T-Stoff) and sodium permanganate (Z-Stoff) combined in the Dampferzeuger, generating in a tenth of second a huge amount of high pressure steam which accelerated the flying bomb to a launch speed of 320 km/h.

The flying bomb launched, the steam piston dropped away at the end of the ramp. It was collected by the crew for re-use.

with a pair of gyroscopes controlling yaw and pitch, while a magnetic compass maintained azimuth. The altitude was controlled by a barometric device. In addition to pressurising the fuel system, the compressed air also drove the gyroscopes and operated the servo motors controlling the rudder and elevator.

A preset air log, driven by the small propeller on the nose of the missile, counted down the numbers on the odometer. Prior to launch, this odometer was set such that it would reach zero when the target area was reached notwithstanding the prevailing wind condition. When the count reached zero, two detonating bolts were fired, severing the connection between the elevator and rudder and their servos, which sent the flying bomb into a steep dive. It was not originally planned to shut down the engine, but the sudden dive caused fuel flow to stop, thereby shutting down the engine.

The warhead consisted of 830 kg of Amatol high explosive. It was triggered by two impact fuzes. In addition, to avoid the risk of the secret weapon being examined by the British, a delayed action fuze set to fire two hours after launch was to destroy the flying bomb in the event of a soft landing.

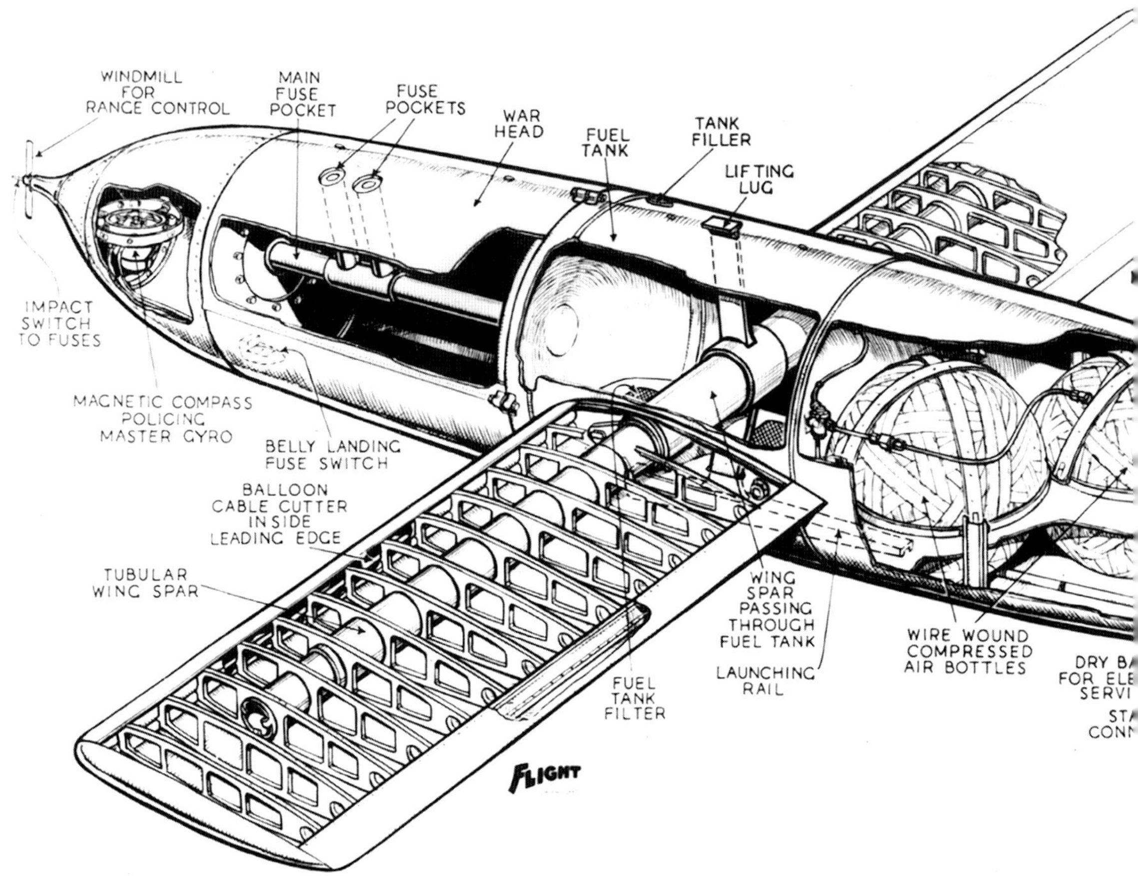

The architecture of the FZG 76, from left to right: the windmill on the nose which counts down the digits of the odometer; the magnetic compass; the warhead; the fuel tank, with the main spar passing through; the two bottles of compressed air; the pulse jet engine; and the tail section housing the gyroscopes, altitude control system and servo-motors.

The downside of the FZG 76 was that it could not take off under its own power and had to be catapulted from a launch ramp. The catapult for field deployment of the missile was developed by Walter. The inclined launch rail was 49 metres long, with a tube running the entire length; a piston connected to the underside of the missile was propelled along the tube by high pressure steam. This steam was produced by the Dampferzeuger, a small gas generator trailer, in which hydrogen peroxide (T-Stoff) and sodium permanganate (Z-Stoff) combined, generating high pressure steam that was fed into the catapult tube. The catapult accelerated the flying bomb to a launch speed of 320 km/h.

The FZG 76 maximum flight altitude was approximately 2,625 metres, but the average operating flight altitude was between 900 and 1,500 metres. Becoming lighter as its fuel burned, the missile gradually accelerated, achieving speeds of 550 km/h when it reached the British coast and 600 km/h when it flew over London.

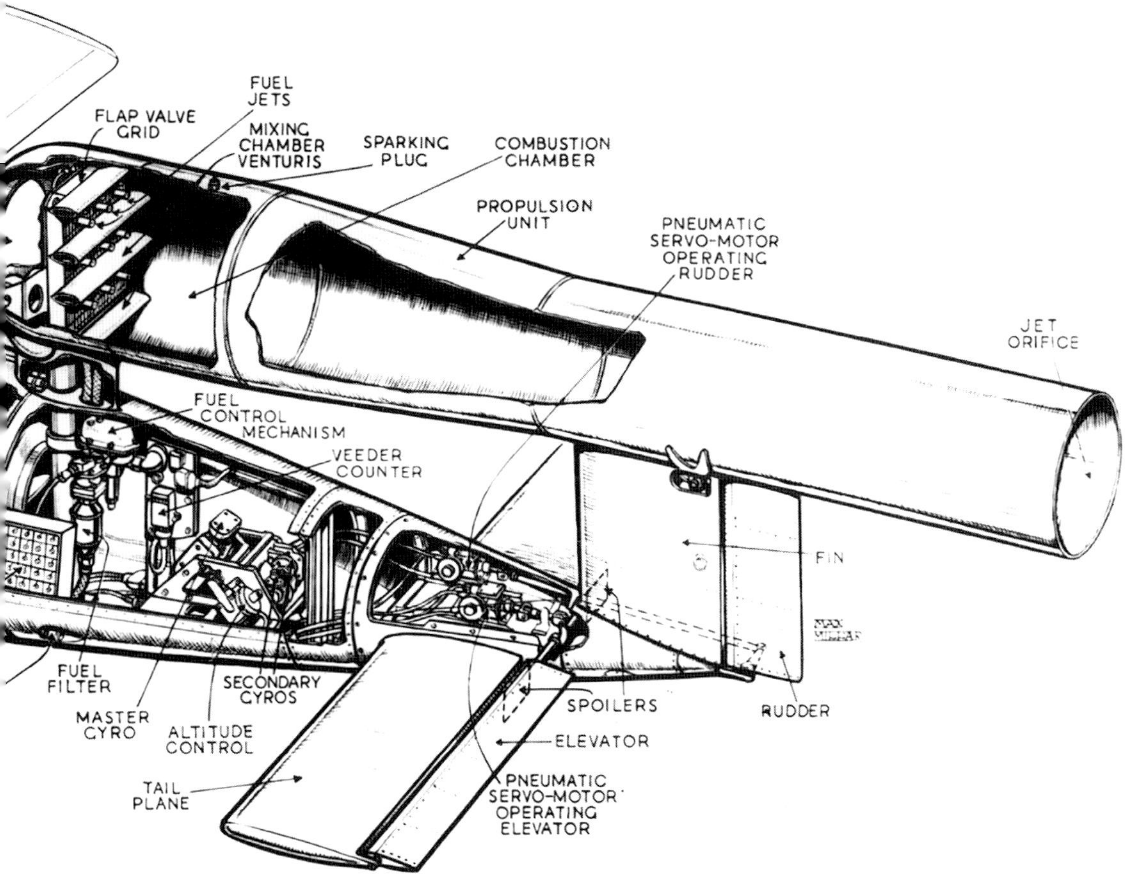

TOWARDS OPERATIONAL DEPLOYMENT

In April 1943, Generalleutnant Walter von Axthelm, the Flak commander at the Reichsluftfahrtministerium (Ministry of Aviation), entrusted Oberst Max Wachtel, an experienced Flak officer, with the military deployment of the FZG 76. The Lehr- und Versuchskommando Wachtel was then established at Zempin, 15 kilometres south-east of Peenemünde, and charged with training of troops and preparing for their future deployment.

Production planning for the FZG 76 was discussed at a meeting of Reichsmarschall Hermann Göring, Generalfeldmarschall Milch and Generalleutnant von Axthelm on June 17-18. The plan was to have 100 flying bombs produced in August, with production increasing to 500 in September, 1,000 in October, 2,000 in December, 3,800 in March 1944, and finally reaching a production rate of 5,000 in May. Alone, the Fieseler Werk at Kassel-Bettenhausen could not achieve such a level of production, so the Volkswagen Werk at Fallersleben was included in the program.

There were two different views regarding the future deployment of the flying bomb against England. Milch proposed a limited number of giant bomb-proof storage and launch bunkers, from which continuous fire could be maintained. Von Axthelm, on the other hand, believed that the Allies would quickly spot the construction work and send their bombers to destroy the bunkers before they were completed. He was in favour of spreading the launch of the FZG 76 over many small mobile sites, a hundred or more. No clear decision was made and both types of construction were launched.

Work began in early August 1943 to build four massive combined storage, assembly, and launch bunkers codenamed Wasserwerk (Waterwork): Wasserwerk Desvres at Lottinghen, Wasserwerk Saint-Pol at Siracourt, Wasserwerk Valognes at Tamerville and Wasserwerk Cherbourg at Couville. Under a five metres thick concrete roof, these bunkers were to store up to 1,000 flying bombs in underground halls, and launch them at a rate of 90 per day. By mid-August, some 40,000 men were working at the various sites, in day and night shifts.

At the same time, research detachments scoured the regions of northern France along the Channel coast to find suitable locations for lighter launch sites. These sites consisted of ten concrete buildings for storing and assembling the flying bombs, each site storing a reserve of about 20 flying bombs. These were not bomb-proof constructions, merely providing protection against aircraft machine guns fire and shrapnel from their

At Siracourt, the massive combined V1 storage, assembly, and launch bunker named Wasserwerk measured 215 metres long and 36 metres wide. This drawing illustrates the report produced by a group of experts led by Colonel Terence Sanders sent to France in November 1944 to inspect the V-weapon sites. Railway spurs from the nearest main line would loop into the south end of the building and wagons would deliver crated flying bombs. They would then be assembled under the bomb-proof roof and fired from inside along an earth ramp pointing at London.
(Sanders' Report)

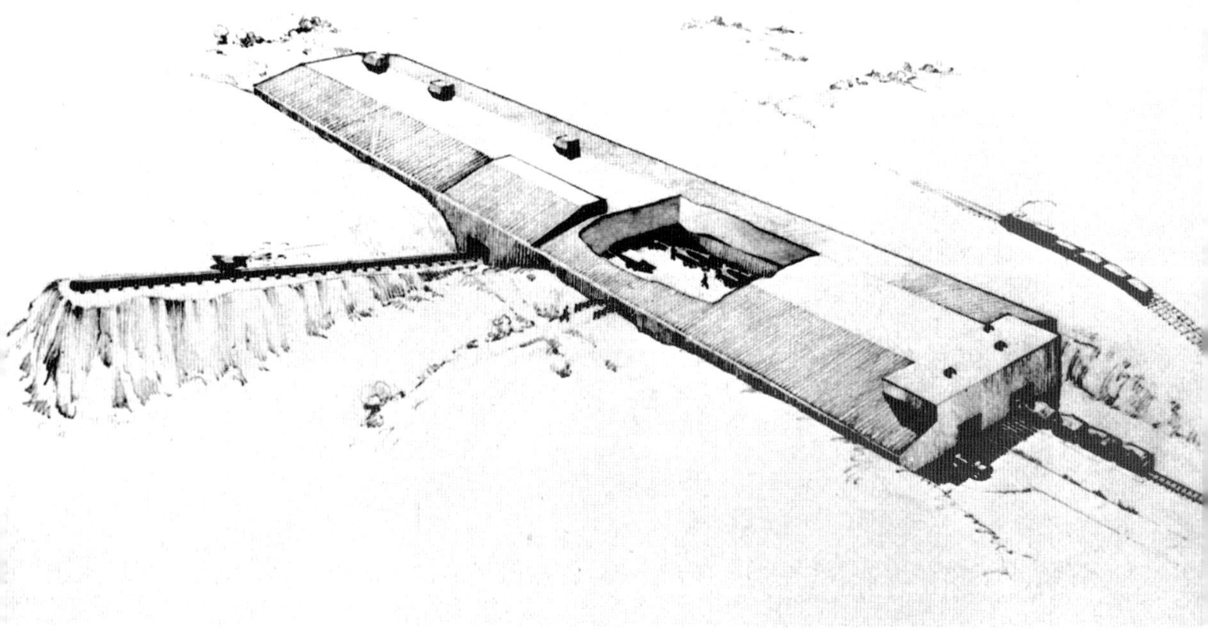

bombs. The storage buildings were ski-shaped, with a curved entrance designed to provide blast protection for the flying bombs stored within. The peculiar shape of these buildings made the sites easily detectable from the air and the Allies soon called them 'ski sites'.

The guidelines required by the FZG 76 catapult launches severely restricted the choice of suitable sites: the ground had to be sloping in front of the catapult, so that the flying bomb, which stalled after launch, would not crash, and there should be no obstacle passing above a 3-degree plane over a distance of six kilometres. Moreover, the catapult had to be aligned in the direction of London, a possibility which was almost never offered by tracks hidden in the woods and, therefore, the sites chosen were mostly in orchards, where the ramps were visible from the sky.

On September 1, the Flak-Regiment 155 (W) was created from the Lehr- und Versuchskommando Wachtel, with four battalions. Each battalion was comprised of four launching batteries, with four launch catapults per battery. In December, two technical batteries were added to each of the battalions to operate a storage depot. The (W) in the name of the unit stood for Werfer (mortar), to mislead about the purpose of the unit.

The plan was to store up to 1,000 flying bombs in underground halls in the bunker and launch them at a rate of 90 launches per day. Remarkably, this *After the Battle*'s aerial shot of 1974 perfectly matches the sketch that appears in the Sanders' report of 1945.

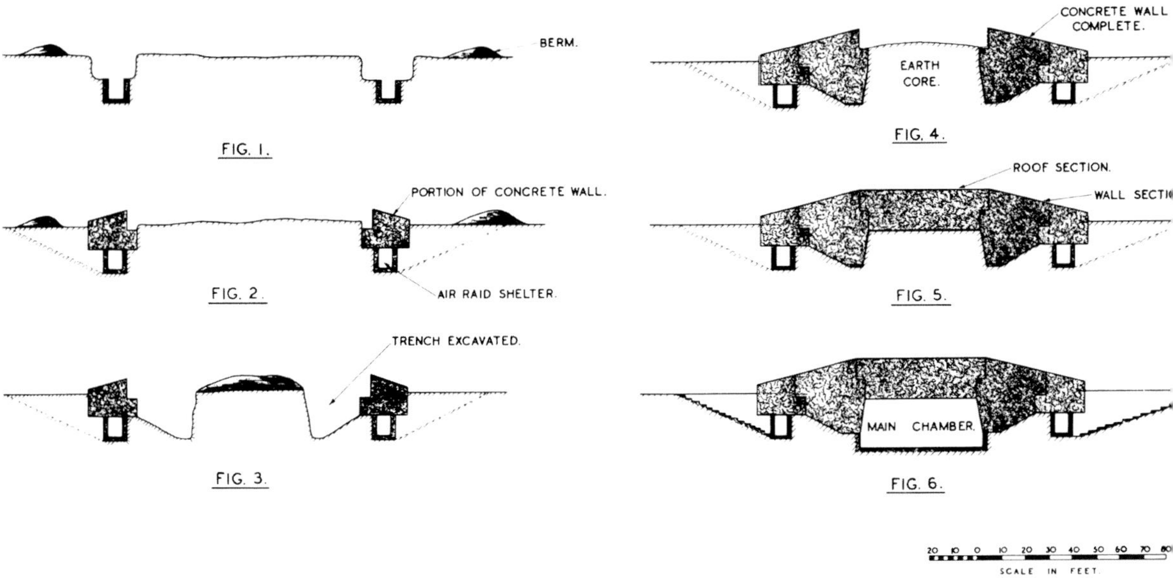

To safeguard the construction work against air attacks, the German engineers devised the Verbunkerung process: first, large parallel trenches were dug; concrete was then poured into the trenches; then a concrete slab was cast flat on the ground between the two trenches, keyed into a recess on each trench side. Then, under the protective cover of this concrete slab, the ground was excavated from beneath it, which itself became the roof of the underground bunker. (Sanders' Report)

Officers arriving to the quickly expanding regiment were introduced to the new weapon by officers of the Lehr- und Versuchskommando Wachtel, and were shown live test launches at Peenemünde. They then attended courses at the factories involved in the production of the FZG 76: Fieseler in Kassel, Askania and Argus in Berlin, Walter in Kiel, or Rheinmetall Borsig in Breslau.

In September, the battalion and battery staffs moved to Brüsterort, north-west of Königsberg, where NCOs and men transferred from various Luftwaffe units gradually assembled. Theoretical and practical training was carried under strict secrecy measures, which hampered the training: no plans or sketches were distributed and even the taking of notes was prohibited. After three weeks of instruction, the launch batteries were transferred to Zempin for live firing of the flying bombs. However, due to production difficulties, the missiles were not delivered as planned. This failure seriously hampered the training program, and Wachtel had to report that the delivery of six units per day was the minimum required to complete the training on time. As a result, the first FZG 76 was launched at Zempin only on October 26.

Production at the Fieseler factory in Kassel-Bettenhausen had just commenced when Bomber Command launched a deadly raid on Kassel on October 22, dropping over 1,800 tons of bombs. The old city centre was destroyed, 10,000 people were killed, and 150,000 residents were left homeless. (The Allies were unaware at the time that preparations for FZG 76 production were underway at the Fieseler factory). It proved impossible to

Construction was first reported at Siracourt early in September 1943, and photographed by 542 Squadron. The work then in progress seems to be building a ramp pointing towards London (the top left corner) but the bunker was finally built a few metres in front of this first construction, as if the German engineers had changed their plan after this first work.

resume production of the FZG 76 at the factory and some of the production equipment was eventually moved to another factory at Rothwesten, north-east of Kassel. However, it was feared that the foreign workers were spying for England and Fieseler was forbidden from moving them to the new production line. Due to the resulting labour shortage, the transfer of the Kassel production line took a long time and for the time being the production of the FZG 76 remained concentrated at the Volkswagen factory in Fallersleben.

The Volkswagen Werk was also severely lacking in skilled workers and machine tools, making it difficult to start production. Additionally, Allied air attacks hit other factories producing guidance and control subcomponents, and as a result, only 30% of planned deliveries were made available at Fallersleben. The factory began production of the FZG 76 in September, but it was only able to deliver two flying bombs per day.

Problems continued in October meaning that the projected production fell so far short that the training program at Zempin could not go ahead.

In the meantime, test launches showed an endless series of problems and the design was constantly evolving to resolve them – since August, 150 modifications had been designed. As a result, production had to be temporarily stopped at the end of November and a whole series of wings and centre sections produced at the Volkswagen factory had to be scrapped.

LXV. ARMEEKORPS z.b.V.

To command the operational actions of the new long-range missiles, the LXV. Armeekorps z.b.V. was created on November 28 under the command of Generalleutnant Erich Heinemann. The Flak-Regiment 155 (W) was subordinate to the corps, and it was planned that the batteries which were to launch the A4 rockets were to join when operational. To ensure the best possible coordination in this unit, two thirds of which came from the Army and one third from the Luftwaffe, care was taken to appoint a Luftwaffe Chief-of-Staff, Oberst Eugen Walter, when the corps commander came from the army.

In northern France, construction work was progressing well and on November 12, the war diary of Flak-Regiment 155 (W) noted that 88 sites would be ready by December 1 in the main operational area of Pas de Calais, east of the Seine, and eight sites in the Cotentin peninsula. Twenty-four other sites, initially planned as dummies to deceive Allied aerial reconnaissance, could be completed, if necessary, as operational sites.

Shortly after taking command, Heinemann toured the development and testing sites at Peenemünde, Zempin and Blizna, the new A4 rocket launch range in south-eastern Poland. Heinemann realised that the A4 was still far from operational and he recommended priority of the FZG 76 program over the rocket. He then visited the operational sites being developed in northern France and saw how easy they were to identify from the air. With French firms and workers at each site, he feared they would be teeming with potential spies.

In October, Michel Hollard, a French agent, sent a detailed report to London indicating that new constructions of a particular type were underway in six locations in northern France. When his reports reached England, specially flown sorties provided photographs of the sites and RAF air reconnaissance

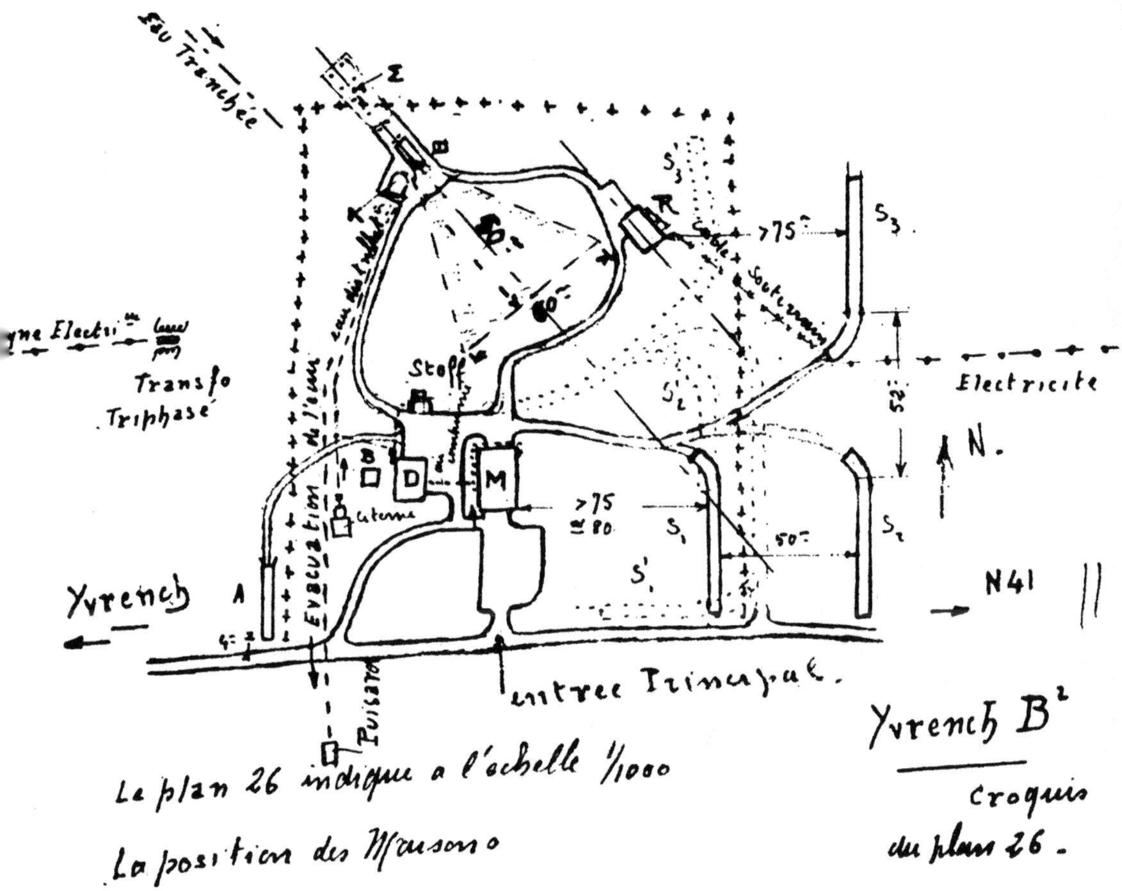

Michel Hollard, a French agent, wrote a detailed report on German construction sites he located and took it himself across the Demarcation Line then through the Swiss border to hand it over to British services. Received in London in October 1943, his report constituted a major contribution to the fight against the German flying bomb offensive. It went to the highest level and Prime Minister Churchill wrote of Hollard's work to President Roosevelt on October 25. Hollard was arrested by the Germans in February 1944 and sent to the Neuengamme concentration camp. On his release in 1945 he was awarded the Distinguished Service Order, the highest British military decoration for which a foreigner is eligible.

interpreters noted that each appeared to have nine buildings, three of which were built like skis on their sides.

At the end of November, after re-examining photographs from across northern France, 95 construction sites were located at different stages of construction. Fighter-bombers began their attacks on 'ski sites' in early December, followed by bomber squadrons and a total of 52 sites were attacked before the end of the year. The British interpreters estimated that 21 sites were destroyed and 15 damaged, when in reality only seven had been put out of action.

In January, after conferences in Paris between the LXV. Armeekorps z.b.V. and representatives of the factories producing the FZG 76, a new system of simpler sites was designed. Natural camouflage should be the

The sites signalled in the Hollard's report were promptly covered by photographic reconnaissance missions. The photo-interpreters of the Central Interpretation Unit at Medmenham recognised that all these construction works were to a standard design, and all similar sites were from then on given the name of Bois Carré, the first of these sites to be studied.

primary condition for choosing the location of a site. The new sites consisted of a prefabricated catapult ramp that could be bolted onto previously prepared foundations. No ski buildings were to be built, only three or four camouflaged huts. The prefabricated catapults would be transported to site just days before the offensive began, since it took only six days to assemble the sections on the previously prepared foundations.

In January, engineering detachments and transport columns of Flak-Regiment 155 (W) arrived in France but, for reasons of secrecy, it was strictly

This low-level photograph of Bois Carré, 10 kilometres north-east of Abbeville, on November 9, 1943, shows how the ski-shaped storage buildings (forefront), which prompted the interpreters to nickname the sites the ski sites, were easily detectable from the air.

In addition to the ski-shaped buildings, the 'Bois Carré' installations all had another noticeable feature in common: a platform lined up in the direction of London. In April 1944, choosing the Maisoncelle site as an example, the Crossbow Committee – Crossbow was the code name in use to describe all German long-range weapons – produced this schematic drawing of a ski site as an aid to identification.

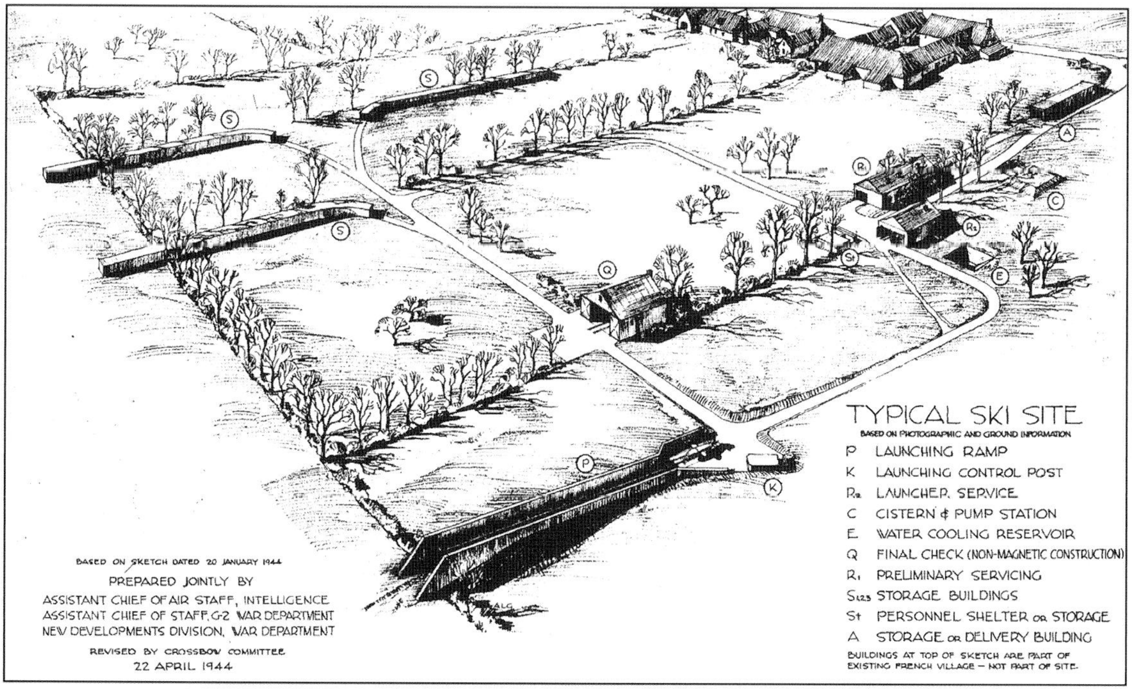

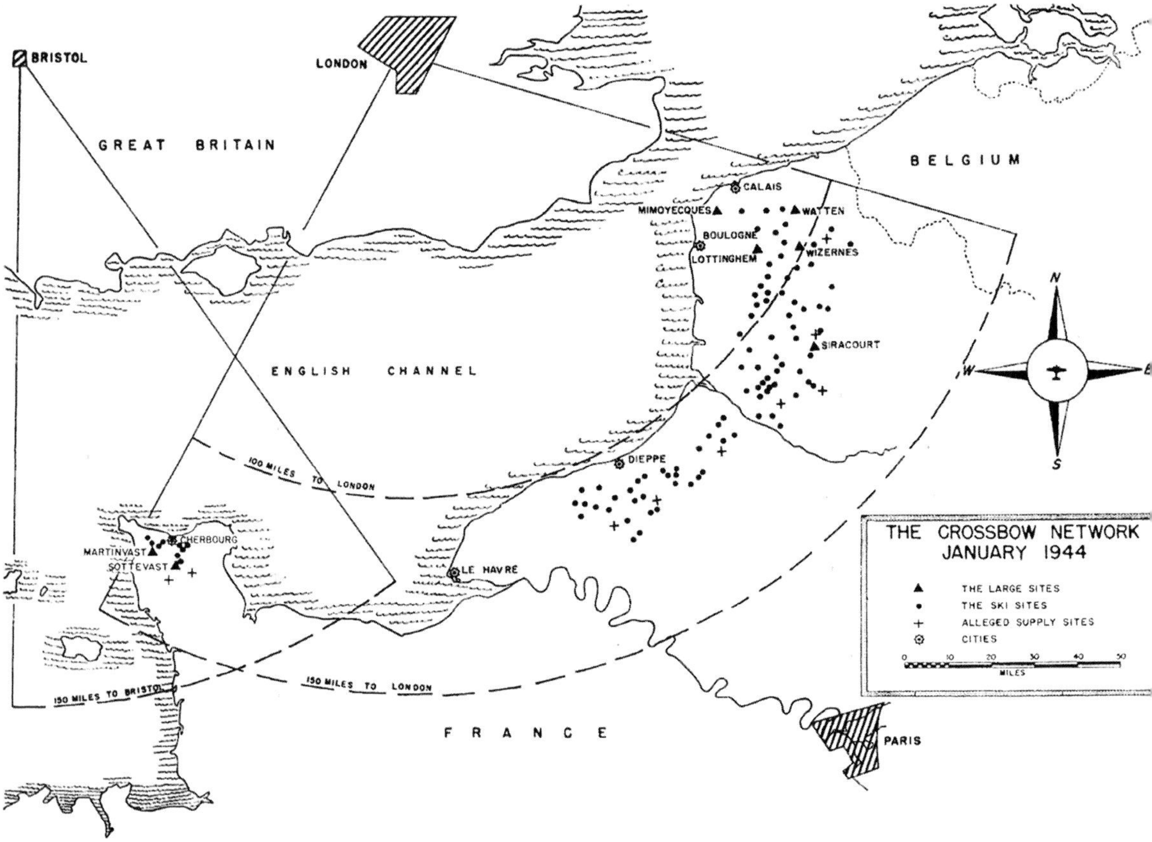

In the weeks that followed, the Crossbow Committee sent dozens of photographic reconnaissance missions and by January 1944, when this map was produced, the total of identified sites was 96. The map also shows seven massive combined storage, assembly, and launch bunkers built for the V-weapons campaign against England: three of the V1 'Wasserwerk' – at Lottinghen, Siracourt and Martinvast –, three of the V2 bunkers – KNW at Watten, SNW at Wizernes, and RLW at Sottevast – and the HPD launch bunker under construction at Mimoyecques.

forbidden to bring flying bombs or elements of the launching device, such as the steam generator and the catapult, in the operational area. They were to remain in Germany to be brought to the launch sites at night within ten days of the start of the attack. As it was feared that British intelligence had spotted Oberst Wachtel, he was given a new name, Oberst Martin Wolf, and he often disguised himself as a civilian.

On December 23, the OKW issued an order to LXV. Armeekorps z.b.V. to begin operations in January 1944, but not a single one of the 1,400 flying bombs ordered for production in January was completed. Testing of an improved version yielded positive results, and the design finally seemed operational in February and Milch ordered mass production to resume. Production accelerated and 1,700 FZG 76s were produced in April and 2,500 in May.

In May 1944, during a training session at Zempin, the 1. and 7. Batterie of Flak-Regiment 155 (W) launched 29 FZG 76s, 24 during the day and five

Created in November 1943, the LXV. Armeekorps z.b.V. established its headquarters at Saint-Germain en Laye in December. The corps commander, General Erich Heinemann (this photo) was from the Army, and his Chief-of-Staff, Oberst Eugen Walter, was from the Luftwaffe. On May 14, 1944, the corps transferred its headquarters to Maisons-Laffitte. (Max Wachtel)

Created at Zempin in August 1943, the Flak-Regiment 155 (W) moved to Merlemont, south-east of Beauvais, on December 3. To hide Oberst Wachtel from the attention of British intelligence, his staff was renamed Sonderbaustab Schmidt, allegedly from the Organisation Todt, in February 1944 and he was given a new name, Oberst Martin Wolf. The staff then took up residence at the Château d'Auteuil, just south of Beauvais, where this photo was taken. On June 9, the headquarters moved to Saleux, south-west of Amiens. (Max Wachtel)

Oberst Wachtel (left) often disguised himself in civilian clothes, as did Oberst Walter (right), LXV. Armeekorps z.b.V. Chief-of-Staff, for this meeting with General Heinemann (middle) at the Château d'Auteuil in May 1944. (Max Wachtel)

at night. By day, the flying bombs were set up to fly at an altitude of 1,500 metres, 18 of them were targeted at a point at a distance of 225 kilometres, the other six at a distance of 185 kilometres; at night, the flying bombs flew at 1,000 metres, and the target was 90 kilometres away. Of the 22 flying bombs whose trajectory and point of impact could be precisely measured, 19 (86 percent) hit within a circle of 15 kilometres radius, including 9 (41 percent) within a circle of 7.5 kilometres.

On March 1, LXV. Armeekorps z.b.V. and Flak-Regiment 155 (W) conducted a map exercise in Paris to rehearse a massive attack on London. The exercise concluded that each of the 64 sites would have launched 12 to 15 flying bombs in the night, for a total of 768 to 960. This was a realistic reduction from estimates made in December, but future operations will soon show that these estimates were still far too optimistic.

The launch sites in the Pas de Calais and the Cotentin peninsula remained

The Siracourt bunker suffered 28 heavy air attacks between January and August 1944, including three raids by 617 Squadron with Tallboy earthquake bombs and an Operation 'Aphrodite' attack with remote-controlled B-17 drones packed with explosives. This photo was taken in April when the bunker had already suffered over a dozen air attacks.

More than 5,000 tons of bombs were dropped on the Siracourt site. This is a view facing north-east, with the church of Croix-en-Ternois in the background.

a priority of the Allied air offensive in the first quarter of 1944. However, the attention paid to camouflage with the new simplified launch sites proved very effective and the LXV. Armeekorps z.b.V. reported in April that air attacks only hit old ski sites, while the well-camouflaged, simplified sites went undetected.

As for the heavy bunkers, they have suffered almost a hundred attacks since the air campaign against them began in August 1943. The bunkers themselves did not suffer as much damage, but the surrounding areas were devastated, making the approaches impractical and the resumption of work impossible. By early June, it was clear that due to incessant air attacks, the heavy bunkers could never be brought into action and the LXV. Armeekorps z.b.V. ceased work on them.

The Lancasters of 617 Squadron claimed three hits with Tallboy bombs on July 6 but when Colonel Sanders visited Siracourt in November, he reported no Tallboy direct hit, only some damage on the western edge of the roof slab where a section had been lifted out of place. Following the publication of this story in *After the Battle* in 1976, Bissell Alderman, a former Eighth Air Force officer, wrote to the editor that he had inspected the site on September 28, 1944, in company with Charles V. Kring, another former Eighth Air Force officer. 'I am happy to confirm that one particular bomb which made a direct hit on the Siracourt roof slab did actually perforate the slab. Being an architect and Mr. Kring being a structural engineer, we were both duly impressed by the perforating of the 16-foot-thick reinforced concrete roof slab.' Mr Alderman provided *After the Battle* this photo of Mr Kring beside the Tallboy perforation and this photo of himself on the roof of the bunker.

The Tallboy crater is arrowed on this oblique reconnaissance photo. As there is no crater visible on the roof today, one can only assume the French authorities later expertly repaired it, although why remains a mystery.

In the Cotentin, south of Cherbourg, the Brécourt site was initially planned as part of the A4 rocket operational plan. However, the office of General Dornberger did not like the idea of installing complex and costly facilities, notably the oxygen liquid plant, so far to the west. Also, they considered the site much too close to the sea, and therefore at risk of being shelled by warships. The Army consequently abandoned the site by the end of 1943 and the Luftwaffe took it over with plans to develop it as a flying bomb launch site. The bunker was to comprise two launching ramps and sheltered storage for 300 flying bombs. Work began in January 1944. A report from the Organisation Todt indicates that works continued until June, just weeks before American troops took the site. The work used some 13,000 cubic metres of concrete, with a peak in April and May. These photos were taken on August 8, 1944, when two Canadian pilots from 403 Squadron, Flight-Lieutenant Andrew Robert MacKenzie and Flight-Lieutenant Walter J. Hill, visited the site.

INTO ACTION: FIRING AT ENGLAND

On May 16, Hitler ordered the flying bomb operation against England to begin in mid-June. The activation of the launch sites, Operation 'Rumpelkammer', was to last ten days, while the catapults and special equipment were to be moved from Germany to depots behind the front, and then installed at each of the sites. At the end of this operation, the code word 'Eisbär' would direct the opening of the attacks.

The FZG 76s fresh from the factory were delivered by rail to two main supply sites at Nucourt and Saint-Leu d'Esserent where they were checked and repaired if necessary. From there, they were taken at night by road to a storage location north of Beauvais where the supply batteries of Flak-Regiment 155 (W) picked them up. Traveling at night, small convoys of two or three lorries delivered the flying bombs to each of the launch sites.

It appeared that some of the launch sites had not been prepared with the necessary care and that the previously prepared foundations did not match the catapult struts. Additionally, Allied air attacks on the lines of communication seriously hampered the supply system, and critical components and supplies were missing at some sites, such as diesel fuel for the compressor or T-Stoff and Z-Stoff fuels. for the steam generator.

Despite these difficulties, the LXV. Armeekorps z.b.V. gave the order on June 11 to attack on the night of June 12, with two bursts at 11.40 p.m. and 12.40 p.m., followed by harassing fire until 4.45 a.m. on June 13. This armchair decision was badly received by Flak-Regiment 155 (W) which had repeatedly warned the corps that the batteries could not be ready for a premature date. On June 12, General Heinemann left his headquarters at Maisons-Lafitte and went to the headquarters of Flak-Regiment 155 (W) at Saleux, south of Amiens.

This hurried start was a real fiasco. Only a few sites were ready to launch at the specified time and Wachtel had first to delay the salvo. When it appeared that there were still not enough sites ready for the planned salvo, at midnight, sites were ordered to fire individually as soon as they were ready for action.

By morning, only 10 bombs were fired, five of which crashed almost immediately. One probably crashed in the English Channel, the other four reached southern England, the first landing at Gravesend at 4.18 a.m. The only bomb to cause casualties this night was the one that landed alongside the railway bridge over Grove Road, Mile End at 4.25 a.m. The bridge and track were badly damaged, several houses were destroyed and six people killed.

After this poor start, Oberst Wachtel blamed the failure on the supply system and postponed the firing until June 15. The flying bombs, fuel and necessary equipment were this time delivered to the launch sites, and 55 of the 64 sites were ready for action by 10 p.m. that evening. The batteries succeeded to launch 244 flying bombs by noon on June 16, 45 of which crashed shortly after launch. Others failed on the way or were shot down

Delivered from the storage area, the V1 had the wing spar and wings attached. In the non-magnetic building, the missile was suspended and pointed at its target and compass adjustment was completed. The autopilot was set, with the flight altitude entered in the barometric height command, and with the range set in the air log.
(Signal and Hans Lächler)

by anti-aircraft guns and only 144 missiles reached England, of which 73 hit Greater London. On the morning of June 16, it was announced in the British Parliament that a new form of warfare had begun.

On June 17, the new weapon was named V1 by Hans Schwarz van Berkl, a journalist with Das Reich propaganda organ. The 'V' stood for Vergeltung, retribution, signifying its function as a means of reprisal against the Allies,

In August 1944, *Der Adler*, the Luftwaffe's biweekly propaganda magazine, published a double-page spread reporting the deployment of the 'barrage of revenge' (Vergeltungsfeuer). London and the south of England 'has for weeks now been the target of our V1'.

Stressing that secrecy was maintained for months and that the men lived day after day in deep bunkers, isolated from the outside world, the article says that it is time to reveal the men of the 'new weapon'.

in revenge for the destruction of German cities by Allied bombs.

On June 18, a V1 crashed onto the Guards Chapel near St. James's Park. The church was packed, with guardsmen, families and friends attending the service. The whole roof collapsed on top of the congregation, 121 soldiers and civilians were killed and 141 seriously injured.

After a few days of experience, the system was established, the teams effectively handled the complex weapon, and Flak-Regiment 155 (W) launched its 1,000th V1 in the early hours

The article describes the men as veterans of the 'Eastern and Western Fronts' and 'excellent specialists'. 'The V1 target accuracy requires precise knowledge of weather conditions' was the caption for this photo of a Leutnant checking wind speed.

Like these two Wachmeister, the men are described as being enthusiastic because 'they knew the effects of the new weapon'.

of June 21. However, technical failures still plagued the missile, with 20 percent of those launched crashing shortly after launch.

On June 26, some batteries fired on Southampton, which was one of the important ports of embarkation for troops landing in Normandy. In total, 53 V1s were launched on this new target before an order arrived the next day to stop this operation and resume the attack on London.

The missile was then delivered to the launching ramp on a loading trolley, the Zubringerwagen.

The missile was slid up the ramp then lowered precisely onto the piston hook at the base of the tube running up the length of the catapult. The trolley was removed and the starter trolley, the Dampferzeuger, was brought up.

By means of a bayonet interface, the Dampferzeuger was locked to the tube base. Compressed air will blast two highly reactive chemicals, Z-Stoff (potassium permanganate) and T-Stoff (hydrogen peroxide), into the reaction chamber where they will combine to form a massive amount of steam that will force the piston over the entire length of the ramp.

The starting device, Anlassgerät, supplied compressed air to the engine intake and electrical connection to the engine spark plug. The pulse jet engine was started, it reached full power after 7 seconds and the catapult then accelerated the missile to its launch speed of 320 km/h. Note that the spark plug was only needed when starting the engine, while the residual flame ignited further fuel and air mixtures throughout the flight.

For the Germans, the Bois Carré site was Feuerstellung (Firing Site) No. 660 of the II. Abteilung of Flak-Regiment 155 (W). Given the Target Code XI/A/39 by the Allies, it received much attention from their air forces and suffered many attacks. Like almost all ski sites, it was never used.

Before the end of June, Flak-Regiment 155 (W) had launched its 2,000th V1 against England. At the beginning of July, due to the advance of the Allied troops landed in Normandy, the sites on the west bank of the Seine were abandoned.

The new, carefully camouflaged launch sites, with reduced catapult foundations and where flying bombs were prepared in simple tents, avoided detection by Allied aircraft. Maintaining activity at the abandoned ski sites proved effective as Allied pilots fell into the trap and repeatedly attacked these inert sites.

However, the Allied air attacks were very effective when they hit the supply system and the two heavily bombed ammunition establishments at Nucourt and Saint-Leu d'Esserent had to be abandoned to be replaced by mobile installations hidden in woods. Supply difficulties therefore did not allow the sites to be used to their full capacity, and the catapult crews launched a flying bomb every hour or hour and a half, when technically they could have launched one every 30 minutes.

At the end of June, the Americans had taken the Cotentin peninsula, and captured all the firing positions prepared for the IV. Abteilung of Flak-Regiment 155 (W). At the hamlet of La Sorellerie, eight kilometres south of Cherbourg, GIs examined the firing bunker and the launch ramp of Feuerstellung No. 17. (USNA)

At another V1 launch site just north of Mesnil au Val, GIs examined the entrance of a heavily camouflaged building. This was Feuerstellung No. 18. (USNA)

The original caption for this photo taken on July 1, 1944, is vague as to the location but this ramp could well be that of Feuerstellung No. 18. This photo shows that the trees in front of this ramp were never cut down, proof that the launch site was never completed. An aerial photo taken in July 1947 by the IGN shows that this was precisely the situation at Feuerstellung No. 18. (USNA)

Two large cave systems were retained for the storage and maintenance of the flying bombs, and to supply the launching sites: Nordpol at Nucourt, south-west of Beauvais, and Leopold at Saint-Leu d'Esserent, south-east of Beauvais. The Allies spotted the activities at the two sites and sent several photographic reconnaissance missions, this photo of Saint-Leu d'Esserent was taken on June 13.

In the late hours of July 4, 617 Squadron attacked the storage site at Saint-Leu d'Esserent. The first 11 Lancasters dropped their Tallboy bombs, but the resulting smoke completely obscured the target and the remaining six aircraft were unable to attack. Almost immediately afterwards, from 1.30 a.m. on July 5, 231 Lancasters and 15 Mosquitos attacked the site with high explosive and incendiary bombs. German efforts to repair the site were observed and Bomber Command returned to Saint-Leu d'Esserent twice. In the night of July 7/8, with 208 Lancasters and 13 Mosquitos, and in the afternoon of August 5, with 450 bombers, Lancasters, Halifaxes and Mosquitos. This is the area named 'St Leu d'Esserent I' on the reconnaissance photo of June 13.

An entrance to the underground complex, a photo taken in September 1944, just after the liberation. (Robert Gallas)

On July 22, the Flak-Regiment 155 (W) launched its 5,000th V1 against England. On August 2 and 3, the regiment reached its maximum rate of fire, launching 316 flying bombs in 24 hours.

In mid-July another V1 launch unit was established, Flak-Regiment 255 (W) with two battalions, each with four launch batteries. The I. Abteilung was new, but the II. Abteilung was in fact the IV. Abteilung of Flak-Regiment 155 (W), which had had to evacuate its positions west of the Seine. This reorganisation was nothing more than a restructure on paper.

In addition to the operations of Flak-Regiment 155 (W) from France, the new weapon was also brought into action by Heinkel He 111 bombers which launched V1s from the air from early July. Tests at Karlshagen in April 1944 made it possible to define the procedure, the FZG 76 being carried under the starboard wing, between the engine and the fuselage of the He 111 twin-engined bomber He 111. Equipment in the fuselage allowed the pulse jet to be started before releasing the missile. The III. Gruppe of Kampfgeschwader 3 was tasked with the mission and its crew trained at Karlshagen in May, the training ending with the air launch of 54 missiles in the first days of June.

The III. Gruppe began operations on July 9 from Venlo and Gilze-Rijen airfields in the Netherlands. After take-off, the plane headed at low altitude for a radio or light beacon on the coast. Once over the sea, they descended to a very low altitude, around 50 metres, to avoid detection by radar in England. Shortly before reaching the launch point, the bombers quickly climbed to an altitude of 600 metres. The pulse jet was then started and was left running

Authors identified this Heinkel He 111 as belonging to Kampfgeschwader 3, but Dieter Hölsken pointed out that the camouflage scheme of the V1 excludes this hypothesis. The plane was probably A1+GA from the Stab of Kampfgeschwader 53. Note the wire from the plane connecting to the spark plug on top of the pulse jet engine. (Hans Lächler)

Silhouettes in the twilight, a Heinkel from Kampfgeschwader 53 and the V1 it has just released.

at reduced power for about half a minute before the missile was released. The pulse jet then automatically switched to full power and the V1 began to climb to its predetermined flight altitude. In a steep turn, the He 111 quickly descended to wave-top level for the return flight.

With the unexpected arrival of missiles from the North Sea, the air launch gave the Luftwaffe the opportunity to outflank the increasingly effective ground and air defences put in place against the V1s launched from France.

With a total complement of 30 aircraft, of which at best five to eight would be ready for action each night, the III. Gruppe managed to launch around 300 V1s against London, 90 against Southampton and 30 against Gloucester when the first phase of this campaign ended on September 5. The III. Gruppe had lost only two planes during this operation.

With V1s continually hitting Greater London, day and night, the

Cleared for publication on August 3, these photos were the first to be released showing a V1 diving on the centre of London. The buildings in the foreground are the Royal Courts of Justice on the Strand. It was June 30, 2.07 p.m., and the missile exploded in the street in front of Adastral House. It was lunch time, the street was crowded, and about fifty people were killed, 400 seriously injured, 200 others lightly.

government ordered London County Council on July 1 to begin the evacuation of mothers of children under five and school-age children. The first parties left on July 3, and by mid-July half a million people had left the capital, including 170,000 under the official program. More followed in August and September and ultimately, it is estimated that between 1.5 and 2 million people left London for safer areas during the flying bomb attacks.

Prime Minister Churchill was so worried that on July 6 he issued a secret memorandum asking his military leaders to 'think very seriously over this

Belts of anti-aircraft guns, barrage of balloons, standing patrols by fighters, and attacks on the storage depots in France, all helped to reduce the number of bombs reaching England. The fighters employed were Tempest Vs, Spitfire XIVs and Mustang IIIs, with Mosquitos flying at night. Unfortunately, the original caption of this remarkable photo of a Tempest chasing a V1 does not say when and where it was taken.

One tactic employed by fighters to combat the flying bombs was to slide the wingtip of the interceptor close of the undersurface of the V1's wing, so that the airflow over the aircraft's wing would tip the wing of the flying bomb upwards. This manoeuvre would over-ride the V1's gyroscopes, sending the flying bomb into an out-of-control dive.

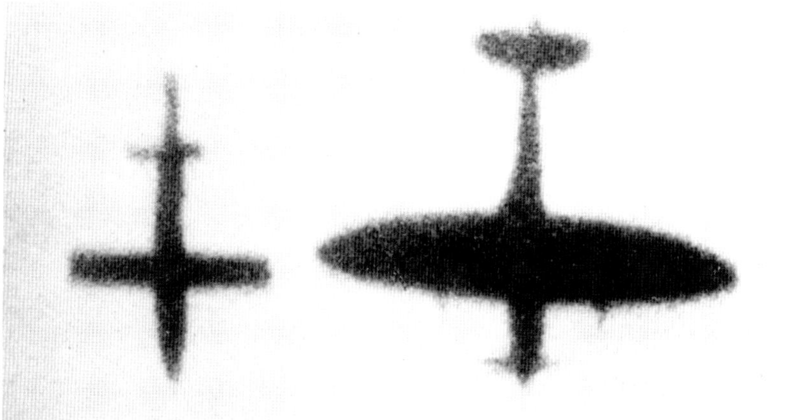

By mid June 1944, Air Marshall Roderick Hill, the commander of Air Defence of Great Britain, ADGB, decided to move the anti-aircraft guns to a coastal strip, thus giving the guns freedom to engage at any time and under any conditions. The fighters could not intervene in the area covered by the gun belt but they had complete freedom of action in front of it, and between it and the balloon barrage. Initially the guns claimed 1 kill per 2,500 rounds fired, but technical improvements, particularly the use of shells with proximity fuses, improved this to 1 kill per hundred rounds fired. This RAF Regiment team manned their Bofors 40mm gun in a rain-sodden emplacement.

After redeployment, on June 30, General Sir Frederick Pile (GOC Anti-Aircraft Command) took Churchill to visit the 481 (H) AA Battery now located on the North Downs, at which the Prime Minister's daughter was serving. They saw the battery engages one flying bomb, but not bringing it down.

question of using poison gas . . . We could drench the cities of the Ruhr and many other cities in Germany . . . We could stop all work at the flying bombs starting points . . . and if we do it, let us do it one hundred per cent.' He argued: 'It is absurd to consider morality on this topic when everybody used it in the last war without a word of complaint.'

The Chiefs-of-Staff, however, advised against the use of gas, as it would inevitably provoke Germany to retaliate in the same way. The Prime Minister replied that he was not at all convinced by this negative opinion. 'But clearly I cannot make head against the parsons and the warriors at the same time. The matter should be kept under review and brought up again when things get worse.'

The crisis quickly passed, however, because by August defences against the flying bombs, through fighter patrols and belts of anti-aircraft guns and balloons, were defeating a large part of them before they reached Greater London. In September, the Allied forces which had landed in Normandy in June crossed the Seine and invaded the Channel coast, soon overrunning the V1 launch sites. Subsequently, only a few air-launched V1s still hit London, and in the autumn, people began to return.

Pleased with the start of the V1 offensive against London, Hitler ordered production of the A4 rocket to be limited to 150 units per month so that the manpower and resources freed up could be used to increase production of flying bombs. The planned production of V1 for December had thus been set at 9,000 units per month.

Allied bombers soon intervened to disrupt this grand plan. On June 20, the Eighth Air Force launched a massive attack on the Volkswagen plant at Fallersleben, with 137 B-17 bombers delivering 305 tons of bombs, and four more raids followed over the summer. These attacks did not stop production, however, because if the presses to form the fuselage were damaged, these parts could

The original captions for these Planet News photos of rescuers recovering casualties give the date of the incident as June 23, but say nothing about the location. There were more than 70 flying bomb attacks in London that day, but the fact that the Planet News office was in Johnson's Court may suggest that this was the incident in nearby Holborn where a flying bomb crashed at 2.30 a.m.

On August 20, at 11.51 a.m., a V1 crashed on the south-east corner of Berkeley Square, Westminster. The main damage was to the Stewart & Ardern car showroom visible in the right background, in the building known as Morris House. The building was redeveloped in the 1980s in a post-modern style and renamed Lansdowne House.

be supplied from similar presses at another factory in Schönebeck, south of Magdeburg. Additionally, most of the flying bomb's sub-components came from other factories elsewhere and their delivery to Fallersleben had not been affected by the bombing of the factory. Assembly of the FZG 76 continued in Fallersleben until February 1945.

However, air raids on the Fallersleben factory prompted consideration of moving part of V1 production to the underground tunnels at Nordhausen. In August, Galleries 43 to 46, 'Werk II', were assigned to the production of the flying bombs. The plan was to start production with 400 pieces in September, increase it to 1,000 the following month, and reach a steady production of 3,000 by December. Delivery had barely begun when in October a new decree ordered the Mittelwerk to stop production of V1s until further notice, and only 238 were produced in November. The V1 soon regained priority and by December production rose to 1,161, followed by 1,491 in January 1945, 2,275 in February and 831 in March. The Mittelwerk produced a total of more than 7,500 V1s.

LIMA

At 8.07 p.m. on October 6, a V1 scored a hit on No. 32 Old Jewry. A fire broke out at Gresham Street and several officers were wounded at the nearby police headquarters. These clerks carrying their typewriters to another office probably belonged to Freshfield Bruckhaus Deringer which owned the damaged building.

At dawn on October 31, a flying bomb scored a direct hit on the St Marie Hotel in Dale Road, Purley, in the borough of Croydon. The hotel was wrecked, and many of the 29 guests were trapped under the rubble. A contemporary account describes the scene: 'The devastation was such as is all too familiar from a direct hit from a flying bomb, and strewn amongst the rubble were the remains of clothing, furniture, suitcases and a grand piano. Lock-up garages adjoining the hotel were destroyed, and the cars inside crushed by the falling masonry, but a surface shelter was still standing.'

An Alsatian dog specially trained to scent out victims helped rescuers dig through the wreckage, and by midday it was known that 13 people had died in the explosion. Four other people died in hospital, and 31 people were injured.

On June 20, 1944, the Eighth Air Force launched an attack on the Volkswagen Werk at Fallersleben where production of the FZG 76 was concentrated. However, as many sub-components of the flying bomb came from factories elsewhere, assembly continued at Fallersleben and production was not significantly affected. This photo was taken during a new attack by the Eighth Air Force on August 5, 1944. (USNA)

The Fallersleben plant was subjected to two more major air raids by the Eighth Air Force, on June 29 and August 5. Original caption of this photo taken in June 1945 when American officers were examining the ruined factory reads: 'This is all that remained of the famous Nazi Volkswagen factory at Fallersleben when US Army ground forces captured the town. Before the Allied air attacks, the plant was capable of monthly production of 1,800 Kübelwagen, 1,000 amphibious jeeps, 1,200 V1 bombs, 100,000 Teller mines and the repair of 30 Ju 88 aircraft wings'. (USNA)

The air threat caused the transfer of part of the FZG 76 production to the Nordhausen underground factory and from August 1944, the southern section of Tunnel A and the first three cross galleries were allocated to the production of V1s. This is how the southern entrance of Tunnel A appeared in April 1945, with a pile of V1 wire-wound compressed air bottles, and tail sections. (Raphaël Algoet)

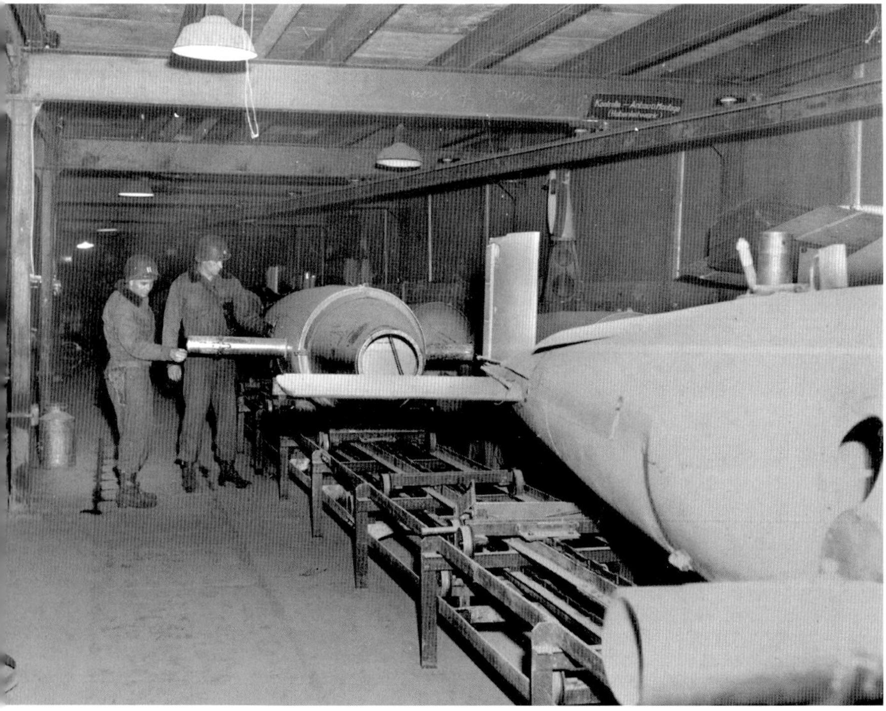

The first missiles left the Mittelwerk assembly line in October, and production reached its peak in February 1945 with 2,275 delivered. The Mittelwerk produced a total of over 7,500 V1s. American officers examine uncompleted V1s on the production line, this was probably Gallery 43 and the panel at top right (Kontrolle - Anbau und Montage - Höhenleitwerk) indicates what was done there: checking the construction and assembly of the altitude control unit. (USNA)

HASTY WITHDRAWAL

In mid-August, due to the threat of the Allied advance, the westernmost units of Flak-Regiment 155 (W), III. Abteilung, had to withdraw from their positions west of the Somme. On August 31, the launch sites in northern France were in turn threatened, and the LXV. Armeekorps z.b.V. then ordered I. Abteilung and II. Abteilung to prepare to withdraw. They were to continue firing V1s until the Allied spearheads were close to reaching the site, with the decision to withdraw left to local commanders. The II. Abteilung was the first to evacuate, then the I. Abteilung launched its last V1s on September 2 before blowing up its sites and retreating to Maria-ter-Heide, north-east of Antwerp.

Oberst Wachtel and his staff withdrew to Maria-ter-Heide on August 31 and to Enschede in the Netherlands on September 4.

On September 3, the British leaders entered Brussels, the Americans liberated Luxembourg on the 10th and reached the Siegfried Line in the Aachen sector on the 12th.

After recovering from the surprise and confusion, the LXV. Armeekorps z.b.V. reorganised in October the men and equipment that had managed to

On the left wing of the Allied armies rushing east after crossing the Seine, the First Canadian Army advanced along the Channel coast in the first days of September and captured abandoned flying bomb launch sites. Was this catapult destroyed by an air attack or was it destroyed by the launch team as they made a hasty retreat just hours before the Canadian leaders arrived?

Sergeant Leo Dubuc, Sergeant Walter Pisz, and Corporal Thomas Guariglia of the Ninth Air Force examine a V1 that crashed somewhere in France. The missing warhead likely separated at the time of the crash, but, as the missile appears to be at an airfield, it is possible that it had already been removed by the squadron's bomb squad when this photo was taken. (USNA)

On September 5, a few days after the liberation, Canadian photographer Harold Aikman took these photos of a Canadian soldier and a French resistance fighter inspecting the wreckage of a V1 near Foucarmont, between Dieppe and Amiens. The missile failed to fly after launch and crashed without exploding. The fuselage had broken apart behind the fuel tank, exposing one of the two compressed air spheres. (LAC)

American soldiers of the VII Corps examine the wreckage of a V1 that came down near Plomion, east of Vervins, on September 2. (USNA)

withdraw and completed its I. and III. Abteilung with four launch batteries and two technical batteries each. The II. Abteilung was reorganised as a Flak rail unit, becoming leichte Flak-Abteilung 1001, as were the two battalions of the short-lived Flak-Regiment 255 (W), becoming leichte Flak-Abteilung 1002 and leichte Flak-Abteilung 1003.

As a deception measure, with resumption of operations, the LXV. Armeekorps z.b.V. was renamed XXX. Armeekorps z.b.V. on October 20.

INTO ACTION, ANTWERP AND LONDON

On October 12, Hitler ordered the firing of V weapons against Antwerp and Brussels. The III. Abteilung opened fire on October 21 from four launch sites in the Eifel region west of the Rhine, and by the end of the month a total of 337 V1s had been launched, 55 against Brussels, the others against Antwerp. Unsurprisingly, 47 of them crashed prematurely, causing havoc in the launch areas and the German population quickly nicknamed them 'Eifelschreck', the terror of the Eifel.

In the last days of October, Flak-Regiment 155 (W) reorganised its forces into three detachments which were to operate from three different operational areas. A new II. Abteilung was created, the I. Abteilung and the III. Abteilung each delivering it one battery, and the three groups were planned to deploy as follows:

- west of the Rhine, in the Eifel, north-east of Wittlich, the III. Abteilung with three batteries,

• east of the Rhine, in the Westerwald, north of Koblenz, the I. Abteilung with three batteries,
• in the Netherlands, in the Deventer area, the II. Abteilung with two batteries.

No need for an army corps to command a single regiment and Ob. West decided to disband the XXX. Armeekorps z.b.V. and establish a division. The 5. Flak-Division (W) was thus set up at Meschede on November 15, with Oberst Walter, the former corps Chief-of-Staff, as division commander.

One of the division's first decisions, on November 18, was to decide that operations from the Westerwald region could not be risked because premature crashes and 'circle runners' would endanger the German civilian population, and it ordered the transfer of the I. Abteilung to the Netherlands to join with the II. Abteilung.

On November 19 at 11.03 a.m., the 10,000th V1 launched since the start of the operation in June was fired against Antwerp by a team under Oberleutnant Roschach from position No. 5 of the 23. Batterie.

On the same day, Heeresgruppe B asked Ob. West to engage the V1 against Liège, an important point of communication at the rear of the American armies advancing towards Aachen, and Ob. West directed the 5. Flak-Division (W) accordingly. Note that aiming for Liège did not require repositioning the catapults, all directed towards Antwerp: the slight course corrections necessary to aim for Liège (or Brussels) were obtained by a corresponding adjustment of the compass. In early December, as the major Ardennes offensive was about to begin, OKW ordered that all batteries should direct their attacks towards Antwerp.

In early December, with the great Ardennes offensive about to begin, the OKW ordered all batteries to direct their attacks towards Antwerp.

On December 6, when more than 2,500 V1s had been launched from sites west of the Rhine, it appeared that nearly 30 percent of them had crashed prematurely. A technical inspection attributed this catastrophic failure rate to a factory defect in the elevator mechanism and a ceasefire was ordered until the defect was repaired. Launch resumed on December 11 once repairs were completed.

In mid-December, the II. Abteilung had completed its deployment in the Netherlands, with the 11. Batterie at Nieuw Heeten, north-east of Deventer, and the 12. Batterie at Laren, south-east of Deventer. The battalion opened fire on Antwerp at 5 a.m. on December 16, the day the Ardennes offensive was launched. As the flying bombs flew almost entirely over enemy-held territory, they were configured to fly very low to evade defences and witnesses later reported having seen V1s flying at an altitude of 100 metres.

On December 20, while the leaders of the 6. Panzerarmee came to a standstill in their attack to reach the Meuse, the OKW authorised the resumption of the attacks against Liège, though Antwerp remained the main target.

The debate on the nature of the V1 weapon then resumed, with Flak-

Antwerp was taken on September 4, but it took three months and an amphibious assault against Walcheren Island to finally open the port and the first convoy entered there on November 28. From October 1944 to March 1945, the Germans maintained the bombardment of the port and for the whole period, the Allies logged 4,248 V1s falling near greater Antwerp. They deployed three anti-aircraft brigades against the V1s, and at their peak the defences of Antwerp had 208 American 90mm guns, 128 British 3.7 guns, and 188 37mm and 40mm guns. The only days of the 175 days of the bombardment when no V1 hit the sector were the six days in December when the 5. Flak-Division had to suspend firing due to defective elevators and March 17, 1945. On January 5, 1945, Signal Corps photographer T/3 Ingledew photographed rescue teams working amidst damage after a V1 hit at around 1 p.m. at the junction of Carnot Straat with Koningind Astridplein (left). (USNA)

Regiment 155 (W) expressing doubts about the effect of the bombings of Antwerp and Liège on the supply and deployment of the Allied armies. Flak-Regiment 155 (W) emphasised that due to its wide distribution, V1s should not be considered as a long-range artillery weapon for attacking military targets, but should be used as a weapon of terror, as they were deployed against London.

However, although German agents or aerial reconnaissance failed to assess its full extent, the V1 bombing of Antwerp effectively limited the port's capacity. In November, SHAEF raised the issue of unloading munitions in the port under incessant attack, and the port authority decided that munitions ships were barred from Antwerp. Except for ammunition intended for the anti-aircraft batteries defending the port, ammunition ships were sent to unload in Cherbourg or Le Havre, respectively 650 and 450 kilometres away.

The III. Gruppe of Kampfgeschwader 3, which had air launched V1s against England in July, was disbanded and what remained was integrated into the

I. Gruppe of Kampfgeschwader 53. The air launches of V1 against England resumed in October with the I. Gruppe and II. Gruppe of Kampfgeschwader 53, and the III. Gruppe joined in November. The groups operated from airfields in northern Germany, like Ahlhorn, Bad Zwischenahn, Varrelbusch, and Vechta.

Difficult weather conditions and severe fuel shortage hampered operations, and at best 20 aircraft could be brought into action in a single night. The British night fighters were chasing the Heinkels and on the night of November 5 to 6, four planes were lost, including 'A1+AM' of the 4. Staffel in which two Ritterkreuz holders were lost, the pilot, Hauptmann Heinz Zöllner, and the observer, Oberfeldwebel Karl Christmann.

Things went from bad to worse in December, when in addition to the losses inflicted by the British night fighters, the II. Gruppe lost 12 planes and their crew during two missions as V1s carried underneath the aircraft inexplicably exploded shortly after take-off. By the end of the year, Kampfgeschwader 53 was worn out and after two light attacks on London in early January, the last air-launched V1 hit the city on January 14.

With the Allied advance threatening to trap them, the launch batteries were directed to withdraw on March 30 and the last V1 missile of the war was launched around 8 a.m. that day, at Antwerp. On April 5, near Almelo, Gunners L.J. Armitage and J. Raffle, Lance-Corporal Don Stover, and Signalman Robert Clarke, of the Royal Canadian Artillery, examined a launching ramp blown by the launch crew before to withdraw. (LAC)

Search parties sent by Operation 'Backfire' in June 1945 to scour northern Germany and recover V2 rockets found a quantity of abandoned V1s along their path. These photos were taken by Major Charles Black, Mechanical Construction Superintendent for the Operation 'Backfire' team. These V1s were destroyed by the Germans when this field depot was abandoned. Note the typical V1 wire-wound compressed air spheres. (Charles Black)

On January 26, the 5. Flak-Division (W) was assigned to Division z.V., a command established in October 1944 under SS-Gruppenführer Hans Kammler to command the A4 rocket launches. The designation 'z.V.' meaning 'zur Vergeltung', derived from the denomination of the so-called 'Vergeltungswaffen'. Kammler realised that further air launches of the V1 were practically impossible due to Allied air superiority and he immediately ordered to halt such operations.

At the beginning of January, in order to shorten the flight route of the missiles, and thus reduce their dispersion at the target, it was decided to install launch ramps as close as possible to the front. The 11. Batterie, II. Abteilung, was thus directed to move its three catapults to the port and industrial area of Rotterdam. The battery opened fire from its new positions on the evening of January 27. Meanwhile, I. Abteilung had completed its move to the Netherlands, in a sector just west of Hengelo and Enschede, and it opened fire on January 25 with its three batteries.

At the end of the month, the Allied advance threatened to trap the three batteries of the III. Abteilung in the Eifel region and Kammler ordered them to withdraw to positions east of the Rhine. The 21. Batterie was the last to withdraw after launching the last V1s from the Eifel sector on February 5, and the 22. Batterie was the first to reopen fire from new launch sites at Schönenberg, north-east of Bonn.

The new longer-range version of the Fi 103, model F-1, made it possible to fire against London from the Netherlands. Kammler ordered the Flak-Regiment 155 (W) on February 5 to build launch ramps south of The Hague to

The compressed air spheres cell of this flying bomb was blown apart, probably a destruction by the depot crew before withdrawing. The six-screw panel was the access to the compressed air spheres. On the undamaged fuel tank, the hole in the side was for the tubular wing span passing through, and on the top right was the suspension lug, fuel cap, and connecting bolt for the warhead. (Charles Black)

target London at a distance of 370 kilometres. The operation was codenamed 'Pappdeckel'.

On March 9, the 12th Battery of II. Abteilung thus opened fire on London with extended-range flying bombs, from launch sites south of The Hague. However, production of the F-1 variant was insufficient and after an opening day with the launch of 49 V1s, the rate of fire had to be reduced as there were not enough missiles available. Kammler promised that the delivery of the F-1 model would improve soon and ordered 155. Flak-Regiment (W) to make operation against London a priority.

The last two V1s to reach London exploded at 7.54 a.m. and 7.55 a.m. on March 28, at Chislehurst and Waltham Holy Cross respectively. The last V1 to fall in England was shot down by anti-aircraft fire near Sittingbourne in Kent at 9.59 a.m. on March 29.

As the Allied advance threatened to trap the launch batteries, on March 30 Oberst Wachtel directed the retreat of all of them toward areas near Bremen. On the last day of operation, March 30, 18 missiles were launched against Antwerp, with the last V1 missile of the war being launched by the 12. Batterie at around 8 a.m. that day.

On May 4, the V1 launch units surrendered to the British near Bad Segesberg, north of Hamburg.

ASSESSMENT

In the absence of reliable data, the number of FZG 76 flying bombs produced can only be approximated and the following figures should be taken as the best estimation from available data. According to statements later made by Speer, a total of 30,257 flying bombs were produced in 1944 and 1945. The number of pre-productions FZG 76s produced for tests and trials from September to December 1943 projected between 2,300 to 2,500. The total production of the FZG 76 flying bomb was thus between 32,600 to 32,800.

The lack of data does not allow an overview of the production of each of the factories concerned, but the Volkswagen plant in Fallersleben accounted for around two thirds of the FZG 76s produced.

In the first phase of the V1 campaign, against England, the four battalions of Flak-Regiment 155 (W) had launched 8,617 flying bombs. In the second phase of the campaign, targeting London and Antwerp from sites in Germany and the Netherlands, the three remaining battalions had launched 12,263 flying bombs by the end of the war. Additionally, Heinkel He 111 bombers had launched some 1,600 V1s against targets in England. The total number of V1s launched into action amounts to some 22,500.

The distribution of this total between the different targets is as follows: London, 10,279; Antwerp, 8,696; Liege, 3,141; Brussels, 151; Southampton, 143; Manchester, 50; and Gloucester, 20.

For the period between June 1944 and March 1945, 5,822 flying bombs hit English soil, of which 2,419 hit Greater London. The defence forces destroyed 3,957 flying bombs, about 1,847 by the fighters, 1,878 by the anti-aircraft guns and 232 by the barrage balloons.

Between September 1944 and March 1945, 2,448 flying bombs hit Antwerp and its suburbs. During the same period Liège and Brussels were struck 1,768 times by V1s and V2s, the majority of these hitting Liège. With less than 30 V2s launched against Liège, it appears that almost all these impacts were V1s. In Belgium, the anti-aircraft guns shot down 2,183 V1s, most of these in the Antwerp sector.

The V1 campaign against England forced the Allies first to divert significant bomber forces from other targets (in July and August 1944, more than a quarter of the Allied bombing effort was directed against V-weapons sites) then to spend massively on defensive measures. In the second period of the campaign, the bombardment of Antwerp severely limited the port's capacity, particularly in terms of munitions.

Simple to produce and using inexpensive materials, the V1 flying bomb proved to be, despite its inherent inaccuracy, a cost-effective weapon. However, despite all the fear and devastation they caused, the V1s could not make a difference in an already lost war.

In the postwar years, the V1s sparked a proliferation of unmanned flying bombs that evolved into elaborate cruise missiles that still feature prominently on battlefields today.

V2, THE FIRST BALLISTIC MISSILE

BEFORE BOMBER COMMAND'S massive attack on Peenemünde on the night of August 17-18, the A4 production plan received its first blow on June 20 when 60 Lancasters of Bomber Command targeting radar production at Friedrichshafen destroyed the A4 production line at the Zeppelin factory (which had by then produced only a few tanks and fuselage sections). A third blow was on August 13, when 60 B-24s of the Ninth Air Force, which were to bomb the Wiener Neustädter Flugzeugwerk (WNF) aircraft factory producing Messerschmitt Bf 109s, seriously damaged the A4 production line under construction at nearby Rax-Werk. The Rax-Werk was again bombed in October and November, and the plan to produce A4 rockets there was abandoned and the machines were relocated.

In a meeting with Hitler on August 19, Speer noted that 'the Führer orders that every effort be made to again speed up the construction of suitable

Dornberger and von Braun take pleasure in reading telegrams of congratulations on their award of the Knight's Cross of the War Merit Cross, which they are wearing in this photo taken at the officers' mess in Peenemünde. They were awarded on October 28, 1944.

The rocket research centre attracted a steady stream of visits from important figures of the Third Reich to Peenemünde. Dornberger (right) shows the test stand of the A4 rocket – the future V2 – to Generalfeldmarschall Wilhelm Keitel and Generaloberst Friedrich Fromm. (DM)

Involved in the bomb plot against Hitler on July 20, 1944, Fromm was dismissed from office (he was tried and ultimately shot in March 1945), after which Reichsführer-SS Heinrich Himmler was appointed to replace him as head of the army equipment and commander of the replacement training army. Here, Dornberger (centre) greets Himmler and a group of SS officers in Peenemünde. This photo was taken in December 1942. (BA)

These A4 rockets pictured at the Pilot Production Plant in Peenemünde Süd in mid-1943 feature different camouflage schemes that were under study at the time: the two rockets in front show two versions of the Gezackt (ragged) scheme, while the one behind shows the Geflammt (wavy) pattern. All three schemes used the same three colours, olive green, earth grey and cream white. (DM)

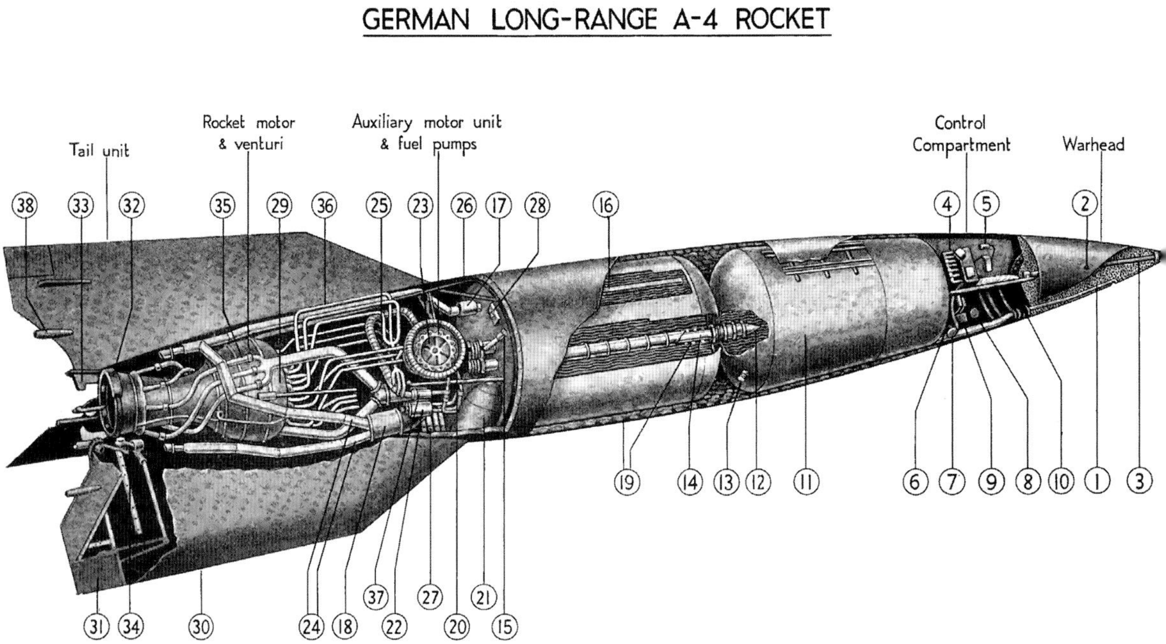

This plan from volume 3 of the Operation 'Backfire' report shows the architecture of the extremely complex A4 rocket. It was made up of 20,000 different components. 1: Alcohol tank pressurising pipe. 2: Slinging point. 3: Central exploder tube. 4: Main distribution box and ground control plug. 5: Alternator and regulator. 6: Time switch. 7: Alcohol fuelling inlet. 8: Air pressure gauge and hand control cock. 9: Automatic pilot. 10: Control amplifier. 11: Alcohol tank. 12: Outlet valve. 13: Drainage valve. 14: Alcohol delivery pipe. 15: Oxygen fuelling inlet. 16: Stack pipe. 17: Oxygen tank vent valve. 18: Heat exchanger unit. 19: Glass wool. 20: Turbine. 21: Hydrogen peroxide tank. 22: Sodium permanganate tank. 23: Oxygen and alcohol pumps. 24: Turbine exhausts. 25: Oxygen main valve. 26: Braced steel frame. 27: Compressed air bottles. 28: Distribution box. 29: Combustion chamber. 30: Stabilising fin. 31: Outer rudder. 32: Thrust ring. 33: Carbon rudder. 34: Servo motor. 35: Alcohol feed pipes. 36: Oxygen feed pipes. 37: Auxiliary combustion chamber. 38: Aerial supports.

production plants, as well as the production of the A4, in cooperation with the Reichsführer-SS, with extensive use of concentration camp inmates'. Immediately, on the next day, Himmler summoned Speer and Saur to his headquarters in East Prussia. Referring to Hitler's instruction which 'you have heard directly from him', he insisted that he expected them to contribute fully. He asked Speer to receive, 'within the next few days', SS-Brigadeführer Dr.Ing. Hans Kammler to whom he had entrusted the execution of the plan.

Kammler met with Speer on August 26 and proposed moving main production of the A4 to an underground factory in the Kohnstein limestone hill at Niedersachswerfen in the Harz mountains. There, from the mid-1930s, the state-owned company Wifo used tunnels in the hill to store oil, gasoline, and chemicals.

The Wifo was ordered to immediately evacuate the complex and a week after the meeting with Speer, on Kammler's orders, the first inmates were moved from the Buchenwald concentration camp to Niedersachswerfen to provide labour for construction of the new factory. This subcamp of

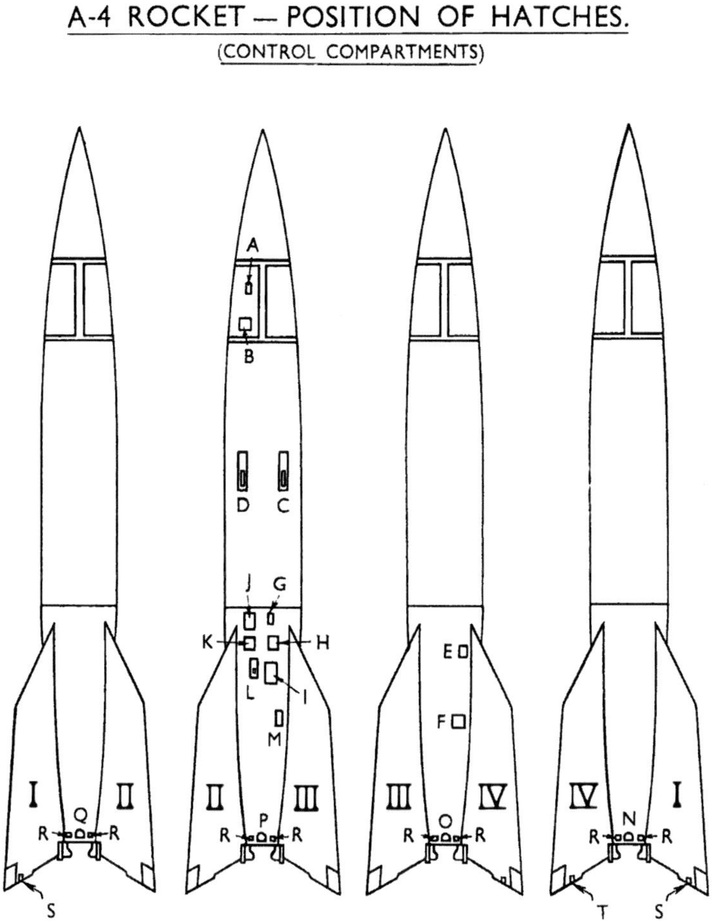

Another plan from the Operation 'Backfire' report showing the various technical hatches in the rocket body and, in the nose, the four control compartments. A: Hatch for distribution box safety switch. B: Spring hatch for Stotz plugs. C: Hatch for alcohol drainage. D: Hatch for leads for alcohol outlet valve. E: Hatch for turbine centrifugal switch. F: Hatch for alcohol main valve. G: Hatch for hydrogen peroxide fuelling inlet. H: Hatch for pressure reducing valve and auxiliary motor unit. I: Hatch for hydrogen peroxide drainage and vent. J: Hatch for oxygen fuelling inlet. K: Hatch for sodium permanganate fuelling inlet. L: Hatch for sodium permanganate vent. M: Hatch for sodium permanganate drainage. N: Cowling for oxygen topping up valve. O: Turbine exhaust cowling. P: Cowling for five-way coupling. Q: Cowling for oxygen tank overflow and turbine exhaust. R: Hatches for servo potentiometers. S: Take-off switch. T: Socket for emergency fuel cut-off lead. The control compartments were identified by the number of the corresponding fin. Compartment I: batteries. Compartment II: electrical distribution box. Compartment III: gyroscopes and control amplifiers. Compartment IV: Alcohol tank air bottles.

Buchenwald was named Arbeitslager 'Dora'. Over the next few weeks, more and more prisoners were brought in on almost daily transports from Buchenwald, and more than 3,000 inmates worked at Kohnstein by the end of September. This number rose to 6,800 by the end of October and to more than 10,500 by the end of the year, mostly Russians, Poles, and French.

Their first task was to remove the Wifo storage tanks and other equipment and start blasting rock to extend the second tunnel all the way through the mountain (the first tunnel was already completed). Most of the work was done manually, even pieces of rocks blasted by the explosive were removed by hand. Slave workers worked 12-hour shifts, six days a week, brutally pressed into work by SS guards.

At first, the inmates slept in a gallery, on straw on bare rock, until wooden bunks four levels high were built in one gallery. Oil barrels cut in half with boards on them served as toilet. Blasting went on day and night, filling the sleeping gallery with blinding and suffocating dust. As food, the slaves only received coffee and bread in the morning, occasionally with a slice of sausage

View of the Mittelbau-Dora concentration camp, photo taken in April 1945 by Raphaël Algoet, official Belgian photographer. This is a view of the western part of the camp, looking south, with the town of Nordhausen in the distance. In the centre of the photo is barracks 112, on the right is barracks 110, and the path seen on the left of the photo leads to barracks 111. (Raphaël Algoet)

When the Wifo evacuated the complex in August 1943, Tunnel B ran all the way through the mountain, but Tunnel A did not. The last 300 metres of Tunnel A were dug, under terrible conditions and hardships, by slave workers during the last months of 1943. They were then housed in four galleries, Galleries 43 to 46, equipped with rows of bunk beds. Noise, dust and noxious gases from explosions and trains carrying blasted rocks away worsened the already inhumane health situation of the slave workers. Tunnel A emerged to the south in January 1944. (Walter Frentz)

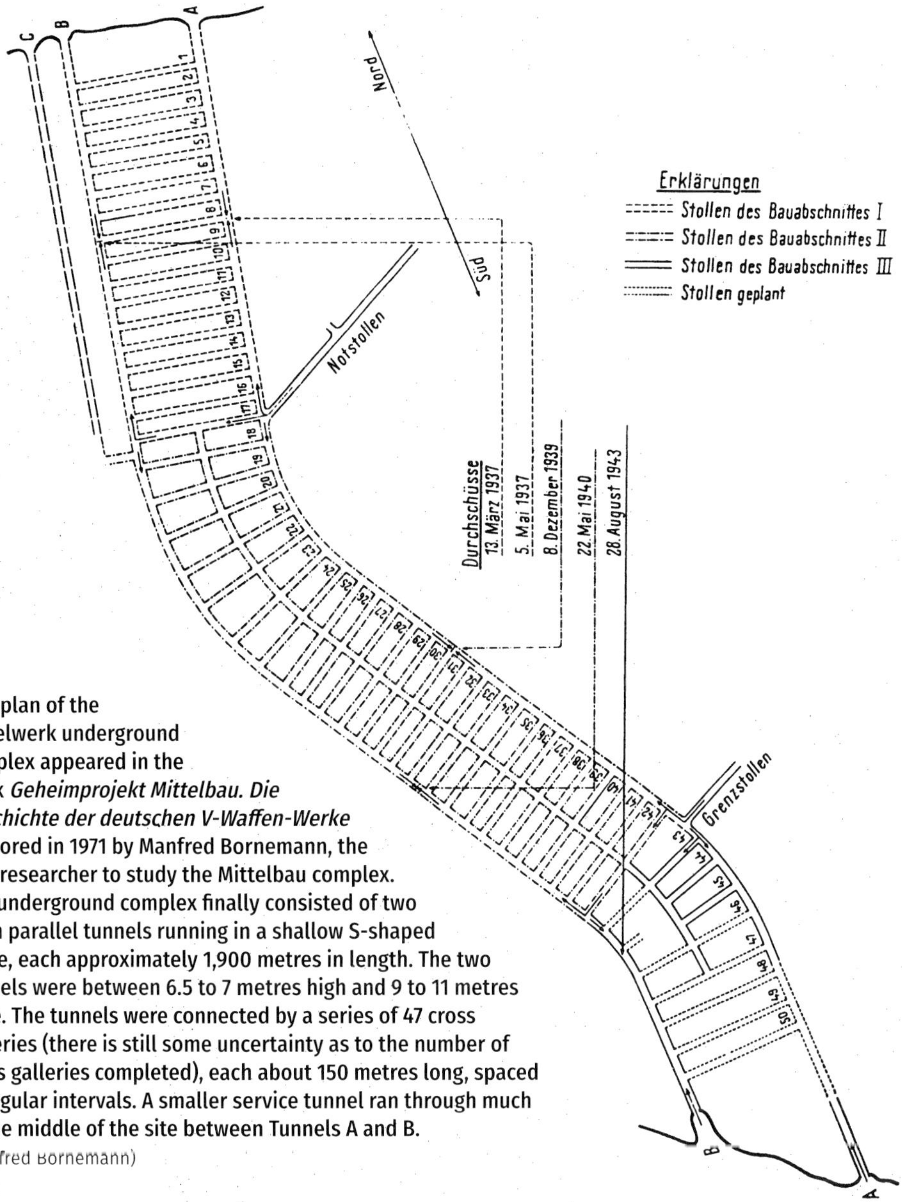

This plan of the Mittelwerk underground complex appeared in the book *Geheimprojekt Mittelbau. Die Geschichte der deutschen V-Waffen-Werke* authored in 1971 by Manfred Bornemann, the first researcher to study the Mittelbau complex. The underground complex finally consisted of two main parallel tunnels running in a shallow S-shaped curve, each approximately 1,900 metres in length. The two tunnels were between 6.5 to 7 metres high and 9 to 11 metres wide. The tunnels were connected by a series of 47 cross galleries (there is still some uncertainty as to the number of cross galleries completed), each about 150 metres long, spaced at regular intervals. A smaller service tunnel ran through much of the middle of the site between Tunnels A and B. (Manfred Bornemann)

or margarine, and a thin soup in the afternoon and evening. It was hell on earth, they were dying of hunger, thirst, cold and overwork and by the end of winter 3,000 of them were dead.

On September 1, the appointed Technical Director, Albin Sawatzki, opened his offices in a cabin next to the tunnel entrance. Arthur Rudolph and ten engineers then arrived from Peenemünde and the transformation of the tunnels for the production of A4 rockets began. Machine tools were brought in, some from previously bombed factories.

On September 24, the Mittelwerk GmbH was founded to manage the underground factory. It was technically a private limited liability company (GmbH), but it was owned by the government. The name Mittelwerk (Middle Work) referred to the location of the works in Mitteldeutschland.

The Mittelbau-Dora Memorial staff identified this photo as the northern entrance to Tunnel B. Today, this entrance has completely disappeared under the tons of rubble dumped there by the gypsum quarry. The situation is the same at the entrance to Tunnel A about 200 metres to the east. (Raphaël Algoet)

On October 19, General Emil Leeb, head of the Heereswaffenamt, signed an order for the production of 12,000 A4 rockets at the Mittelwerk, with an estimated price of 40,000 Reichsmarks per rocket. A new production program was put in place, with planned production of 200 rockets in December, 300 in January 1944, 600 in February and 900 in March.

On December 10, Speer came to Nordhausen with some of his colleagues to inspect the complex together with Kammler and Degenkolb. They saw the terrible conditions in the tunnels and the corpses lying on the ground, and some members of Speer's team were reportedly shocked. Speer was

The V2 production line was installed in Tunnel B, running from north to south. The rocket being built moved along the tunnel from north to south, and the southern exit was the way out of the factory for the completed rockets. The first three rockets rolled off the assembly line on January 1, 1944. This is the south entrance to Tunnel B as it appeared to Signal Corps photographers in April 1945. (USNA)

The southern entrance to Tunnel A as it appeared to Captain Georges Phillips in May or June 1945. He was an officer in the 5th Armored Division which took over the Nordhausen region at the end of April. He privately took remarkable photos of the underground Mittelwerk factory. (Georges Phillips)

Detainees and German workers worked together on the assembly line, about two prisoners to one German worker. In June 1944, 2,500 Germans and 5,000 forced workers worked at the factory. This photo of a team of German workers arriving at Tunnel B was taken by Hanns Hubmann, a journalist for the propaganda magazine *Signal*, who was commissioned by the OKW in 1944 to take photos of the Mittelwerk production plant. (Hanns Hubmann)

Charles Sadron, a French inmate, later described how they transported the oxygen and alcohol tanks from the freight trains parked in front of the entrance to Tunnel A to the storage gallery: 'Three of us stood on either side, spread out along the length of the cylinder. Each man on the left side reached out with his right hand and took hold of the left hand of the man facing him on the other side. The load lay on these three pairs of extended arms. And off we went. In the beginning, it worked, but very soon, it became unbearable. The sweat made our hands slippery. Our shoulders were aching and the hearts of all of us undernourished men were beating fast. There was no question of slowing down. One of the men in front tripped and dropped to his knees. The others continued holding up the enormous load, which gradually slipped and fell, making a huge racket. An SS was there in a second, laying into the man with kicks and blows from his club as he stood up slowly and shakily, with the look of torture victim on his face.' The liquid oxygen tanks seen here were stored in Gallery 25 or 26.

not too moved by the misery of the enslaved workers, and a week later he wrote to Kammler, congratulating him on his success 'in transforming the underground facility . . . from its raw condition two months ago into a factory . . . I take this opportunity to express my appreciation for this truly unique achievement . . . '

Construction of barracks had begun near the southern entrance to the tunnels, but it was not until January 1944 that the first prisoners moved into this surface camp; many had to sleep in the tunnels until May.

In January 1944, the number of prisoners at Arbeitslager 'Dora' stood at 12,000. The most educated and technically skilled prisoners, mainly from Western Europe, were selected to work in the Mittelwerk factory, while the others were sent to the more demanding outdoor, transport, and construction Kommandos.

At the end of the year, production began at Mittelwerk, with the first three rockets rolling off the assembly line in Tunnel B on January 1, 1944. The first

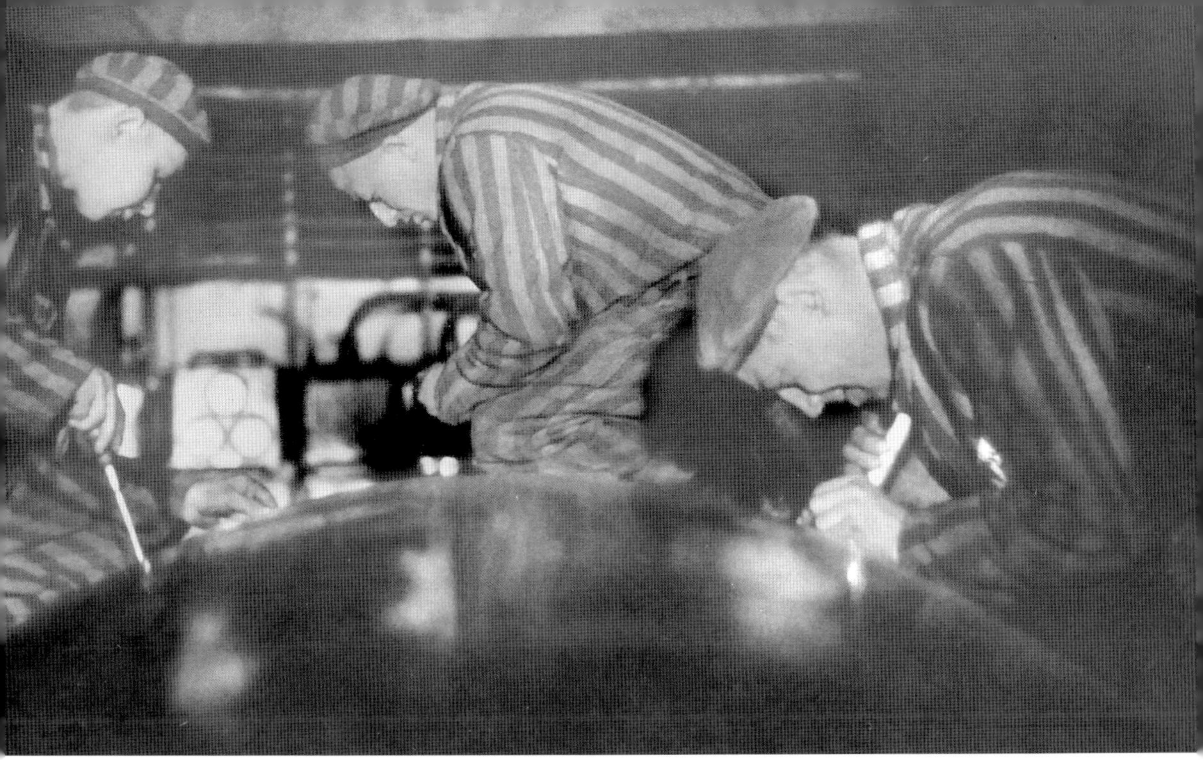

Research has shown that of the 60,000 inmates who passed through the Mittelbau-Dora camps during the whole period of activity, at least 20,000 died there. Historians have pointed out that the Mittelwerk's production lines employed only a small part of the Mittelbau-Dora inmates: of the approximately 40,000 prisoners in the complex in March 1945, of whom 16,000 were in the main camp, less than 6,000 at the main camp were employed in the Mittelwerk production lines, as well as a few from some smaller sub-camps. This photo shows inmates working at the half-sections that composed the central part of the rocket body. (Walter Frentz)

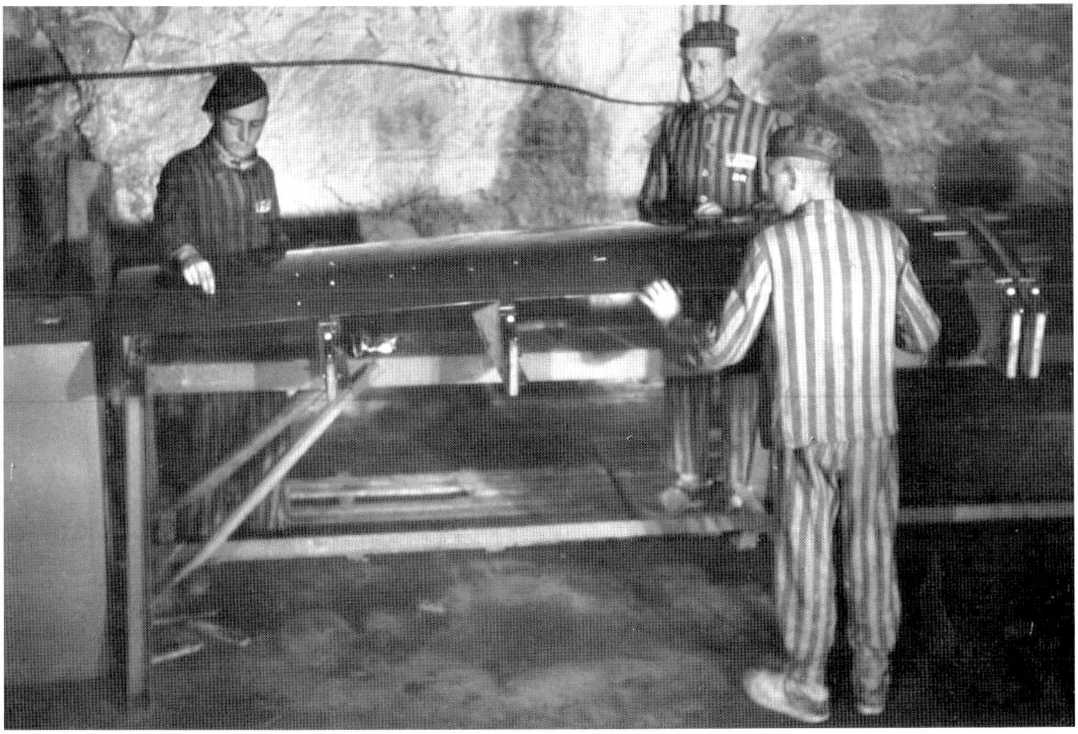

The rocket production line ran from north to south along Tunnel B. Another genuine photo, of slave workers working on the central part of the rocket. A Belgian inmate later recalled how one hundred very young Hungarian Jews were employed in this sector to pad the half-shells with glass wool in the summer of 1944, before the last of them were sent to Auschwitz to be gassed there. (Walter Frentz)

rockets produced were delivered without electrical equipment and the missiles were transported by train to the Demag factory in Falkensee, west of Berlin, where the electrical equipment was completed. A special dust-free workshop was built in one of the underground galleries and from May the rockets were delivered with installed wiring.

With the slave workers now housed outside the tunnels and the camp's facilities gradually improving, life had become less horrible by the spring of 1944, although the hard work and ruthless brutality of the SS kept the death toll high.

When completed, the central part of the rocket was over six metres long and, in a vertical position, it almost touched the ceiling of the gallery.

Subcomponents produced in distant factories, such as the combustion chambers produced by Linke-Hofman-Werke AG or the turbopump and steam unit produced by Wumag Abteilung Maschinenbau, were delivered to the Mittelwerk by railway trains. They were stored and assembled in cross galleries before being delivered to the main assembly line in Tunnel B. This is Gallery 29, where the propulsion units were assembled.

Metal-press workshops were in Gallery 32 and 33 and the assembly of the rocket tail units was done in Gallery 37 where welding jigs made it possible to precisely fit the fins to the fuselage. When completed, the tail unit stood four metres high. This shot may have been taken in Gallery 35 where completed tail units were stored.

The GIs discovering the underground factory reported that the assembly line was as if the work crews had gone out to lunch and would return soon. This production board as of March 22, 1945, was photographed in Tunnel B in April 1945. (Raphaël Algoet)

In mid-1944, the Ministry of Armaments and War Production sent a photographer to document V2 production at the Mittelwerk. The propaganda photographs were intended to show the high-tech factory producing rockets and the Mittelwerk staff had prepared the workshop and workers for the photographer. Model work crews were to be seen at work and inmates pictured on assembly lines were all clean shaven, with clean striped uniforms and caps, and shoes or clogs. The conditions in which the detainees lived and worked were carefully hidden and no photos were taken at the 'Dora' concentration camp. Here the inmates installed and wired the servo motors in the rear unit. (Walter Frentz)

These inmates assembled electrical control and regulation equipment in the rocket's control compartments. The control compartments were located at the top of the rocket, immediately aft of the warhead. It was a truncated cone divided into four equal sections by radial sheets of plywood. (Walter Frentz)

An idealised image of a prisoner and three Germans working together to test a rocket. One wonders what Speer, who knew the barbaric realities of forced labour, expected from these cynical photos. Propaganda photos for the attention of the German people, or document testifying for the history a 'unique achievement' of the Nazi regime? (Walter Frentz)

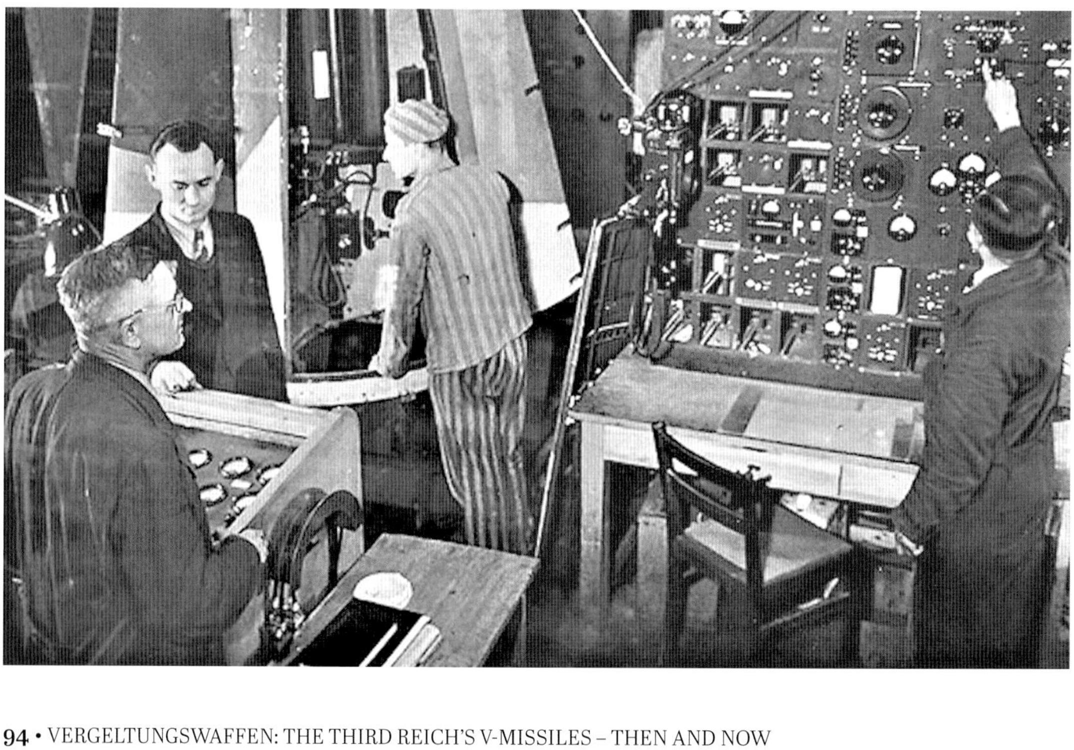

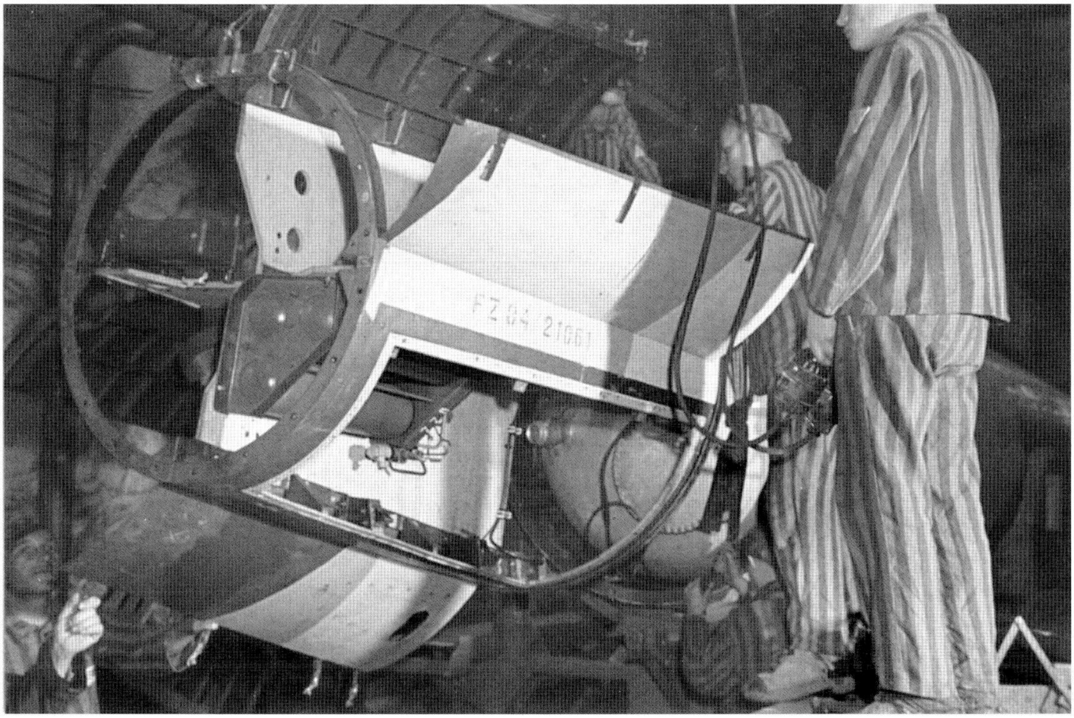

On the main assembly line, inmates prepared the control compartment before bolting it to the top of the rocket. On the right, the top of the alcohol tank. The compartment at the bottom of this photo is Compartment IV, with the three air bottles which, in flight, pressurised the alcohol tank, and above it is Compartment I. (Walter Frentz)

At the end of the assembly line in Tunnel B, this rocket was almost finished, with only the tail remaining to be installed. This photo was taken after the Americans occupied the underground factory in April 1945. (USNA)

At the end of the assembly line, the completed rocket would reach Gallery 41 where a crane would lift it into a vertical position for final testing. Gallery 41 had a deepened floor giving it a ceiling height of 15 metres, the only place in the tunnels and galleries high enough to accommodate the 14-metre-high missile. (Walter Frentz)

LAUNCH BUNKERS

Convinced that due to the complexity of the A4 rocket, the Peenemünde scientists believed that only qualified technicians working in a large support structure could launch them successfully. They therefore campaigned in favour of the construction of large bunkers from which the rockets could be prepared and launched. On the other hand, many, like Dornberger and his staff, were convinced that these large bunkers would be bombed by the

Allies and rendered unusable before they were even completed. Instead, they argued for deploying mobile batteries that would move the rockets on special trailers and launch them from camouflaged positions hidden in forests.

In November, Hitler approved the construction of massive storage and launch bunkers in northern France to operate the A4 rockets, and Generalfeldmarschall Gerd von Rundstedt, C-in-C West, was soon tasked with preparing the 'long-range combat against England' by selecting launch sites and securing their construction.

The first site was quickly chosen and work began in March 1943 for the construction of KNW, Kraftwerk Nordwest (Power Station Northwest) at Watten, north of Saint-Omer. The construction of a second bunker, RLW, Reservelager West (Reserve Store West) at Sottevast, south of Cherbourg, was ordered in June and the construction of the third, Ölkeller Cherbourg (Oil Cellar Cherbourg) at Hainneville, just south of Cherbourg, in July.

In addition, it was decided to build 30 to 50 field sites, as Dornberger envisioned. These consisted of a concrete platform sunk into a track, with

Work began in March 1943 for the construction of the KNW, Kraftwerk Nordwest, in Watten, north of Saint-Omer. The bunker was designed to launch 36 rockets per day. It was to have a liquid oxygen production facility and store enough rockets and fuel for three days of launch operations. The Bomber Command launched two attacks on the Watten bunker with Tallboy bombs, 17 bombs being dropped on June 19, and 15 on July 25. Only one Tallboy hit the bunker, hitting on the northern lip of the roof, but causing hardly any damage to the structure. The Germans began to repair the damage as can be seen (left in this photo) on this photograph taken by the Canadians after their capture of the site on September 6, 1944.

On August 27, 187 B-17s of the Eighth Air Force attacked the site with devastating effect, and 20 more raids followed through August. This low-level reconnaissance photo shows that the bunker itself did not suffer as much damage, but that the surrounding area was devastated, making approaches impassable.

trenches dug on either side to protect vehicles and men from air attacks.

Dornberger's warnings were soon confirmed when 187 B-17s of the Eighth Air Force attacked the Watten site on August 27. The raid was particularly destructive in the northern part of the bunker where the concrete had just been poured. Dornberger later wrote that the site was 'a desolate heap of concrete, steel, props and planks. The concrete hardened. After a few days, the bunker was beyond saving. All we could do was roof in a part and use it for other work.'

As an alternative, the Germans then decided to construct another bunker

This is how the damage to the roof on the southern side of the bunker appeared to *After the Battle* in 1974.

Construction of a second massive storage and launch bunker to operate the A4 rockets, RLW, began in October 1943 at Sottevast, south of Cherbourg. Reconnaissance missions were sent to study the site, this photo was taken on December 2. Remarkably, this aerial shot from *After the Battle* in 1974 perfectly matches the reconnaissance photo from December 1943.

The Sottevast site was bombed in February and April 1944, but during both attacks, thick cloud cover prevented most of the bombers from dropping their bombs. Three more raids hit the site in the first days of May and work was halted. American troops seized Sottevast on June 22. (USNA)

in the hillside overlooking a quarry at Wizernes, just south of Saint-Omer. SNW, Schotterwerk Nordwest (Gravel Work Northwest), was to comprise a colossal concrete dome, 71 metres in diameter and five metres thick, and a series of tunnels and galleries would be excavated beneath the dome and into the hillside.

The Allies repeatedly attacked the bunker sites in July and August, particularly Watten and Wizernes which suffered 20 and 15 air attacks respectively, including several raids with Tallboy earthquake bombs and one 'Aphrodite' attack with remote-controlled B-17 drones packed with explosives.

The rail and road network around the bunkers being totally ruined, work could no longer continue and on July 3, Ob. West ordered a halt in construction of the heavy bunker sites.

General Eisenhower visited Sottevast on July 6 with General Bradley, the commander of the First US Army, as part of his Independence Day tour of the Normandy front. (USNA)

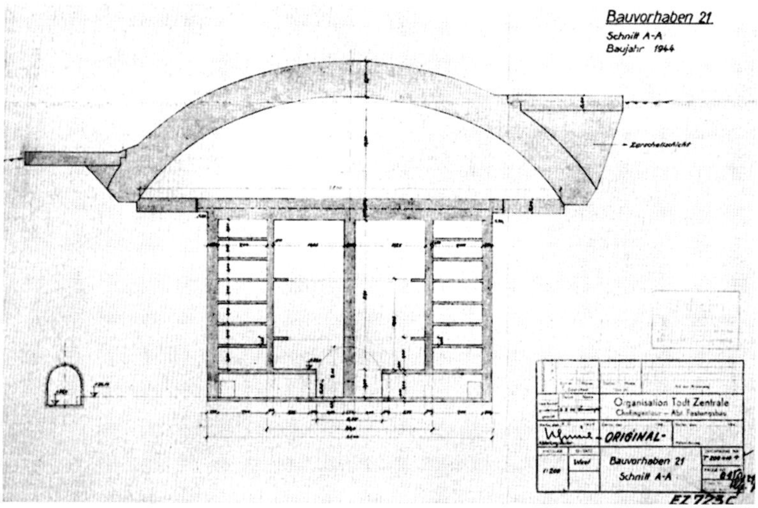

After Allied bombing interrupted construction of the Watten bunker in August 1943, the Germans turned to the Wizernes quarry as an alternative prospect for A4 rocket operations. The plan was to build a colossal concrete dome, 71 metres in diameter and 5 metres thick, on the hillside overlooking the quarry, and a series of connecting tunnels and galleries would be dug beneath the dome and into the hill. This plan of the octagonal central part of the bunker bears the stamp of Werner Flos, Chief Engineer at the Organisation Todt in Berlin. The chamber would have a diameter of 41 metres and the height under the dome would be 24 metres.

Beginning in March 1944, the Eighth Air Force launched five raids against the Wizernes site, with B-17s and B-24s dropping 680 tons of bombs. The bunker suffered no damage, but, as this photo taken on April 23 by 542 Squadron shows, the entire area was cratered, the railway lines and road access were all disrupted.

Nine more raids were to hit Wizernes, first five attacks by the Eighth Air Force, then Bomber Command took over with a first raid on June 24 by 16 Lancasters of 617 Squadron and their Tallboy bombs. Bomber Command launched four further attacks with Lancaster, Halifax and Mosquito bombers between June 27 and July 20, dropping 1,800 tons of bombs, as well as a further raid by 617 Squadron dropping 16 Tallboy bombs. This photo was taken from a Lancaster of 617 Squadron, just after the Tallboy bomb was dropped during the attack on June 24. The town of Wizernes appears at the bottom right of the photo and the target of this bomb, the quarry, is just to the right out of the photo. This photo shows that the Lancasters were flying from west to east to drop their bombs.

On July 10, a Mosquito Mark XVI from the 540 Squadron took off at 11.40 a.m. from RAF Benson, Oxfordshire. Flight Lieutenant King was the pilot, Flight Sergeant Bowden the navigator. Their mission: 'low level recce of rocket site at Wizernes'.

The crew reported: 'Visibility was poor but we sighted Boulogne and turned in at Hardelot, flying at 20 to 50 feet. Just before estimated time of arrival at Wizernes we plotted position over little village of Lumbres, we circled, and then proceeded to Wizernes, nipping over the railway line with the camera nose oblique, we then continued on to the rocket site. We were at 2,850 revolutions, at +12 (loud), which really made the froggy workmen duck and run. One guy took a header into a hedge. After covering the target, we set course for Bradwell, staying on the deck until we were over the Channel, and then up to 1,500 feet. Landed at base 13:30.'

The Mosquito camera brought back this amazing low view of the concrete dome. A Tallboy bomb exploded just under the dome, another exploded at the mouth of a tunnel, and three next to the tunnels. The hillside collapsed, undermining the dome.

TOWARDS OPERATIONAL DEPLOYMENT

In August 1944, the A4 Special Committee established by Speer in his Ministry of Armaments and War Production became Sonderausschuss V-Waffen, often referred as Sonderausschuss z.b.V., a cover name.

In an effort to maintain Army control over the rocket program, on September 4, Generaloberst Fromm appointed Dornberger as his direct subordinate with the title of Beauftragter zur besonderen Verwendung Heer or B.z.b.V. Heer (Army Commissioner for Special Tasks). Dornberger thus had control over the development of the A4 rocket, the recruitment and training of the future rocket batteries, as well as the establishment of the logistics supply system for operational units. On October 4, he received command of Arko 191 (Artillerie-Kommandeur), which would put him in

Training at Blizna. Here, a crane lifts the warhead container and the rocket on the Vidalwagen is man-handled forward to face the warhead, then the securing studs are inserted and tightened. (Walter Frentz)

charge of the future tactical deployment of the rocket. In December, the adjective Höhere (Higher) was added to the command, making Dornberger Harko 191.

However, Generalfeldmarschall von Rundstedt, C-in-C West, wanted to have command of the military deployment of the new long-range weapons and, so that field command would not be given to Dornberger, he proposed the creation of a special interservice corps under his authority. He soon succeeded and the LXV. Armeekorps z.b.V. was created on December 1 to command 'preparation and waging of the long-range fight against England with all special weapons.' The corps had command of the Flak-Regiment 155 (W) which was soon to launch the FZG 76 flying bombs. It was also to control the batteries which were to launch the A4 rockets when operational.

A first rocket battery, the Lehr- und Versuchsbatterie 444 (Training and Experimental Battery 444) was created in July 1943 and two launch battalions

At the transshipment point, the technical team practiced hoisting a rocket from the Vidalwagen with the Strabo crane. The vehicle pulling the Vidalwagen was a Hanomag SS-100 tractor. (Walter Frentz)

began to assemble in the autumn: Artillerie-Abteilung 836 in September and Artillerie-Abteilung 485 in November. Each was to have three launch batteries and three supply columns.

To train the launch troops, a Fernraketen-Schule (Long Range Rocket School) was established in Köslin, on the Pomeranian coast, 150 kilometres east of Peenemünde. The Fernraketen-Schule provided two different training courses: Course A was intended to train the officers and men who needed technical qualifications, and Course B was intended to train men who did not need technical knowledge to do their job. Very strict secrecy measures surrounded the training.

In November 1943, a new testing range was established in Blizna, south-eastern Poland, at SS-Truppenübungsplatz Heidelager, an SS training area with a nearby concentration camp. The SS had 2,000 concentration camp inmates build the secret facility, then 400 men from the Army under Oberst Gerhard Stegmaier took control of the testing range.

After the transfer of the tests to Blizna, only the development remained in Peenemünde. Buildings and workshops were rebuilt in the ruins of the destroyed buildings, with elaborate camouflage measures giving the appearance of destroyed buildings.

Although launch tests showed that the rocket was far from fully developed, production was underway: 24 rockets were produced at Peenemünde in December, and 50 in January while the first 56 rockets were produced at Mittelwerk. Production at Mittelwerk increased rapidly and figures for February, March and April were 86, 170 and 253, while production at Peenemünde was 50, 40, 20 respectively.

The A4 rocket, a machine of great technical complexity, at the cutting edge of technologies of the time, was rushed into production while still plagued by technical problems. Consequently, when the Lehr- und Versuchsbatterie

At the transloading point, the rockets were taken over by the Launching Troop. Cameraman Walter Frentz filmed them practicing receiving the rocket on the Meillerwagen and securing it in the clamps. (Walter Frentz)

One rocket had just been fired when this photo was taken at Blizna, and the smoke trail from another appears at upper left. The two rockets in the foreground were painted in the so-called Geflammt (wavy) camouflage in three colours. Note that the fabric tail cover was also camouflaged in this same wavy pattern. (Walter Frentz)

444 began test launches at Heidelager (three rockets were launched in November and December, 11 in January and February 1944, 11 in March and 30 in April), the results were very disappointing. There were numerous premature engine cut-offs and 60 percent of rockets broke up before reaching the target area.

The explanation for this is simply that the quality of the first rockets produced at Mittelwerk was poor, with leaks, cracks, ill-fitting parts and incorrect connections. How could it be otherwise when two-thirds of the workforce on the assembly line were slave workers forced to labour six days a week on two 12-hour shifts and suffering from hunger, cold and the constant threat of violence. In an effort to obtain better quality work, the Mittelwerk instituted a bonus system, through which vouchers could be earned for use in the camp canteen, and provided shoes and other items to the assembly-line workers.

Experts sent from Peenemünde to investigate the reasons for the failure of the rockets found numerous instances of sabotage.

Measures to improve quality were taken, technical simplifications were progressively introduced. Anti-sabotage measures were strengthened, and informants were planted among the prisoners to identify sabotage groups. Slave workers were hanged for sabotage, often with little evidence,

In mid 1944, the Allies were able to recover parts from two A4 rockets. On May 30, a rocket launched from Blizna crashed on the marshy banks of the Bug River near Sarnaki, more than 250 kilometres from the launch point. Members of the Polish resistance pushed the wreck into deeper water, and a farmer drove a herd of cattle into the river, which kicked up mud, further hiding the rocket before Germans arrived. That night, the Poles brought six horses to pull the remains out of the mud and took them to a nearby barn. A few days later, Polish engineers dismantled equipment and studied them. On the night of July 25, an RAF Dakota landed at an abandoned airfield and collected some of the parts. The Allies thus obtained important components of the rocket, detailed reports from Polish underground scientists, as well as numerous photographs, describing the parts which could not be transported by the plane.

and executions reached greater proportions in February and March 1945, including a number of mass hangings in the tunnels.

By the end of March 1944, the assembly of Artillerie-Abteilung 836 was almost complete in men and equipment and it was hoped that it would be fully equipped by April 15. The second launch battalion, Artillerie-Abteilung 485, would be ready for action in six or seven weeks.

By March 21, the first battery of Artillerie-Abteilung 836 had launched six rockets, of which only two recorded a successful flight; the second battery had launched 12 rockets, none of which functioned properly; the third battery had launched five rockets, only one of which succeeded in its flight.

A new battery, SS-Werfer-Batterie 500 was established on May 1 and spent the summer training with the rocket. It had a special status, being assigned directly to the Reichsführer-SS.

In March, the decision was made to move the entire aircraft industry to bomb-proof factories. As a result, the Mittelwerk was directed to hand over the northern part of the complex, Galleries 1-20, 'Nordwerk', to the Junkers company to produce Jumo 004 jet engines. Another blow came in late June when, impressed by the start of the V1 offensive against London, Hitler ordered an immediate reduction in production of the A4 rockets, so that manpower and resources could be used to increase the production of V1s. As a result, when A4 production in May had been 437, it fell to 132 in June and 86 in July.

Allied air attacks against the Fallersleben factory in June prompted the transfer of part of the V1 production to the Mittelwerk and in August, Galleries 43-46, 'Werk II', were assigned to the production of V1s.

Production of A4 rockets was then reduced to 22 galleries, Galleries 21-42, but production soon increased to 374 in August, and 629 in September. By the end of the month, a total of over 2,000 rockets had been produced at Mittelwerk.

On June 13, rocket V-89 was launched from Peenemünde under radio control. It was supposed to crash into the sea off Bornholm, but the controller lost sight and control when the rocket disappeared into the high cloud layer. Out of control, the lost rocket went well beyond its intended aiming point and ultimately broke up over neutral Sweden during re-entry, scattering fragments in Bäckebo county, 350 kilometres from the launch point. Two tons of wreckage were recovered and transported to Stockholm for examination by the Military Aeronautical Research Institute. Although Sweden was neutral, two RAF officers were allowed to come and inspect the recovered parts at the end of June. They returned with 100 kilos of components for examination, while heavier items were flown to Britain in late July. The Royal Aircraft Establishment at Farnborough then began rebuilding the missile.

During the summer of 1944, the Eighth Air Force launched three major raids against Peenemünde to attempt to destroy suspected hydrogen peroxide production. On July 18, Mission 481 sent 377 B-17s to bomb Peenemünde, the scientific headquarters at Zinnowitz, and the marshalling yards at Stralsund. Mission 512 returned to Peenemünde on August 4 with 221 B-17s, and Mission 570 on August 25 with 146 B-17s. This photo of a B-17 of the 401st Bomb Group was taken on August 25, centre left is Prüfstand XI, the acceptance test stand for series production, with road and rail connections from F1 pre-production hall. (USNA)

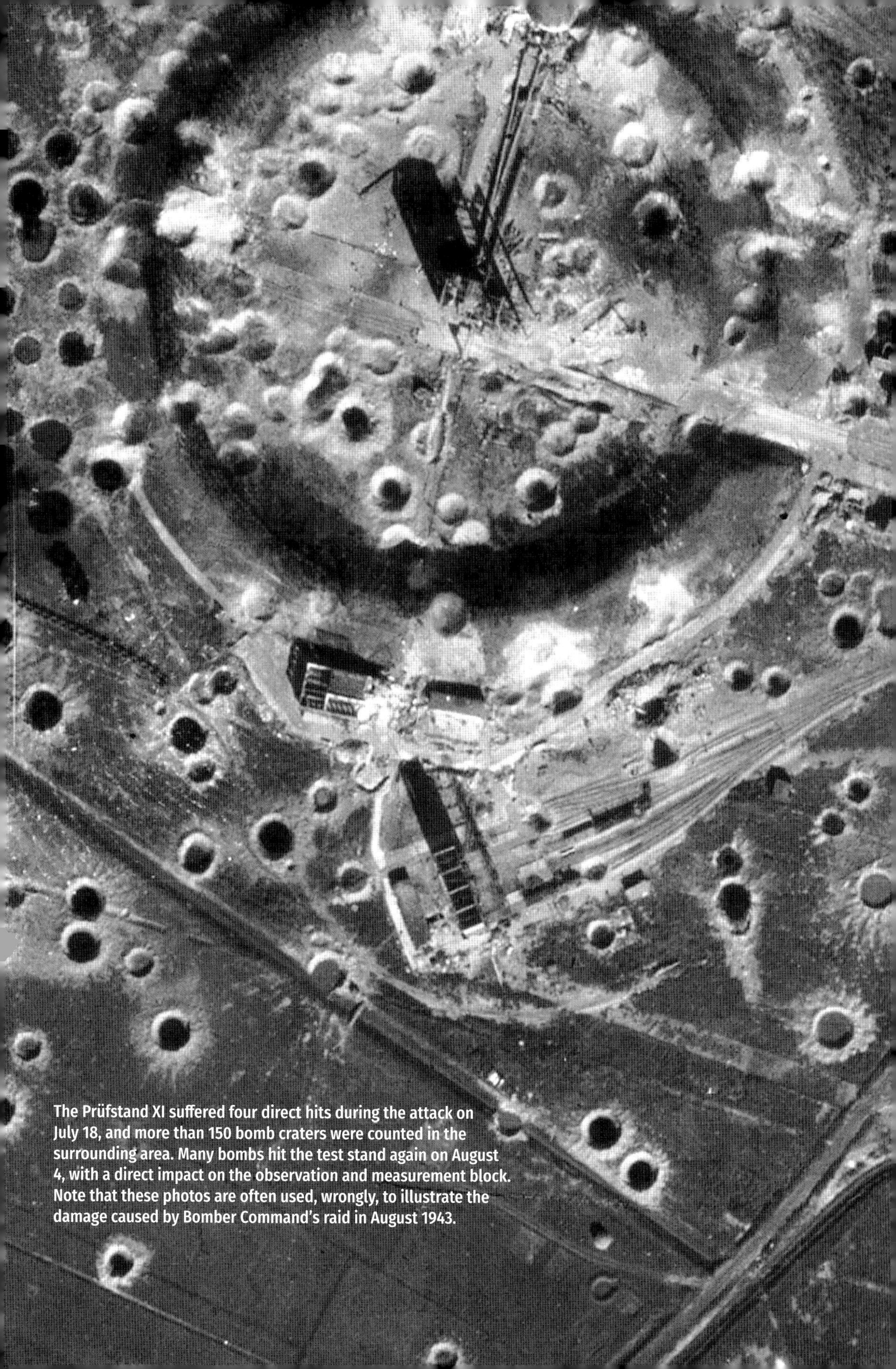

The Prüfstand XI suffered four direct hits during the attack on July 18, and more than 150 bomb craters were counted in the surrounding area. Many bombs hit the test stand again on August 4, with a direct impact on the observation and measurement block. Note that these photos are often used, wrongly, to illustrate the damage caused by Bomber Command's raid in August 1943.

Peenemünde South was hit on August 4, the office and laboratory wings were badly damaged, and the large F1 pre-production hall was hit. (USNA)

A planned test launch from Prüfstand VII was cancelled when the alarm sounded on July 18. The test stand was damaged (this photo shows the mobile tower used for static tests of the A4 rocket engine), but repairs reportedly allowed launchings to resume just six weeks after the raid.

CHAOTIC COMMAND SITUATION

In March 1944, relations between the LXV. Armeekorps z.b.V. and Flak-Regiment 155 (W) were tense, the two staffs having different points of view regarding the operational concept of the flying bomb.

Just named Höherer Artillerie-Kommandeur 191 (Harko 191) after Dornberger, Generalmajor Richard Metz asked in April to be relieved of his command, emphasising that, the A4 rocket being far from ready for action, this position was useless. Fearing that his retirement would fuel tensions and lead to additional command problems, LXV. Armeekorps z.b.V. refused.

The assassination attempt on Hitler on July 20 had major consequences

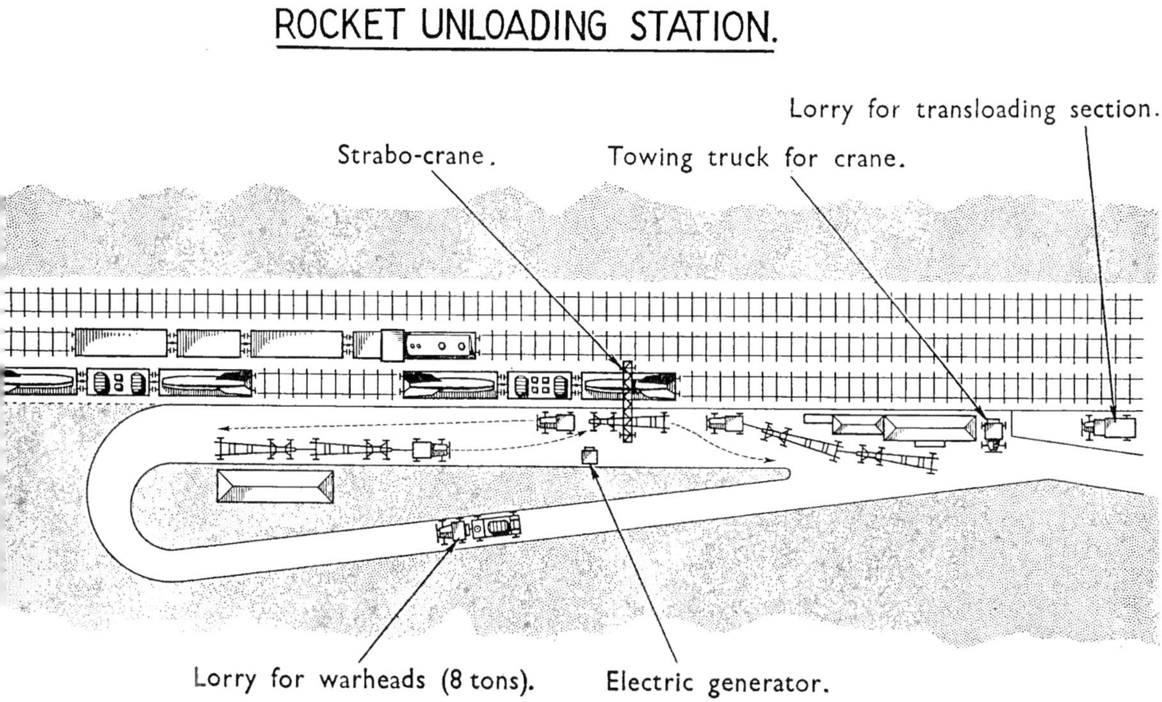

Thanks to the impressive 5-volume report produced by Operation 'Backfire', we can follow each stage of the launch of a V2 rocket. The report explains how the trains delivering the rockets to the launch batteries were made up of sections, with each section made up of three wagons: two wagons each carried one rocket, without a warhead, and these rockets were loaded nose to nose so that their noses overhung the third wagon in between; this third wagon carried the two warheads.

for the A4 program when Himmler succeeded Generaloberst Fromm, implicated in the coup and removed from all command, as Commander-in-Chief of the Replacement Training Army. On August 6, Himmler appointed SS-Gruppenführer Kammler as his special representative for A4 affairs, Sonderbeauftragter 2 des Reichsführers-SS or Sb2 for short. Dornberger, who would have been much more suited to the position, deplored the new arrangement: 'The first two months after Kammler's appointment were hard and bitter ones. I had to endure a whole series of humiliations. I had to submit to a chaotic flood of ignorant, contradictory, irreconcilable orders from this man who was neither soldier nor technician. They took the form of as many as a hundred teletypes a day.'

On August 31, the LXV. Armeekorps z.b.V. asked for clarification, and OKW answered that the corps would be responsible for command of A4 rocket operations. This would have been without Himmler's ambition to take control and two days later the correction was made and the corps was informed that SS-Gruppenführer Kammler would command operations, while the corps would supervise him with regard to tactics. This decision placed the LXV. Armeekorps z.b.V. in an impossible situation. Being at the same time not subordinate to Kammler and unable to give him orders,

When the train arrived at the delivery station, the Technical Troop started to remove the camouflage covers from the wagons while the Strabo crane was erected. With an overall length of 11 metres and a height when erected of 6.25 metres, the gantry crane could lift loads up to 16 tons.

The Strabo crane was positioned above the warhead wagon and successively lifted the two warheads to load them onto lorries. The wagon also contained two sodium permanganate containers and two crates, each crate containing four carbon rudders. All this was man handled to lorries which then went to their assigned parking ground.

A Vidalwagen road transporter was then moved into position alongside a rocket wagon and the Strabo crane lifted the rocket from the wagon to the Vidalwagen. The rocket was secured with clamps and the Vidalwagen was towed away to its parking ground.

Heinemann called for the dissolution of his command. The OKW refused, however, as the corps was still needed to conduct V1 operations, but relieved it of A4 rocket operations command. Another consequence was that on September 20, Generalmajor Metz resigned his command as Harko 191, and the command was subsequently disbanded.

At the end of July, the Russian advance forced the abandonment of the Heidelager firing range at Blizna and the test launches were transferred to a new firing range established at the Truppenübungsplatz Westpreussen at Tucheler Heide, now Tuchola Forest in Poland. The last test launches from Blizna took place in July, when 24 rockets were launched, and the first launches at Tucheler Heide, codenamed Heidekraut, took place in August, with 47 launches.

The first test launches in August and September were intended to test changes implemented in the production to address issues affecting the rockets' reliability. The rocket's disintegration at altitude was diagnosed as being caused by frictional heat as the rocket entered the atmosphere, and to remedy this, glass wool insulation was placed in the space between the tanks and the body shell. Also, steel sleeves were riveted to the tanks to reinforce the structure. The cause of the premature engine shutdown was attributed to fuel lines rupturing due to vibration, and a redesign of the fuel lines resolved the problem.

It took months before these improvements were introduced into the production and by October two-thirds of launches still ended in airbursts, and only a third were an impact explosion.

Another Vidalwagen was then moved into position, the second rocket was unloaded and the Vidalwagen was towed away. The procedure of unloading the warhead wagon first and then the two rocket wagons was repeated until unloading of the entire train was completed. (Frank Micklethwaite)

Where possible, fuels were delivered to different railway stations from where the rockets were delivered. An alcohol train normally consisted of 15 tankers (B-Stoff Eisenbahnwagen), each containing 24,000 litres of alcohol. A battery launching six to nine rockets per day required four tank cars per day, and alcohol trains had to arrive every three days at the unloading station. Alcohol was pumped from the rail tankers into road tankers (B-Stoff Strassenkesselwagen). When a road tanker was full (their capacity was 2,900 litres), they left for a specific parking ground. More road tankers then came up, and the same procedure was followed until all the rail tankers were empty.

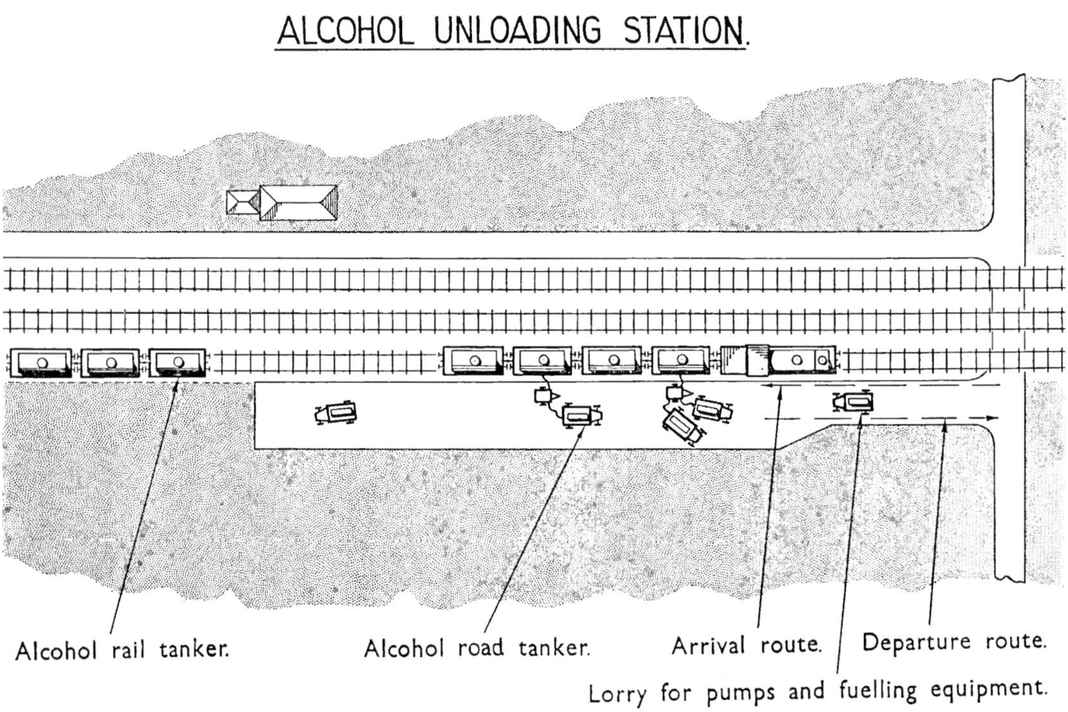

The alcohol road tankers were of two types, either a trailer or a truck, and both were originally designed as airfield refuelers for the Luftwaffe. The procedure was to have four dispersed parking grounds for the fuel tankers but this photo taken during Operation 'Backfire', when there was was no reason to adhere to security measures, shows all tankers parked at one same place. In front of the column was an alcohol tank trailer towed by an Hanomag SS-100 tractor.

At the liquid oxygen unloading station, one oxygen train normally consisted of four rail tankers (A-Stoff Eisenbahnwagen), each holding 23,500 litres of liquid oxygen. One battery launching six to nine rockets a day will require two rail tankers of oxygen per day and consequently oxygen trains arrived every other day. The liquid oxygen road tanker (A-Stoff Anhänger) held 6,000 litres of liquid oxygen, which, taking into account evaporation, was enough to fill a rocket.

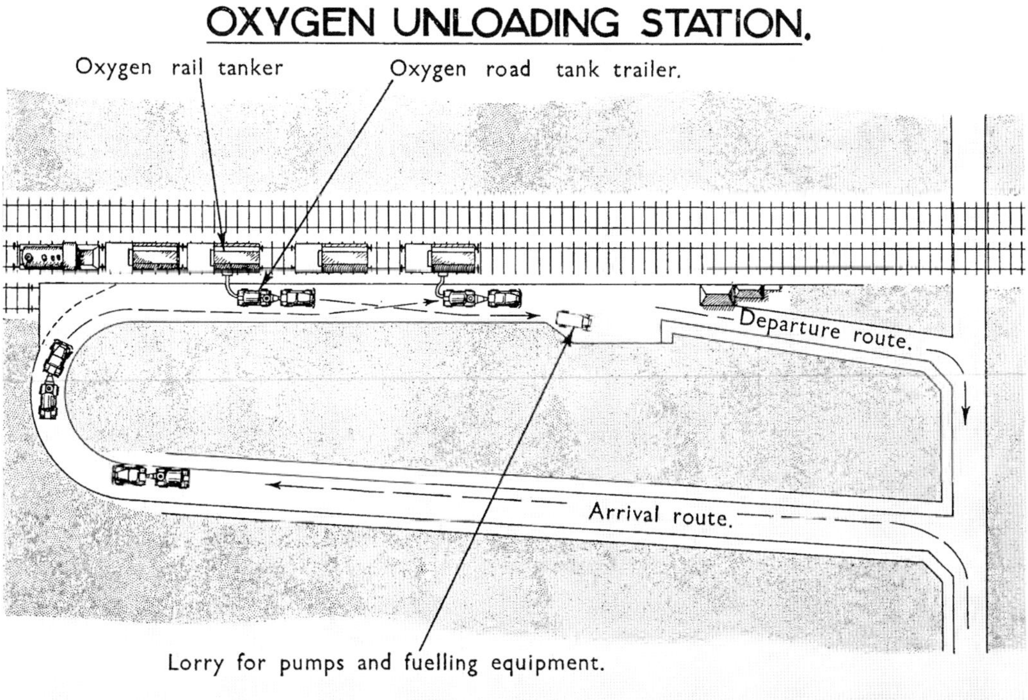

For five minutes, the oxygen gas was allowed to flow through the entire hoses and pump system to cool it before the pump clutch was engaged and pumping began. The very low temperature of liquid oxygen condensed the moisture in the air and frost soon covered the hoses and attachments. When the tank trailers were full, they would head to their parking lot and two more would arrive, and so on. (Charles Black)

At the hydrogen peroxide railhead, there was normally only one hydrogen peroxide tank in a train. Hydrogen peroxide burns the skin and troops handling it wore protective clothing, gloves and googles, and special care was taken to keep the equipment clean from contamination. Adequate supplies of water were always available to dilute the spilled liquid. Considering the day's temperature and using a specific chart, water was added to adjust the hydrogen peroxide concentration to 1.34. When the road tanker was full at this concentration, it was driven to its specific parking ground. A second road tanker came up, then a third, and the same procedure continued until the rail tanker was empty.

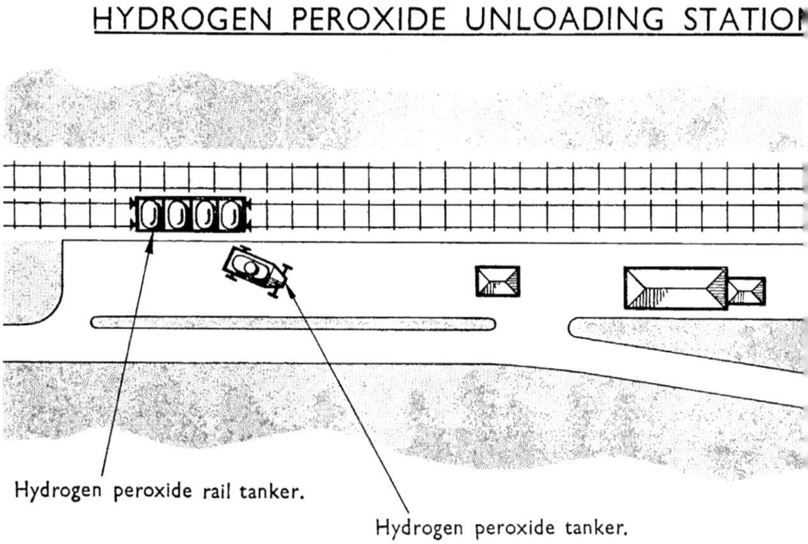

The hydrogen peroxide road tanker (T-Stoff Strassenkesselwagen) had a capacity of 2,100 litres, which was enough to fill 16 rockets. This photo of the hydrogen peroxide tanker shows (from left to right) the pump compartment situated at the rear of the vehicle, the hydrogen peroxide tank, and the 300-litre needed to supply water to adjust the hydrogen peroxide concentration and to rinse pipes and connections. (Frank Micklethwaite)

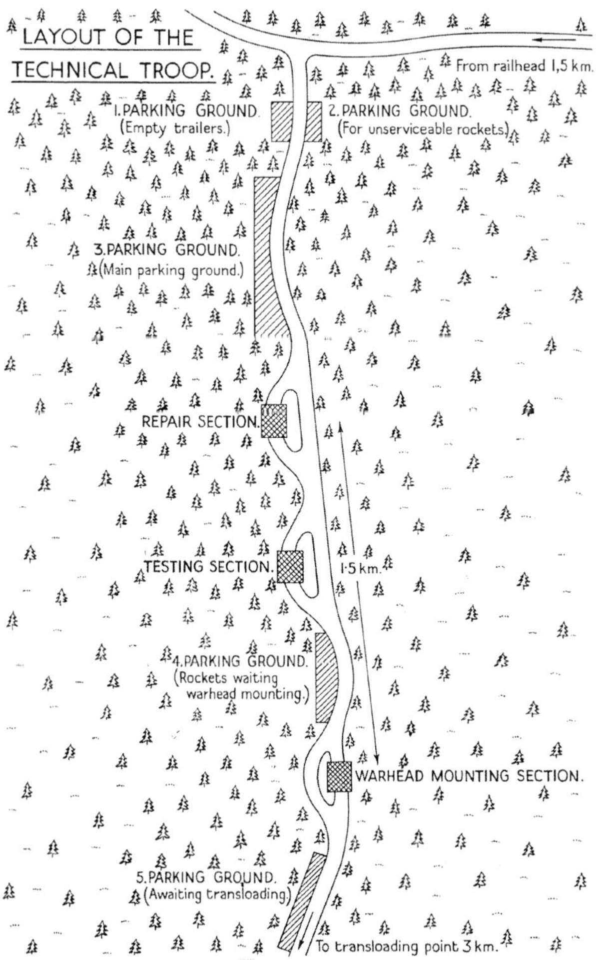

Layout of the Technical Troop at the launch site. The rockets were tested by the Technical Troop team on their arrival: the rocket on the Vidalwagen was driven into a tent 18 metres long and 7 metres wide by the side of a by-pass road (Testing Section in this sketch). The tests took about three hours for each rocket.

With the tests successfully completed, the rocket was towed to the warhead mounting section established into another tent on a by-pass road. Lifted by a crane, the warhead container was positioned in front of the rocket's control compartment and the 20 securing studs were inserted and tightened in the order 3 o'clock, 9 o'clock, 12 o'clock and then laterally in both directions from 12 o'clock downwards. The fuzes were inserted.

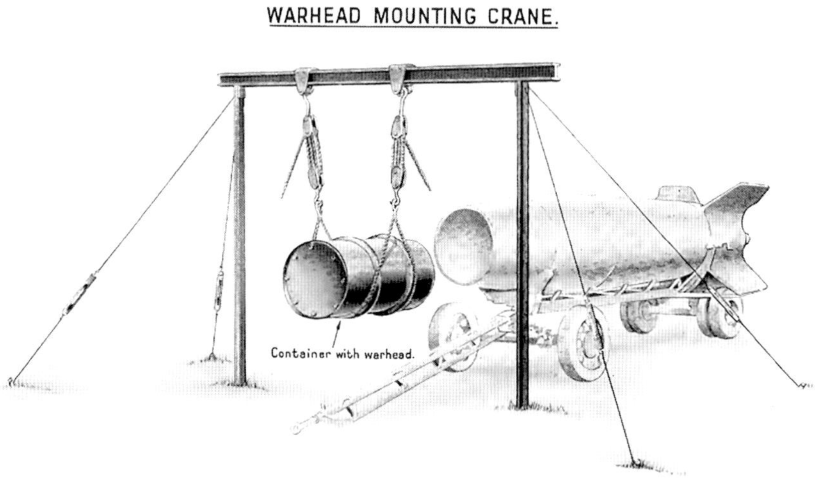

The towing vehicle, a FIAT SPA TM 40 in this photo taken during Operation 'Backfire', then towed the Vidalwagen out of the tent to another parking ground, the transloading point. The rocket was then ready to be delivered to the Launching Troop.

The Launching Troop came with its Meillerwagen, the transporter erector trailer, to the transloading point. With towing arm but without camouflage frame, the Meillerwagen was 14.7 metres long and 2.8 metres wide.

The Technical Troop pulled the Vidalwagen with the rocket under the Strabo crane, and the Firing Troop pulled the Meillerwagen alongside. The crane moved the rocket from the Vidalwagen to the Meillerwagen, where it was secured in clamps. The Meillerwagen was then driven to the final parking ground about 200 metres from the launch point.

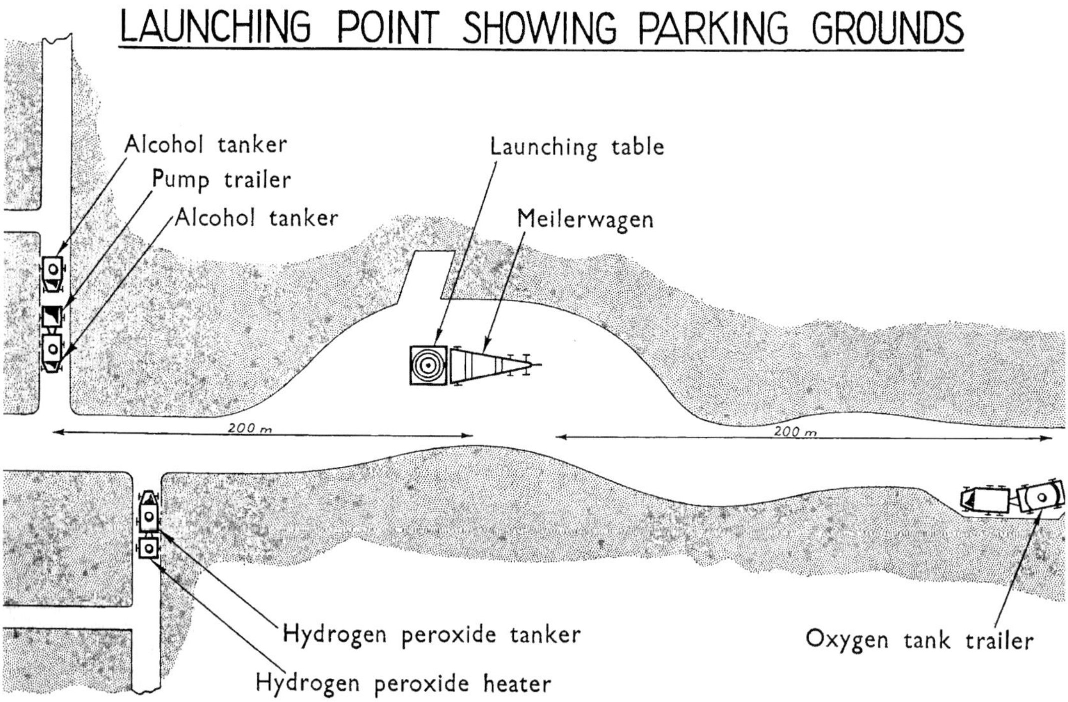

The ideal configuration for the final parking grounds: one each for the oxygen tank trailer, the hydrogen peroxide tanker, the two alcohol tankers and the three Meillerwagens. The recommendations were to choose them so that there was no risk of congestion between the various lorries and trailers en route to the firing site.

The launch table (Abschusstisch) was towed behind the fire control vehicle on to the launch point. Four jacks allowed the table to be raised, lowered, and levelled. The rocket rested on four adjustable support plates on a turntable mounted on a ball race. The turntable can be crossed by means of a moving handle and can be tightened by four screws. The blast deflector was of heavy steel sheet in the shape of a pyramid, the sides being slightly concave.

The fire control vehicle (Feuerleitpanzer) was armoured as a protection against rocket blast. At the front, the driver's compartment was not armoured. On both sides there were catches and fittings for accessories and on the front end of the control compartment were boxes with sockets for telephone lines and plugs for power cable.

The launch table was wheeled to the launch point and then detached from its trailer which was moved away. The launch table was levelled and the Meillerwagen was winched aft, two guide blades on the Meillerwagen engaging with two brackets on the launch table. The side girders of the Meillerwagen were swung outwards. The small gasoline engine that drove the hydraulic pump was started and the hydraulic rams raised the lifting frame, and the rocket on it.

The hydraulic pump operator manoeuvred the pressure control handle, the cross in the centre of this photo. As the lift frame reached vertical, as was shown by a plum line, he had to precisely stop the move. The report of Operation 'Backfire' insisted that this operator 'must have considerable experience in raising and lowering the lift frame'. This operation lasted approximately 12 minutes. (Charles Black)

The rocket thus suspended upright just above it, the launch table was raised by means of the jacks so that the weight of the rocket rested (on its four fins) on it. The centre strap and bolts securing the rocket to the Meillerwagen were removed, along with the upper clamping collar.

The Meillerwagen was man-handled 90 centimetre as measured by a rod that length, away from the launch table to allow the three platforms on the lifting frame to be lowered into position. The launch table was then rotated 90 degrees counter-clockwise to bring the rocket fuelling connections opposite the working platforms.

The lifting frame was then raised again until it was vertical, taking care to ensure that the working platforms did not foul the rocket. The cable mast was placed in its socket at one corner of the launch table, the cables were attached to it and it was raised by means of the screw jack and ratchet. (Frank Micklethwaite)

Three of the four carbon rudders were carefully removed from their travel crate and attached to their brackets. Standing on a ladder, one man examined the interior of the combustion chamber, removed the protecting covers from the fuel nozzles and checked that they were free of dirt. This completed, the fourth carbon rudder was secured.

Using a dial sight attached to the base plate on which the gyroscopes was mounted and a collimator on the survey point, the rocket was laid on the line of fire. In the forefront, Oberstleutnant Weber, the German senior officer during Operation 'Backfire'.

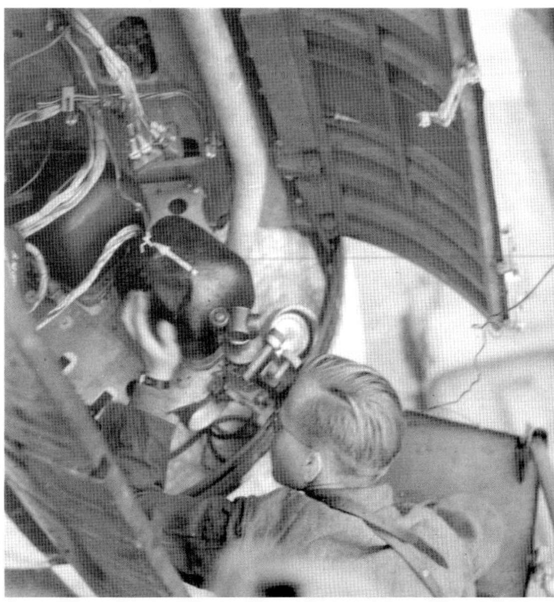

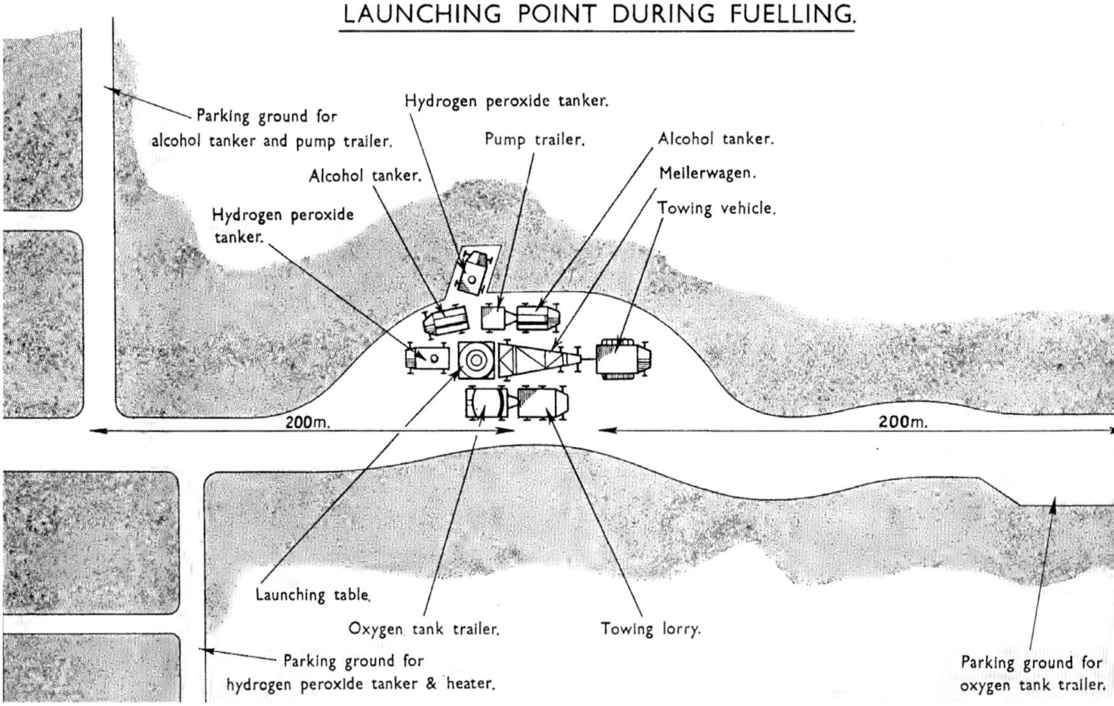

The rocket was once again thoroughly tested (for the second time after delivery to the launch battery), this time vertically and by the Launching Troop. At the beginning of the tests, the headquarters of Launching Troop ordered the Fuelling Troop to bring their vehicles to the launch position so that all preparations for tanking could be made while the tests were going on. The vehicles were precisely positioned, all so that the lengths of hose between the tankers, pump and rocket were as short as possible. The men of the Oxygen Section put on their protective clothing, as did those operating the hydrogen peroxide.

Another photo taken during Operation 'Backfire'. Note that one of the alcohol tankers was of the trailer type, and the second was a Kfz 385 tanker lorry. After the final tests were successfully completed, the rocket was reported ready. After inspecting all the hose connections, the NCO commanding the Fuel Column ordered alcohol fuelling to begin. Alcohol fuelling took from 10 to 20 minutes.

After 1,000 litres of alcohol had been tanked into the rocket, the connection of the oxygen hoses and the pre-cooling of the oxygen pump was started, which required five minutes. Liquid oxygen was then pumped into the rocket. Oxygen tanking took from 10 to 12 minutes. (Charles Black)

Approximately five minutes after oxygen fuelling began, the T-Stoff (hydrogen peroxide) was manually pumped into a pre-measured container, which was then emptied into the rocket T-Stoff tank by gravity. The Z-Stoff (sodium permanganate) fuelling was left until last, the container then being hauled up on to the lower working platform where a man poured it into a funnel until the tank was full. Once fuelling was completed, all vehicles and trailers, tankers and pumps were driven away. The lifting frame of the Meillerwagen was lowered and the trailer was towed away. The cable mast was adjusted, and those parts of the cables which were near the launch table were buried to prevent them from being burned. Assembling, servicing, and testing a V2 rocket before launch required 32 vehicles and trailers. The time required to assemble and service the rocket was four to six hours.

INTO ACTION

According to a report by LXV. Armeekorps z.b.V. on July 18, the operational deployment of the A4 rocket in France included 45 launch sites, 20 storage facilities, 17 alcohol storage stations and seven liquid oxygen production facilities. However, the installations west of the Seine had to be abandoned due to the advance of Allied troops.

The Allied armies soon reached the Seine, which they crossed on August 20. The 21st Army Group crossed the Somme on August 31 and rushed towards Antwerp, which was captured on September 4. On the left flank, the First Canadian Army overran all the V-weapon sites in northern France in the first days of September.

Having no prospect of resuming the V1 offensive soon, Hitler ordered on August 24 to open the attack with A4 rockets on September 15.

After moving his headquarters to Brussels, Kammler conferred with Dornberger there on August 31 and ordered him to prepare the rocket units for action. Dornberger reports that six batteries were to be ready by September 15: the Lehr- und Versuchsbatterie 444, the 2. and 3. Batterie of Artillerie-Abteilung 836, the 1. and 2. Batterie of Artillerie-Abteilung 485 and the SS-Werfer-Batterie 500, although the latter had not yet completed its training.

On September 1, the two batteries of Artillerie-Abteilung 485 and two technical batteries (1. and 2. Batterie of Technische-Artillerie-Abteilung 91) were ordered to move to the Kleve area to form a Gruppe Nord, and the Lehr- und Versuchsbatterie 444, the two batteries of Artillerie-Abteilung 836 and one technical battery (3. Batterie of Technische-Artillerie-Abteilung 91) were ordered to move to Euskirchen to form a Gruppe Süd. Major Bernd von Ploetz took command of Gruppe Nord on September 9 and Major Wolfgang Weber took command of Gruppe Süd on September 18.

On September 2, the Lehr- und Versuchsbatterie 444 was ordered to move south and fire against Paris. On September 4, the two batteries of Artillerie-Abteilung 485 advanced towards an operational zone west of Antwerp but the next day, due to the rapid advance of the Allied armies, Kammler had to order them to withdraw to Burgsteinfurt. On September 6, the 2. Batterie was ordered to move to The Hague to fire against London.

On September 6, the Lehr- und Versuchsbatterie 444 fired two A4 rockets aimed at Paris from a position one kilometre east of Samrée in Belgium. Both rockets misfired at 9.00 a.m. and 9.40 a.m., respectively: the rockets reached full power, but faulty integrating accelerometers directed premature engine cut off. Both rockets had to be drained and evacuated. On the morning of September 8, the battery successfully launched two rockets against Paris, at 8.40 a.m. and 11 a.m., from a new position near the village of Sterpigny. The first rocket disappeared without a trace and the second hit Maisons Alfort, just south-east of Paris, killing six people and injuring 36. It is the first ballistic missile attack in history.

That same day in the evening, from Wassenaar in The Hague, the 2.

After a failed start on September 6, when two rockets misfired, Lehr- und Versuchsbatterie 444 successfully launched two rockets against Paris on the morning of September 8 from a position near the village of Sterpigny. The first, fired at 8.40 a.m., disappeared without a trace, having probably exploded in flight, and the second, fired at 11 a.m., hit Maisons Alfort, south-east of Paris. It was the first ballistic missile attack in history.

Batterie of Artillerie-Abteilung 485 launched the first two A4 rockets towards England. The first rocket hit Staveley Road, Chiswick, killing three people and wounding ten, and the second landed on open farmland near Epping.

That evening too, Kammler ordered Lehr- und Versuchsbatterie 444 to join with Gruppe Nord and attack London from the island of Walcheren.

After joining the 2. Batterie in The Hague sector, the 1. Batterie of Artillerie-Abteilung 485 opened against London on the 10th. On the 16th, in

Here I must recount a personal memory from one of my many research projects for *After the Battle*. I set myself the objective of identifying the place from which the first operational V2s were launched, a real challenge because no historian, not even the local press, had yet reported on these launches. I first studied original German maps and discovered that one of them circled the launch site in the Sterpigny region. To meet as many witnesses as possible in the small villages and hamlets in the surrounding area, I asked for help from the local priest. He agreed for me to attend a meeting of parishioners one evening and I was thus able to find three witnesses. It was in 1989. I am proud to have interviewed these last witnesses before they left us. Thanks to their memory, we now know precisely where the first ballistic missiles in history were launched from. I met François Catin who in September 1944 went to the launch site a few hours after the departure of the German launch team. He showed me (this photo) precisely the place where he saw the roadway melted and blackened by the jet of flames from the rocket. Unfortunately, due to a layout error, I was devastated to find that the location of the launch site I had plotted was incorrectly marked on the map when it was published in Volume 3 from *The Blitz Then and Now*, but I am glad I can now correct this error here.

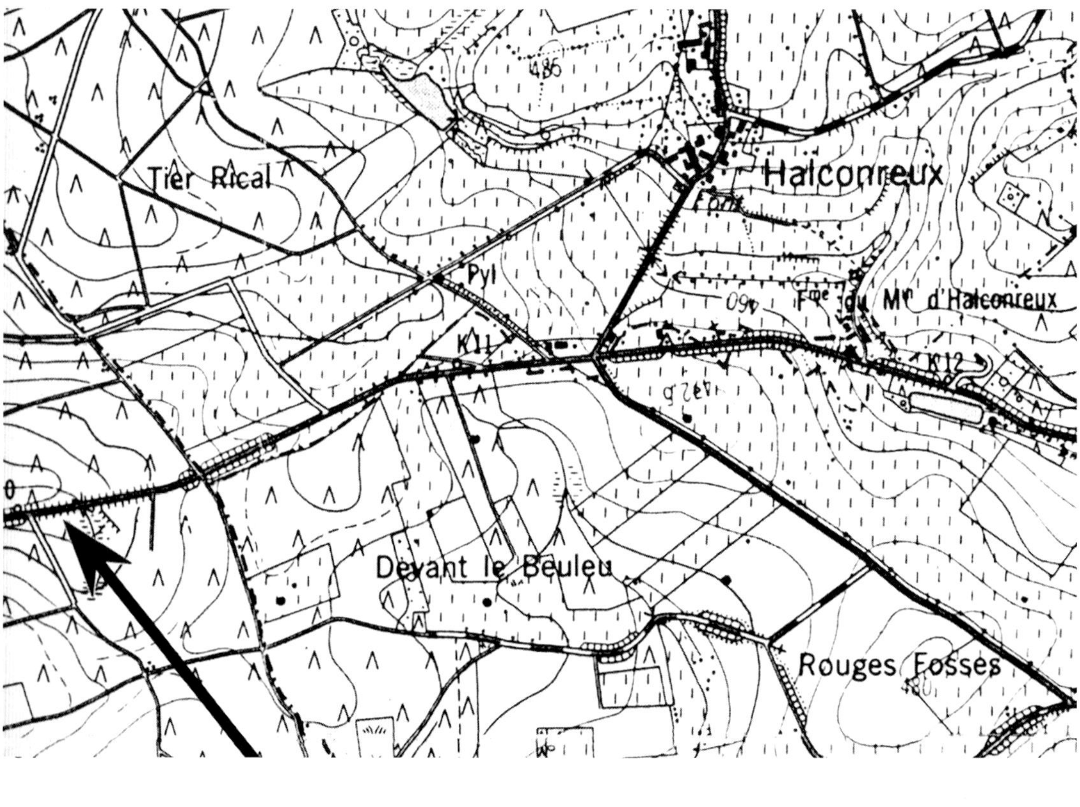

Louis and Marcelle Nissen, a brother and a sister, showed me where they had seen a long trailer parked on the side of the road, with something very large wrapped under a camouflaged tarpaulin, while German sentries waved at them not to stop there. They then led me to the field where they were when the V2 suddenly came roaring up from the Bois de Beuleu, just a few hundred metres away. Terrified by the spectacle, they threw themselves to the ground.

the presence of Kammler, who had gone to Walcheren to see for himself, the Lehr- und Versuchsbatterie 444 opened fire on London.

On September 15, Gruppe Süd resumed fire and the 2. and 3. Batterie of Artillerie-Abteilung 836 opened fire against Lille from sites in the Euskirchen sector. In the following days, Mons and Charleroi were also designated as targets.

The start of Operation 'Market Garden' on September 17 brought the operations of Gruppe Nord to an abrupt halt. Allied paratroopers nearly captured Kammler and his headquarters in Berg-en-Dal, and they hastily pulled back to Darfeld near Burgsteinfurt. To avoid the risk that the two

The explosion took place behind the houses on rue des Sapins and rue des Ormes (today rue Arthur Dalidet). Several houses were destroyed, many others seriously damaged. Six people were killed, including a baby, and 36 were injured, 17 of whom had to be hospitalised. (AMAH)

batteries of Artillerie-Abteilung 485 and the Lehr- und Versuchsbatterie 444 would be trapped by the Allied advance, Kammler ordered the former two to withdraw to the Burgsteinfurt area, and the latter to move to Gaasterland on the north-eastern bank of the Zuider Zee.

Installed in new positions near Burgsteinfurt, the two batteries of Artillerie-Abteilung 485 opened fire against Liège on September 21. In the Netherlands, Lehr- und Versuchsbatterie 444 took up position in the Rijsterbos, a small wooded area near Bakhuizen. From there it was not possible to target London, out of range, and from September 25 the battery fired against Great Yarmouth and Norwich.

The War Cabinet imposed a total blackout on anything related to the rocket attacks, partly to leave the Germans in uncertainty, partly to avoid damaging the morale at home. However, British censorship had no control

This original map reports the operation of 'Action A4' until September 17. From Sterpigny (the circle centered on Stavelot is clearly too far north), the Lehr- und Versuchsbatterie 444 is reported having launched three rockets against Target 303 (Paris); from The Hague, the two batteries of Artillerie-Abteilung 485 had launched 24 rockets against Target 101 (London) and one against Target 103 (Liège); from sites in the Euskirchen sector the two batteries of Artillerie-Abteilung 836 had launched 7 rockets against Target 102 (Lille) and 4 against Target 109 (Mons). Having moved to Walcheren (this map shows the movement, dated September 14), the Lehr- und Versuchsbatterie 444 opened fire on London on September 16 and reported 6 rockets launched in two days.

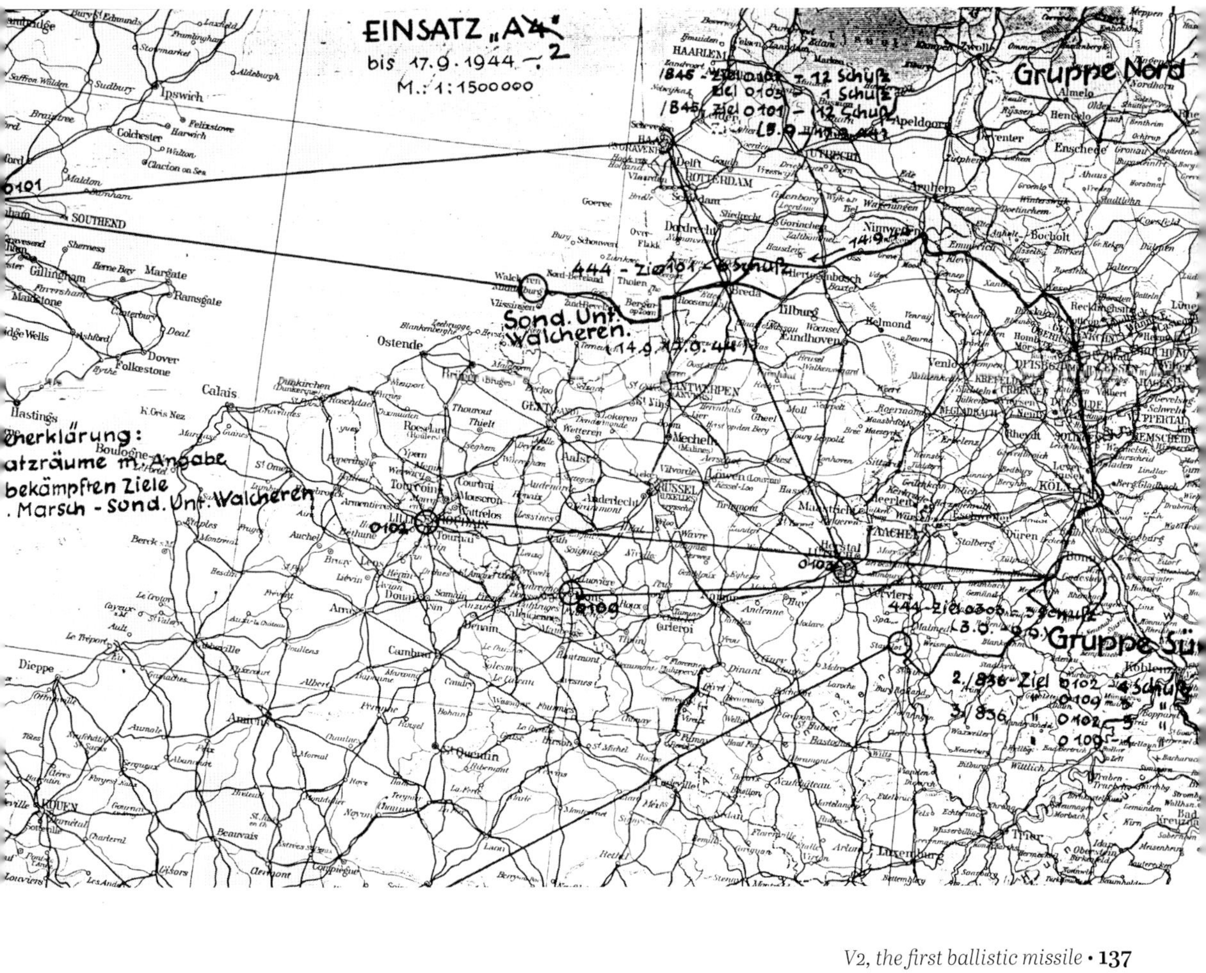

over the American press and on August 21, the New York Times revealed the 'V2 rocket bomb' attacks. Nevertheless, the War Cabinet decided to retain the ban, although oral reports circulated in London and the name V2 was common in the British press.

In the last days of September, Artillerie-Abteilung 836 moved its batteries to new launch sites near Hachenburg, the 2. Batterie in Helferskirchen and the 3. Batterie in Rossbach. They opened fire from the 26th (3. Batterie) and the 27th (2. Batterie) against Lille, Tourcoing, Arras, Cambrai, Hasselt, Mons, and Maastricht. Artillerie-Abteilung 836 was then ordered to operate from a new area near Merzig. The 2. Batterie moved first and on October 2, it fired three rockets at Paris from sites at Greimerath: rocket no. 19016 impacted near Bouillancy, rocket no. 19021 near Silly-le-long, and rocket no. 19026 near Brégy. The battery fired 15 more shots at the French capital over the next three days. None of them hit Paris, all crashing to the north-east of the city. The 3. Batterie opened fire on the 7th from sites near Rimlingen, north-east of Merzig, targeting Tourcoing.

DIVISION z.V.

The Division z.V. was created on October 1 to command the A4 rocket launches. SS-Gruppenführer Kammler, who had come up with the name for his command, was its commander. The designation 'z.V.' meaning 'zur Vergeltung', derived from the denomination of the so-called 'Vergeltungswaffen' (for retribution/retaliation).

At the beginning of October, the Allied offensive having been checked, Kammler directed the batteries he had withdrawn to return to The Hague. The 2. Batterie of Artillerie-Abteilung 485 arrived at Ockenburgh on the morning of October 3 and launched two rockets against London in the evening. The second one exploded shortly after liftoff, lighting up the whole area.

The 2. Batterie of Artillerie-Abteilung 485 opened fire from a new site at Ockenburgh, just west of The Hague, on the evening of October 3, launching two rockets against London. The 1. Batterie remained in the Burgsteinfurt sector, firing against Liège, and later against Antwerp.

After having launched 43 rockets towards East Anglia and, from October 13, 26 rockets against Antwerp from Gaasterland, the Lehr- und Versuchsbatterie 444 returned to The Hague on October 22. The battery set up a launch site at Rijswijkse Bos and opened fire two days later.

The operational deployment of the A4 units was completed in October with the arrival of three new batteries: the 3. Batterie of Artillerie-Abteilung 485, which opened fire against Antwerp on October 21 from sites near Burgsteinfurt; the 1. Batterie of Artillerie-Abteilung 836, which opened fire against Antwerp on October 27 from Reinsfeld near Hermeskeil; and the SS-Werfer-Batterie 500, that launched its first rocket on October 10 from positions near Burgsteinfurt, aiming for Hasselt (however, the still poorly

In October 1944, the Division z.V. was established under SS-Gruppenführer Kammler to command the A4 rocket launches. This photo was taken earlier in the summer when Kammler paid a visit to the command post of Flak-Regiment 155 (W) at Saleux on August 10. (M. Wachtel)

trained battery could only launch three rockets over the next ten days). At the end of the month, Division z.V. had seven operational batteries.

On October 27, a launch record was set by Lehr- und Versuchsbatterie 444, now complete with its third firing platoon: a total of nine rockets were fired that day from Wassenaar and Rijswijk, three of them in 45 minutes.

As of November 1, the V2 units had launched some 500 rockets against 14 targets: some 220 against Antwerp, some 150 against London and East Anglia, 28 against Lille, 26 against Liège, 22 against Paris...

After firing a final rocket against Antwerp on November 3, the 2. Batterie of Artillerie-Abteilung 836 was sent back to Peenemünde where it was to test the possibility of launching A4 rockets from specially fitted railway equipment. The battery would not return to action in the West before February 1945.

Throughout November, Lehr- und Versuchsbatterie 444 was the only battery to target London, while six batteries targeted Antwerp: two batteries from Artillerie-Abteilung 836 from the Hermeskeil sector, and the three batteries from Artillerie- Abteilung 485 and the SS-Werfer-Batterie 500 of the Burgsteinfurt sector. On November 13, SS-Werfer-Batterie 500 began the transfer from Burgsteinfurt to the sector near Hellendoorn in the Netherlands from where it resumed fire on the 16th, targeting Antwerp.

On November 25, 1944, a V2 launched by Lehr- und Versuchsbatterie 444 hit Warwick Court, a small alleyway off Holborn, at 11.16 a.m. Rescue workers search the rubble and wreckage for survivors. Five residents were killed and 40 injured in the attack.

Warwick Court was close to Fleet Street, where most of Britain's national newspapers operated, and several photographers were soon there to photograph how those trapped on the top floor were rescued from the roof of the White Hart.

V2 OPERATIONS

History will show that November was the month of records for the A4 rocket units. More than 615 rockets were launched that month, more than any other month. The daily launch record had been set at 29 on October 30. This was beaten on November 17, with 30 launches, and again on November 26 with 33 launches. On November 25, the 1000th A4 rocket was launched.

After waiting two months to announce the deployment of the rocket, German propaganda finally announced its entry in action on November 8. This day, the Wehrmachtsbericht (daily Wehrmacht communiqué) reported: 'After the Greater London area has been under the fire of the V1 with only a short interruption and varying intensity since June 15, this bombardment has been intensified for a few weeks by the use of an even more effective explosive weapon, the V2.'

The ban, still in force in Britain, could no longer be maintained and the

On January 27, 1945, about 4 p.m., a V2 launched by the 1. Batterie of Artillerie-Abteilung 485 hit Battersea. The explosion took place in the back gardens formed by Usk Road, Petergate and York Road, killing 17 residents and seriously injuring 44. Twenty houses were demolished, and 30 badly damaged. The photo was taken by Toni Frissell, an American photographer who travelled to the European front twice as the official photographer of the Women's Army Corps. This photo would have been taken after the bombing on January 27. (LC)

Report of the incident of January 27, Incident No. 625: 'At 19.00 hours, three persons were unaccounted for, Mr Robert Owen of 8 Usk Road and two boys (James Roberts, 11, and Anthony Wildbore, 9) who were known to have been in a wood shed in the rear of York Road shortly before the explosion, and the search for them continued. At 7.40 hours on Sunday the remains of the two boys were found. At 13.45 hours on Monday Mr Owen's body was found. The incident was then closed'. This other photo taken by Mrs Frissell is said to have been taken in Battersea that same day, but there appears to be no original caption to confirm this. (LC)

On December 29, Signal Corps photographer T/3 Ingledew photographed the damage caused when a V2 hit Lombarden Vest in central Antwerp. In the background on the right appears the roof of the Saint-Augustin church, which today houses the AMUZ concert hall. (USNA)

Prime Minister admitted the bombing of England by a 'new weapon, the long-range rocket' in a speech in the House of Commons on December 10.

In the Hermeskeil sector, Allied air attacks having severely affected the production and supply of liquid oxygen, Artillerie-Abteilung 836 had to cease fire for a few days at the end of November. The 1. Batterie was then ordered to move to the Hachenburg area, and on December 8, the 3. Batterie was ordered to follow. Snow was a nuisance on the poor roads in the area, and in consequence, the rockets were transported further afield on the lighter carrier Vidalwagen, so that their transfer from these to the Meillerwagen took place as close as possible to the firing point. On the 9th, the 1. Batterie launched its first rocket from the new sites, targeting Antwerp, and the 3. Batterie opened on the 15th.

As of December 31, rocket troops had fired a total of nearly 1,600 rockets, including some 950 against Antwerp and some 500 against London and East Anglia.

On January 12, in an effort to shield Dornberger from SS influence, Speer

Launched from Hermeskeil by the 1. Batterie, Artillerie-Abteilung 836, on November 27, the V2 rocket No. 20251 impacted ten minutes after midday at the intersection of Frankrijklei, Keyserlei and Teniersplaats, the busiest intersection in Antwerp.

A British convoy coming from the docks was caught in the blast, several of the vehicles caught fire. One of the MPs regulating the traffic was disintegrated and the charred body of another was found sometime later the roof of a nearby hotel.

A city water main burst, the water bubbled up, and the entire place was soon filled with water. Floating on the water were dismembered corpses, clothing, and all kinds of debris. A total of 126 people were killed, including 26 allied soldiers, and more than 300 people were injured. (Another source, which includes in the count the wounded who died in hospital in the days following the bombing, puts the death toll at 157, including 29 allied soldiers.)

appointed him chairman of an 'Arbeitstab Dornberger' within the Ministry of Armaments and War Production. This staff of around ten experts was responsible for developing different types of guided rockets for anti-aircraft use, to break the air superiority of the Allies. Kammler quickly reacted and induced Göring to name him head of the 'Brechung des Luftterrors' (Program to Break Air Terror) on January 26. This done, Kammler managed to subordinate Dornberger and his work team to himself. The SS finally won the battle for control over all aspects of the rocket program.

This remarkable photo was taken from a B-17 of the 860th Bomb Squadron, 493rd Bomb Group, on February 19, 1945. Three V2s launched simultaneously soared straight into the sky towards Antwerp. Such scenes were not uncommon after November 1944 for Allied air crews, who reported rockets speeding past their aircraft, a meteor with a trail of flames. (USNA)

For some unclear reason, probably simply because Kammler wished to increase his command stature, the operational rocket units were renamed in January and February. Although the new names suggest an expansion of the units, it was nothing more than a restructuring on paper: Artillerie-Abteilung 485 became Artillerie-Regiment z.b.V. 902, and Artillerie-Abteilung 836 became Artillerie-Regiment z.b.V. 901, their batteries becoming Abteilung; the SS-Werfer-Batterie 500 became SS-Werfer-Abteilung 500 and the Lehr- und Versuchsbatterie 444 became Lehr und Versuchs Abteilung z.V.

On January 20, the 3. Batterie of Artillerie-Abteilung 485 which had fired against Antwerp from sites near Burgsteinfurt for November and December, was ordered to join the group's two other batteries in the bombardment of London from The Hague sector. The battery moved quickly and fired its first rocket against London on the 26th.

Directed to Karlshagen from where it was to undertake trial launches to resolve the remaining faults in the rocket, the Lehr- und Versuchsbatterie 444 departed on the 26th.

While the Gruppe Nord recorded regular operations in March, with an average of ten rockets fired daily against London during the first half of the month, the Gruppe Süd suffered from serious supply difficulties, notably lack of liquid oxygen, and its average rate of fire against Antwerp was only six rockets per day.

On March 16, Kammler ordered the SS-Werfer-Abteilung 500 to target the Remagen bridgehead that the Americans had just established east of the

Rhine, in an attempt to disrupt their crossing of the river. From its positions in the Hellendoorn sector, at a target distance of about 210 kilometres, the SS-Werfer-Abteilung 500 fired 11 rockets targeting Remagen on March 17.

Shortly after 3 p.m., after the first three rockets crashed, the bridge collapsed into the Rhine. Hitler sent his personal congratulations to the men of SS-Werfer-Abteilung 500, and at Hellendoorn the rocket crews boasted of their achievement to Dutch civilians.

It was a strange coincidence that the bridge collapsed into the Rhine after three V2 rockets targeted it, but the bridge had every reason to collapse: its upstream structure was seriously weakened by the explosion of the German demolition charge, it had been shaken for days by the incessant artillery bombardments pounding the area, and it was overloaded by the decking of the railway by American engineers. However, we can imagine that the shocks of the V2s crashing were the last straw which made the overall stress too great for the weakened structure.

At Remagen on March 7, the local German commander waited until the last minute to blow up the railway bridge to allow more of his troops to escape to the eastern bank of the Rhine. Engineers finally detonated the charge, but the explosion failed to bring down the bridge. The GIs then rushed to the bridge and secured its eastern end. A constant flow of soldiers, tanks and equipment crossed the Rhine for ten days. This photo of engineers working to repair the bridge is believed to have been taken just four hours before the bridge collapsed into the Rhine. (USNA)

The SS-Werfer-Abteilung 500 fired 11 rockets aimed at Remagen on March 17. No rockets hit the bridge, but the closest one crashed about 300 metres away, killing three American soldiers. Except for one short shot that crashed 40 kilometres east of Cologne, all the rockets struck in a circle 20 kilometres in diameter. Shortly after 3 p.m., after the first three rockets crashed, the bridge collapsed into the Rhine. Of the 200 engineers and welders then working on the bridge, 28 were killed, 18 of whom drowned in the fast current of the Rhine and disappeared, and 63 others were injured. (USNA)

THE END

Supply difficulties, notably the lack of liquid oxygen, and the threat of the Allied advance, led to the early cessation of operations of Artillerie-Abteilung 836 (Artillerie-Regiment 901 z.b.V.) from the Hachenburg area. The 2. and 3. Batteries (II. and III. Abteilung) launched their last rockets against Antwerp on the afternoon of March 16 and the two batteries then withdrew, taking along their vehicles and equipment, as well as the remaining rockets. They were first ordered to assemble at Bramsche, west of Osnabruck, and were then ordered to move to Celle, north of Hanover.

The operations of Artillerie-Abteilung 485 (Artillerie-Regiment 902 z.b.V.) continued for a few days, with the 1. and 3. Batteries (I. and III. Abteilung) targeting London from the Hague sector, while the 2. Batterie fired against Antwerp from the Burgensteinfurt sector. On March 27, the 1. Batterie launched its last three rockets, the 3. Batterie its last four, and both retired to Fallingbostel. The SS-Werfer-Abteilung 500 also launched its last rocket

Under Kammler's orders, at the end of March 1945, the officers and men of Division z.V. shot more than 200 Russian and Polish workers, including women and children, in three shootings in the Arnsberg Forest. The 95th Infantry Division reached Suttrop in early May and was informed by locals of two of the massacres (the third came to light in 1946). Outside Suttrop, a German civilian relays to a captain of the 95th Infantry Division information found on the body of one of 57 Russians, including women and a baby, exhumed from a mass grave. (USNA)

They Americans forced the townspeople to exhume the grave, after which Russian displaced persons in the area helped identify the bodies. The victims were reburied in individual graves, and a US Army chaplain conducted burial services. (USNA)

on the 27th and the end of the V2 campaign came on the 28th when the 2. Batterie of Artillerie-Abteilung 485 launched its last two rockets against Antwerp.

On March 27, the Wehrmachtsbericht mentioned the V-weapons for the last time, when it was reported that 'the harassing fire of our retribution weapons on London continued'.

On March 20, while the division headquarters was established in Suttrop, 50 kilometres east of Dortmund, Kammler found himself caught in a traffic jam caused by a crowd of foreign workers. According to later testimonies, seeing the local authorities unable to control the chaotic situation, he mobilised his staff and indicated that the number of wandering foreigners posed a threat to the security of the headquarters and to the civilian population. 'Under the utmost secrecy', he ordered his subordinates to 'drastically decimate the number of foreign workers', and this 'regardless of their gender'. He then left Suttrop due to other duties, and officers of the Division z.V. staff took responsibility for carrying out the order.

Officers and men of the Division z.V. shot dead 208 Russian and Polish workers, including women and children, in three shootings in the Arnsberg Forest. The first murder took place on March 20 near Warstein, two kilometres west of Suttrop, when a firing squad under the command of SS-Obersturmbannführer Wolfgang Wetzling, divisional judge, shot dead 71 civilians, 14 men, 56 women and one child. The next morning, 80 people were taken in groups of 15 to 20 to an execution site near Eversberg, where they were shot. A third massacre took place near Suttrop on the 23rd, when 35 men and 21 women housed in the local school in the immediate vicinity of the Division z.V. headquarters were taken to a forest and shot.

The Artillerie-Abteilung 836 reached the Celle area as ordered, but the order to fire the remaining rockets against the Russian forces attacking the fortress of Kustrin (the present Polish Kostrzyn, about 100 kilometres north-east of Berlin) fell through due to the general collapse and the battalion finally destroyed its equipment on April 7.

The 1. and 3. Batterie of Artillerie-Abteilung 485 withdrew to Fallingbostel, taking back their equipment and vehicles, although many of them were abandoned en route due to exhaustion of fuel. They arrived on April 1 and, coming from the Burgsteinfurt region, the 2. Batterie joined them the next day. A few days later, what remained of the battalion's vehicles and equipment, along with some remaining rockets, were destroyed at a storage area near Leese.

Having fallen back to the north of Fallingbostel after the launch of its last rocket on the 27th, the SS-Werfer-Abteilung 500 destroyed its equipment and vehicles there in the first days of April. The men were then divided into groups, some were given combat assignments, while others formed Nebelwerfer batteries equipped with 150mm Nebelwerfers. But chaos was everywhere and these units were quickly dispersed.

At the beginning of April, the Lehr- und Versuchsbatterie 444 moved to

When the rocket units withdrew in the final days of March, they began evacuating their field equipment, but as gasoline supplies ran out and the chain of command broke down, they gradually abandoned their vehicles and equipment along the way. Here, photographed in June, an abandoned V2 on a Vidalwagen near Leese.

Search teams sent to recover rockets for Operation 'Backfire' found a large quantity of abandoned rockets and equipment. They reported that the Germans carried out their destruction half-heartedly and randomly. However, weather and looting combined to add even more damage.
(Charles Black)

Lüneburg Heath and the last few test firings of the A4 rockets took place on April 5. The unit then moved to Steinhorst, north-east of Hamburg, where they destroyed some of their equipment. A few days later, some of them were sent to Welmbüttel in Schleswig-Holstein from where they were to fight as infantry soldiers. The remaining rockets, vehicles, and equipment, were towed into the bog at Welmbüttel and were blown up. The war diaries of the Lehr- und Versuchsbatterie 444 were burned.

ASSESSMENT

The shipping slips for the rockets sent from Mittelwerk to Demag factory at Falkensee provide a reliable source for calculating the production at Mittelwerk: 4,128 in 1944 and 1,669 in 1945, with the production in March 1945 not known. Mittelwerk Managing Director Georg Rickhey's estimate of March production at 700 units seems somewhat high, other sources put it at 138 or 362. The total production of A4 rockets at Mittelwerk can only be an approximation, between 6,000 to 6,200. Additionally, 300 rockets were produced at the pilot production plant in Peenemünde, this figure representing a minimum estimate. Total production of A4 rockets would thus be between 6,300 to 6,500 units.

Of these, around 3,200 were fired in operation, and about 600 were launched in test and training at Peenemünde, Heidelager, and Heidekraut.

During the V2 operational campaign, the rocket units launched a total of about 3,170 rockets, including about 1,600 against Antwerp, 1,400 against London and East Anglia, and over 150 against 12 others sites.

For the period September 1944 to March 1945, 1,262 V2s hit Antwerp and its suburbs, and 1,054 hit English soil.

Germany wasted a lot of resources and technical expertise on the development and production of the A4 rocket.

Michael Neufeld, in *The Rocket and the Reich: Peenemünde and the Coming of the Ballistic Missile Era, 1995*, provided a detailed analysis of the cost of the V-weapon programs, V1 and V2 included. He calculated that, given the relatively smaller size of the German economy compared to that of the United States, the V-weapons programs represented an industrial effort equivalent to but slightly less than that of the Manhattan Project which produced the atomic bomb. The development and production of the V2 rocket made up the largest part of this enormous effort. An effort out of all proportion to the final military result, which was only to share with the V1 the effective nuisance of unloading at the Antwerp docks between November 1944 and March 1945.

However, the A4 rocket was a revolutionary and pioneering design and it provided the Americans and Soviets with invaluable experience with large liquid-fuelled rockets. On both sides, the Peenemünde rocket led to the intercontinental ballistic missiles of the Cold War, and to the rockets of the conquest of space.

HOCHDRUCKPUMPE, THE 'ENGLAND CANNON'

THE IDEA OF A MULTI-CHAMBERED gun had reappeared from time to time since the middle of the 19th century and in 1918 a patent for such a long-range weapon had been registered in France to retaliate against the German 'Paris Cannon' which had been shelling the French capital from March that year. However, the German armies soon withdrew, the Armistice was signed and that cannon never materialised. However, the tables were turned in June 1940 when, following the French defeat, the Germans came across the old patent and in 1942 the chief engineer of the Röchling Eisen- und Stahlwerk, August Coenders, adapted the concept. He produced plans for a smooth-bore multi-chambered gun which consisted of a very long barrel with pairs of lateral chambers at periodic intervals. After the shell was loaded in the breech, a first charge started the projectile up the barrel. As the shell passed each pair of lateral chambers, additional propellant charges were ignited by the flash, thus adding a fresh quantity of gas and further accelerating the shell until a very high muzzle velocity was achieved.

By early 1943, Röchling approached Speer, the Minister of Armaments and Munitions, and told him of their plan for a multi-chambered gun which would be able to fire fin-stabilised shells of 140kg over a distance of 160 kilometres. A 50-barrel battery of that kind, with a rate of fire of one shot per barrel every five minutes, could fire 600 shells at London every hour. Speer was favourably impressed and in May he informed Hitler about the proposed long-range cannon which would be able to bombard London. The idea of an 'England Cannon' captured Hitler's imagination and he demanded its immediate development.

The project was given the code-name HDP (Hochdruckpumpe – high pressure pump) and the construction of two 150mm cannons was started for development and testing, the first at Hillersleben, an artillery test range about 20 kilometres north-west of Magdeburg, the second at Misdroy (now Miedzyzdroje in Poland) on the western side of the Wollin island.

HDP BUNKER AT MIMOYECQUES

In the summer of 1943, with the FZG 76 flying bomb still suffering technical problems and the A4 rocket far from being fully developed, Hitler's interest in the England Cannon was confirmed. Speer's minutes of a meeting in late August read: 'On the basis of my proposal, the Führer commands that it is

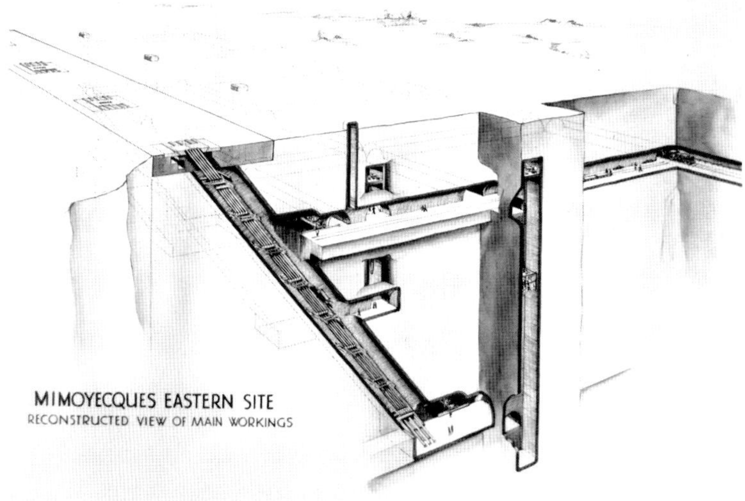

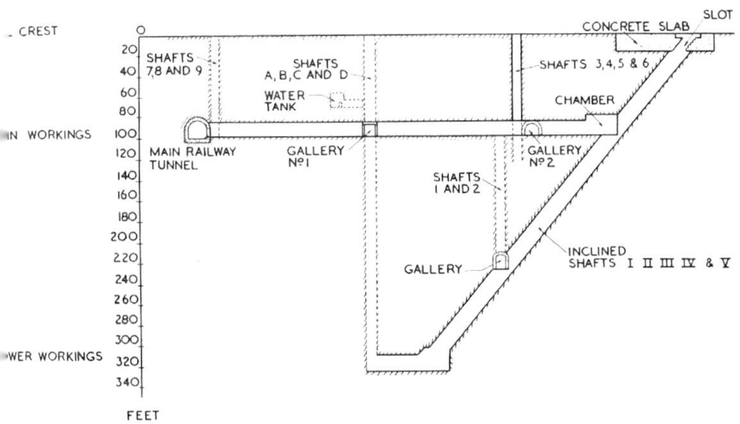

The HDP multi-chambered cannon undoubtedly remains as one of the Third Reich's most bizarre weapons. A survey team led by Colonel Terence Sanders inspected the huge HDP site at Mimoyecques late in 1944 and produced these sketch plans. The shafts were inclined at 50 degrees from the horizontal, each housing a cluster of five 127-metre-long barrels. The main service floor [Main Workings] was 30 metres below ground. It comprised the railway tunnel. In the centre, about 250 metres long, the tunnel was wider to provide an unloading platform beside the line. Parallel to the tunnel, and about 250 metres apart, there was another gallery [Gallery No. 2] and between the two, and perpendicular to them, were eleven galleries numbered 3 to 13. Galleries nos. 6, 7, 8, 9 and 10, served the five inclined shafts numbered I, II, II, IV and V. At their lower ends [Lower Workings], 100 metres underground, the shafts were serviced by another level of galleries and there was also a third intermediary level of service gallery. There were several vertical shafts, both between the various levels and to the surface. Some were intended to accommodate lifts to move personnel, powder charges and ammunition down to the lower levels while others were to ventilate the fumes when the breeches were opened after firing.

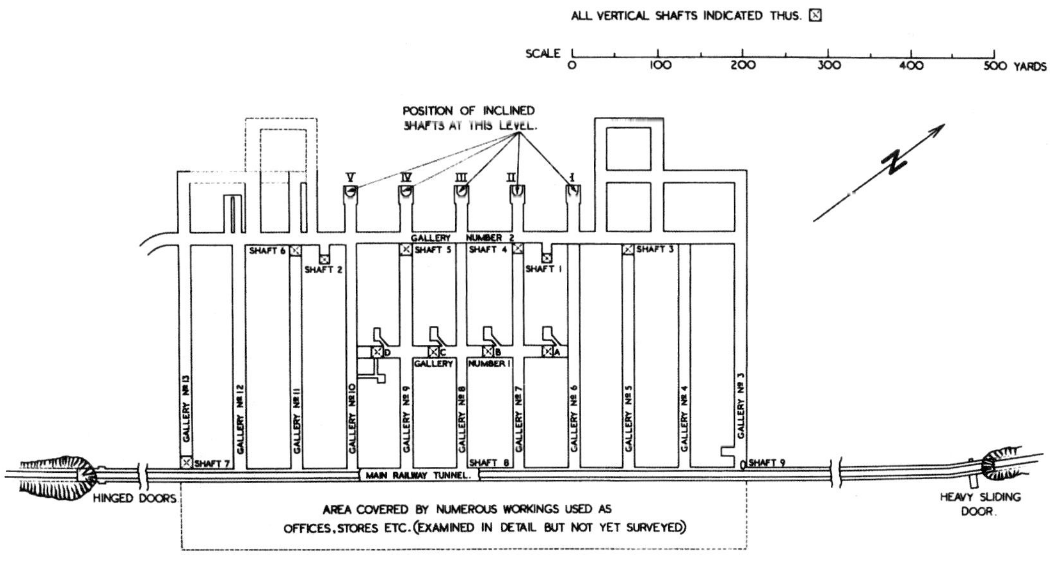

MIMOYECQUES EASTERN SITE.

RECONSTRUCTED PROBABLE PLAN OF MAIN WORKINGS AT 100 FT. BELOW SURFACE.

In May 1945, the Royal Engineers packed tonnes of explosives in the galleries to destroy the facilities but in spite of their efforts, most of the underground complex survived. A mushroom farm was installed in the galleries in 1969, and then a museum was opened in 1984 in the main service floor, 30 metres underground. This is the main gallery as it appears today, looking towards the north entrance.

Gallery No. 9 with the railway tunnel in the background. Shaft No. IV is just behind the photographer.

essential to order the Hochdruckpumpe immediately, without waiting for the results of a test-firing. Test stands at Hillersleben and Misdroy, as well as the immediate construction of a permanent operational site, must be given full support.'

Speer kept Hitler regularly informed of the tests of the 20mm HDP prototype and after a conference with him on September 30 and October 1, he noted: 'After successful tests with the 20mm barrel of the Hochdruckpumpe the Führer wants to be informed continuously about results of the test of the 150mm barrel at Hillersleben and Misdroy. Contrary to planning hitherto, the tests are to be given priority under all circumstances and with considerable support.'

The construction of an operational site in the West was decided and a new code-name was chosen: 'Tausendfüssler' ('Millepede'). Excavation of a huge underground launching bunker was begun in the summer of 1943 under a limestone hill at Mimoyecques in the Pas-de-Calais, about eight kilometres from the Channel coast from where the range to London was 160 kilometres. Five batteries, comprising a total of 25 guns, each approximately 130 metres long, were to be installed in five shafts inclined at an angle of 50 degrees. The bunker would have two floors to service the weapon, at 30 metres and 100 metres, respectively, below the surface. A concrete slab five metres thick was designed to protect the openings of the shaft on the surface.

To complete this gigantic work code-named 'Bauvorhaben 711' (Construction Plan 711), the Organisation Todt engaged 5,000 skilled workers and, according to a note of November 25, the first battery was scheduled to be completed by March 1, 1944, although, at this stage, neither a full-scale HDP gun nor even a projectile had yet been made to work.

On September 18, the suspicions of aerial interpreters at RAF Medmenham had been aroused by railway loops being constructed at Mimoyecques, the lines leading to two parallel tunnels. Further reconnaissance in October showed evidence of shafts being dug from the top of the hill, camouflaged by false haystacks. The site was attacked on November 5 by 150 Marauders of the Ninth Air Force, but bad weather caused one group to miss the target. The RAF in turn arrived on November 8 with some 75 Bostons from the Second Tactical Air Force. Bursts were reported on the railway tracks and at the tunnel entrance.

Work on the west tunnel was abandoned but work on the east tunnel continued without interruption throughout the winter and on January 6, 1944, the Organisation Todt reported that the first inclined shaft was to be completed by February 15. Three weeks were scheduled for mounting the barrels and the first five HDP cannons were to be ready by March 15. The same report stated that 5,000 rounds could be stored there and that from April the first battery would be able to fire an average of 120 shells at London each day.

The first 150mm HDP cannon was ready at Hillersleben at the end of October 1943 when trial firings started. The projectile of Röchling's design

For testing, the first 150mm HDP cannon was built at Hillersleben, an artillery test range on the Colbitz-Letzlinger heath, 20 kilometres north-west of Magdeburg. (USNA)

was about three metres long and weighed 140kg. This prototype, however, had a shortened barrel as it was only intended to test the internal ballistics and other basic technical problems so the range reached during these early experiments was less than ten kilometres.

Nevertheless, Hitler pressed on as the minutes of his meetings with Speer held between January 25-28 at the Führerhauptquartier disclose: 'The Führer has read with great interest the report on the trial firings of the Hochdruckpumpe which

The gun was under repair when this picture was taken. The breech had been unscrewed from the barrel (off the picture to the right) and turned upside down, consequently, the rear of the breech is facing the barrel. (BA)

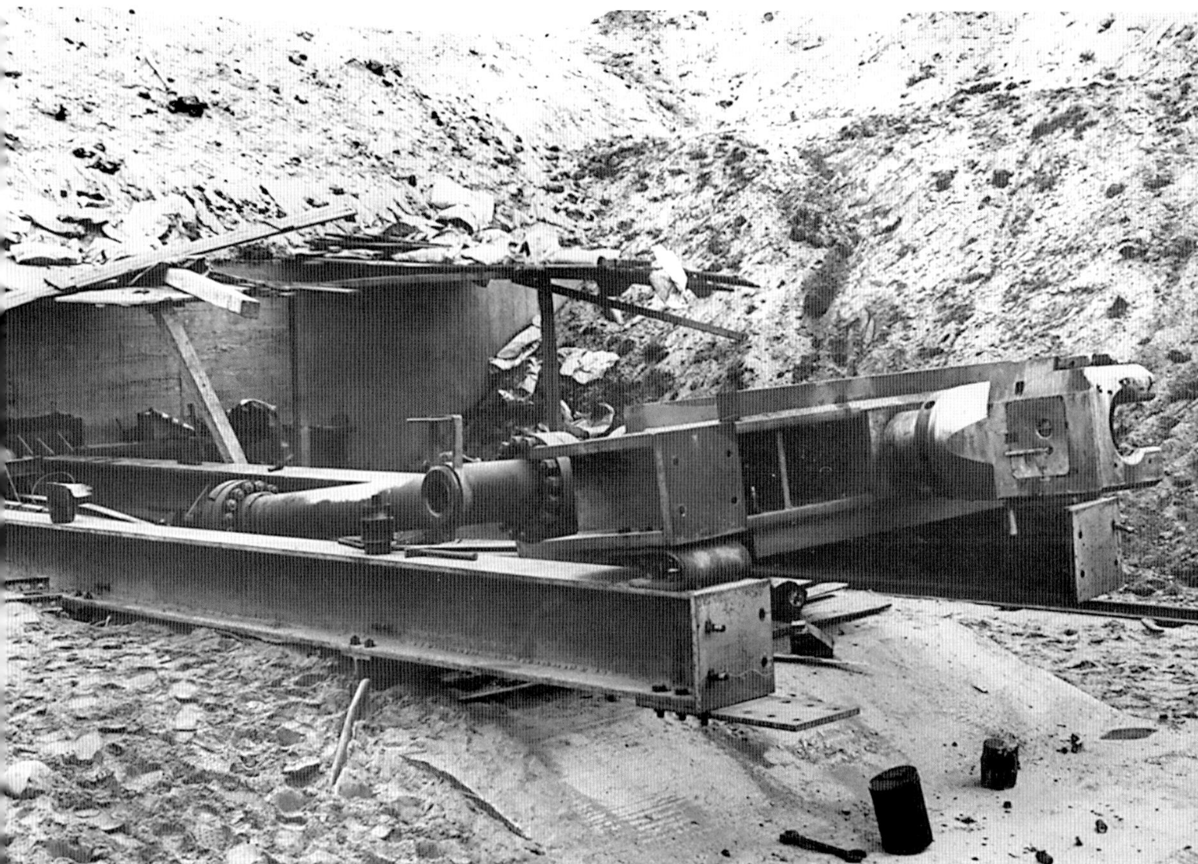

At the Hillersleben test range, the US Ninth Army captured two HDP test cannons in relatively good order, one with ten cross-sections, the other with five. The latter was of a new type, with the side chambers angled at 45 degrees so that a plan view resembles a herring bone. This gun caught the attention of Signal Corps photographers and their photos have led historians to believe that operational HDP guns had firing chambers inclined at 45 degrees. They did not, and all their side chambers were perpendicular to the barrel.

took place January 18-19, 1944. He orders development as well as production to be pushed ahead vigorously, and demands that output of ammunition be shortly increased from the 2,500, which until now was reported as the maximum possible, to 10,000 rounds per month, as had been ordered a long time ago.'

FIRING TRIALS AT MISDROY

On January 15, a special unit – Artillerie-Abteilung 705 – was set up with two batteries to operate the HDP. This was under the command of Oberstleutnant Georg Borttscheller who had previously taken part in the development and testing of the weapon as a member of the Heereswaffenamt, the Army ordnance department responsible for weapon design.

By mid-January, the full-length barrel for the HDP erected at Misdroy was ready. It was 130 metres long and consisted of 32 cross-sections (each with two side chambers). The first trial firings were disappointing for not

For development and testing of the HDP, two full-length barrels were erected near Misdroy on the west side of Wollin island.

In 1944, the Wollin area was German but now it is in Poland and Misdroy was renamed Miedzyzdroje. An old postcard of the Kleiner Vietziger See, now the Wicko Male, with, on the right, the hillside above Weissgrund, today Zalesie, where the HDP prototypes were tested.

Three HDP ramps were built at Weissgrund. The centre and south ramps were for full-length guns, but the north ramp (the test ramp for the shorter operational version of the HDP) was half the length of the other two. Today, the centre and south ramps are still clearly visible from the air. (Google)

only were the muzzle velocities only 1100 metres per second – far from the 1500 metres per second needed to reach England – but the projectiles themselves appeared to be unstable in flight.

The chief of the Heereswaffenamt, General Leeb, had observed some of the trials and he soon drafted in ballistics experts to tackle the defects of the Röchling design. The Reichsforschungsrat (RFR – Reich Research Council) was called in to solve the stability problem of the projectiles and from April wind-tunnel measurements were conducted at the Aerodynamics Research Institute at Göttingen. There, Professor A. Walchner commented critically on the work carried out so far by Röchling: 'Until now there has only a lot of nonsense been done in the development of projectile designs. With such matter, one must use a bit of common sense and it will all go well.' When the chief of the development

By mid-January, the first cannon was ready for testing. It was 130 metres long and consisted of 32 cross-sections each with two side chambers.

branch of the Heereswaffenamt, Generalleutnant Erich Schneider, looked further into the results achieved so far, he made it clear that in his opinion the project was a total failure and that it should be cancelled forthwith. However, with Hitler fully supporting the HDP, nobody dared to endorse his recommendation.

Nevertheless, Speer's deputy (Speer was ill), Karl-Otto Saur, had also become cautious and he broached the subject to Hitler on April 6-7. The Führer agreed to reduce the HDP operational site in the Pas-de-Calais to only three batteries instead of the five originally planned and he also approved the reduction of shell production to 5,000 rounds.

At the end of April, two sections of the barrel exploded at Misdroy after having fired only 25

A careful examination of the two photos taken in 1944 proves that they both show the cannon installed on the south ramp. The long concrete slab that supported the lower part of this ramp ended in the middle, from which point the concrete supports took over.

The three ramps were each of a different design. In 2001, Alvin Gilens took these photos of the south ramp, which consisted of a long, one-piece concrete slab poured directly onto the ground, then a series of massive concrete blocks that, in 1944, supported wooden (or steel?) supports.
(A. Gilens)

rounds and an investigation quickly revealed the cause of the failure: because of faulty heat treatment during its manufacture, the barrel was not strong enough to withstand the multiple explosions. This failure lay with Röchling but the firm appeared unable to produce barrel sections with the specified strength and the Reichsforschungsrat refused to spend more effort on such an immature project. On May 8 the chief of the RFR's planning office, Professor Werner Osenberg, wrote to Reichsleiter Martin Bormann: 'I regard it as my duty to draw your attention to the Hochdruckpumpe project, which is being carried out by order of the Führer at this moment. In my view, it has to be regarded as a failure as far as barrel construction, projectile shape and uneconomical use of explosive material is concerned. For that reason, the use of personnel at the present time cannot be justified.' There is no recorded reaction from Hitler and it is probable that Osenberg's analysis was not even made known to him.

The centre ramp was built with the lower part of the ramp laid directly on the ground in a series of steps and with large concrete supports to carry the upper part of the cannon. The centre ramp was built at a 50-degree angle, steeper than the south ramp which had a 40-degree angle. (A. Gilens)

This was, in 2001, the series of nine concrete supports which supported the upper part of the centre ramp. When compared to what had happened to the south ramp, the foundations were of better quality here and none of the supports have given way. (A. Gilens)

The northern ramp is only visible today as an earthwork on the hillside. This was the test ramp for operational versions of the HDP, half the length of the full-length gun, for testing wood and steel frame supports. It was built at a 34-degree angle. At the bottom of the ramp, by the side of the road, pieces of metal from the base of the cannon were recently unearthed.

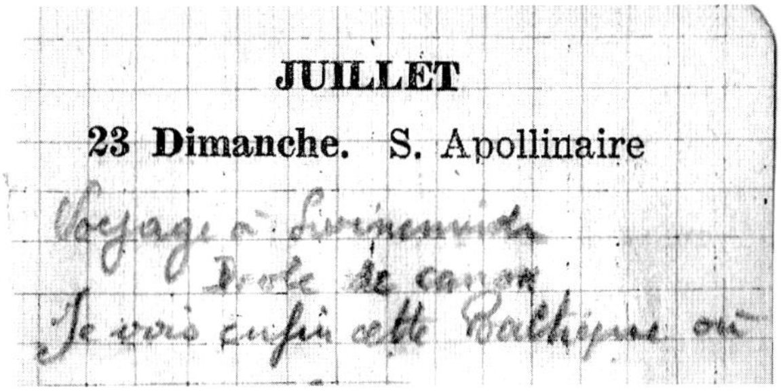
JUILLET

23 Dimanche. S. Apollinaire

Voyage à Swinemünde
Drôle de canon
Je vois enfin cette Baltique où

In May 1944, Pierre Drémont, a Frenchman, was called up for forced labour in Germany as part of the so-called STO measure (Service du Travail Obligatoire – Compulsory Labour Service). He was sent to the Portland Zement-Fabrik at Stettin (now Szczecin in Poland) where he was assigned to work in a quarry at Kalkofen (now Wapnica). Sundays were a day off, Pierre would go hiking in the hills or to the beaches of the Baltic, a long walk through the villages of Vietzig (now Wicko) and Weissgrund (now Zalesie) and back. Pierre provided us with the diary he carefully kept of his deportation to Germany. On July 23, 1944, he scribbled: 'went to Swinemünde, a queer cannon', and on August 13: 'a lot of fuss at the cannon'. One day, he heard an explosion coming from the direction of the cannon – an accidental explosion destroyed a cross-section of the gun during one of the test shots. Some time later, when things returned to normal, Pierre walked to Weissgrund and stopped at the local café for a beer. He saw the locals busy working to repair damage to roofs and windows, helped by a team of workers from the Organisation Todt. The damaged houses were just at the base of the cannon, about 50 metres from the south ramp. It was impossible for him to walk around and take a closer look at the mysterious gun for 'there were a lot of armed guards around'.

A new series of test-firings was carried out at Misdroy between May 20-24, when different shell designs were tried, including the one from Röchling, with others from Deutsche Faserstoff, Bochumer Verein and Witkowitz Eisenwerk. Reaching a muzzle velocity of 1370 metres per second, the latter design – 1.8 metre long and weighing 65kg in flight – attained a range of 90 kilometres. By the end of the month, the Heereswaffenamt reported

Pierre remained in Kalkofen until March 5, 1945, when the quarry was closed and he was then transferred to Stettin where Russian troops liberated him. He brought back this old postcard from the Gasthaus August Berndt in Weissgrund where he stopped for a beer in August 1944. In 2000, Pierre told the author: 'It was like in a Jules Verne book. The cannon was very long, impossible for me to tell the length. There was a wooden staircase on the right-hand side. The bottom end of the barrel was in a small bunker, and on each side there was a bunker with a facade at a slight angle to the road. The installation was in the middle of the forest, the cannon and the bunkers were all painted dark green, and the whole was meant to be invisible from the air.'

By the end of June, the HDP bunker at Mimoyecques had already suffered 13 air attacks when the Bomber Command launched another raid on July 6. Exploding bombs sent smoke and clouds of dust into the air as a Halifax was pictured over the site.

confidently that it was possible that the required range would be reached.

Having attended a demonstration of the HDP at Misdroy, Generalmajor Dornberger wrote: 'An enormous number of gunners was required to service the weapon, standing on the staircases that ran to right and left sides of the barrel, and reloading the T-pieces with propellant charges between rounds.'

After further meetings with Hitler during the course of May 22-25, Saur recorded: 'Have informed the Führer about the result of the latest trial firings with the Hochdruckpumpe at Misdroy. He expects the continuation of tests in view of the special task as England Cannon, as well as for the possible employment of the principle of the Tausendfüssler for other purposes.'

However, the 'England Cannon' was destined never to fire any shots in anger. The Allies had kept a close watch on the construction at Mimoyecques and a dozen heavy attacks by B-17s and B-24s of the Eighth Air Force hit the HDP bunker in March, April, May, and June 1944.

Then, on July 6, 617 Squadron came in with its 'Tallboy' bombs. They scored one direct hit on the concrete slab at the top of the hill, through which the muzzles of the guns would have fired, and four near misses. This caused one of the gun shafts and some tunnels to collapse. In August, the Allies launched further attacks on the site with radio-controlled B-17s and B-24s (loaded with explosives) from Operation 'Aphrodite'. On August 4, the first mission was flown using four B-17s but none of the targets, including Mimoyecques, were hit. In the second such attack, on August 12, a B-24 targeted at Mimoyecques exploded prematurely over the Blyth Estuary, killing the US Navy crew, Lieutenant Joseph P. Kennedy Jr. – the older brother of future US President John F. Kennedy – and Lieutenant Wilford J. Willy.

Bomber Command launched a final heavy raid on Mimoyecques on August

The 617 Squadron dropped 16 Tallboy bombs this day. One clipped the concrete slab and five near misses caused the collapse of one of the shafts and some of the galleries. After inspecting the damage, German engineers reported next day that installation of the HDP barrels was now impossible. However, aerial reconnaissance indicated that work appeared to be continuing (the Germans were repairing the railway tunnel entrance) so the Bomber Command launched yet another heavy attack on August 27. Less than ten days later, on September 5, the 3rd Canadian Division overran the abandoned site.

Colonel Sanders' mission was on site for four months. This was the southern entrance to the railway tunnel as it appeared late in 1944. Note the pipe bottom right, probably used to pump out flooded chambers.

Another photo taken by Colonel Sanders' team, of one of the firing slots in the concrete slab. In his report dated February 21, 1945, Sanders concluded that the installation could be repaired and consequently posed a threat to London. It was therefore decided to destroy the underground installations and the Royal Engineers packed ten tons of explosives in the galleries. The resulting explosion on May 9 failed to close the entrances and a further 25 tons was blown at both end of the railway tunnel on May 14.

This remarkable aerial shot was taken in May 1974 when *After the Battle* visited Mimoyecques. The Editor then reported: 'The top of the hill is an overgrown lunar landscape with the tremendous 'Tallboy' craters and the shattered 18ft slab broken up at all angles.'

27 and in the first days of September, Canadian troops overran the abandoned site. More than 4,100 tons of bombs were dropped on Mimoyecques, more than on any other V-weapons site.

From June 1944, the subject of the HDP was no longer raised by Speer at the regular armament conferences with Hitler. At the beginning of July another defect caused another section of the barrel to rupture at Misdroy as a result of which a third of the barrel had to be replaced. Consequently, Röchling was directed to use a steel richer in nickel and to pre-test each section to a pressure of 2,500 atmospheres in the factory.

From August, a muzzle velocity of 1500 metres per second was known to be unrealistic so a shorter range was accepted as being practical for purposes other than what was originally intended. The development of the long HDP barrel – the 130 metres as envisaged for the England Cannon – was abandoned and instead shortened versions were planned. It seems that plans were made for a 60-metre-long cannon and an 80-metre-long cannon and by mid-August a plan was agreed for the LRK 15 F 58 (LRK, Langrohrkanone – long-barrelled cannon) which could be brought into action at the fighting front. This version comprised 12 cross-sections and was about 50 metres long.

A demonstration of this 12 cross-section HDP cannon was held at Misdroy on November 14 and it went off without any unusual occurrences. Plans were already being made for the deployment of the weapon and two days

The concrete slab protecting the openings of the shaft on the surface did not survive the Royal Engineers' demolitions. This is a surviving corner at the top of shaft No. V. In the background, the crater of the Tallboy which clipped a corner of the slab.

after this demonstration a report gave the basic data for the construction of an operational firing site. To build a site for one gun would need 40 men working for ten days; three to ten tonnes of steel; about ten cubic metres of wood, with 150 to 200 cubic metres of earth to be excavated. The hillside on which the gun was to be set should be at an angle of 30 degrees, or better 34 degrees, and 30 to 50 metres long and, of course, facing the enemy front. As the dispersion of shots was reported as being three kilometres in length and up to 800 metres laterally, it was recommended that the target area should be at least five kilometres long and one kilometre wide. The rate of fire was to be two to three shots per hour. In this report, the gun was referred to as 'Fleissiges Lieschen' (Busy Lizzie).

Although the report said that 700 rounds of ammunition would be produced before January 13, 1945, and a further 800 rounds by February 1, as late as the end of November no decision had been made as to the type of shell to be used. The minutes of a discussion between SS-Gruppenführer Kammler and Generalmajor Dornberger in Berlin on the 29th read: 'Results of the HDP firings at M[isdroy] must be received as soon as possible in order to determine the type of projectile to be used'. On December 22, ten rounds of the 0-Serie, the pilot production batch, were test-fired at Hillersleben and the result was reported as good. The following day, Major Axster (who at B.z.b.V. Heer, Dornberger's staff, had assumed responsibility for the HDP and Rheinbote projects) reported to Kammler that 50 rounds of ammunition would be available at the front on December 29, and another 150 rounds by the end of the first week of January.

INTO ACTION: FIRING AT LUXEMBOURG AND BELFORT

By mid-November, Röchling had delivered two shortened HDP cannons and Kammler ordered their immediate deployment in support of 'Wacht am Rhein', the major offensive then planned in the West. The chosen operational site was at Lampaden, 12 kilometres south of Trier, and work began to install the two cannons on the slope on the western side of the Ruwer river. Their target was to be Luxembourg, 42.5 kilometres away.

Under Kammler's Division z.V., Artillerie-Abteilung 705 took over and, as from November 30, the men of its 1. Batterie (7 officers, 33 NCOs and 96 men) started to assemble at Zerf, a town five kilometres to the south of Lampaden. From mid-December the battalion was under the command of Hauptmann Patzig.

The transport system in the West – railways and roads – was overstrained by the preparations already in hand for the coming offensive with the result that the parts for the HDP arrived piecemeal. When the offensive commenced on December 16, neither of the two guns was ready for action nor was any ammunition available. Nevertheless, two days later, Kammler sent a telex to Generalleutnant Siegfried Westphal, Chief-of-Staff of Ob. West, to describe the operations planned: 'The HDP will be brought into action with two barrels in a troop trial at the operational area of Ruwer at Trier, with the target being Luxembourg. Both barrels have been ready for action since December 15, 1944. During the month of December, 50 rounds will be made available. Operational and target areas have been chosen with regard to firing range (60km) and spread (2.5 - 5km), as well as the angle of inclination of the barrels, which are rigidly installed upon mountain slopes with special trestles (34 degrees). The shells weigh 90kg, of which 7 to 9kg for the explosive charge. Request agreement in principle with making of first attempt from December 20.'

Hitler had high expectations of the HDP's operations, and in early December he announced to Goebbels the deployment of a new weapon. Goebbels then announced the appearance of a new V weapon, the V3, a name which was however never used officially.

Anticipating that the left wing of the 7. Armee might soon reach the Luxemburg sector, Ob. West immediately replied: 'Regarding the current fighting of Heeresgruppe B, Ob. West ask that the target for the HDP, which has been mentioned in the telex, not be used, as this could endanger own troops. In any case, it is requested that an inquiry be made on December 20 regarding the continued possibility of firing against that target.'

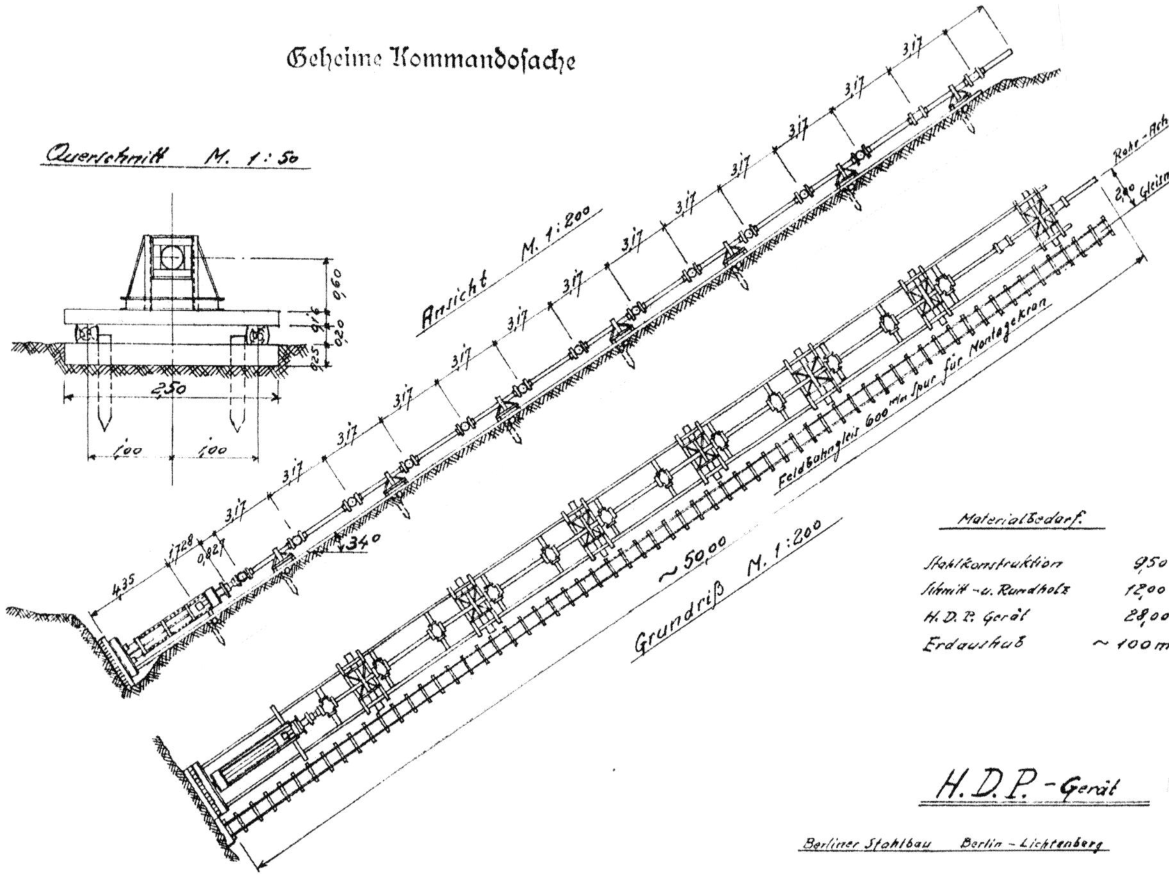

This plan of an operational HDP cannon was drawn on November 26, 1944. It shows the breech block in a pit dug out at the bottom of a slope, the 12 cross-sections of the cannon, the wood framework and the seven steel substructures that supported it. To the right of the barrel can be seen the 60cm rail track for the mobile crane used to assemble the gun.

Equipment and material had still not arrived at Lampaden by December 20 so Artillerie-Abteilung 705 had to report that construction of the HDP had not made any progress. The breech and the first five cross-sections were finally in place by the 25th and three days later the first cannon was ready for action although no shells were available. Construction of the second gun was at a standstill because many parts for it were still on board a train that was caught up in the bombed-out Trier railway yards.

Delivered by the Heeresmunitionsanstalt (HMA – Army Ammunition Establishment) at Feucht near Nuremberg, the first 44 shells finally arrived at Lampaden on December 29. On the 30th, at 11.16 p.m., in the presence of Kammler, Artillerie-Abteilung 705 opened fire with five shots against Luxembourg. The HDP resumed firing early next morning with 12 shots until at 9.44 a.m. it appeared that the barrel needed to be re-adjusted. That work took most of the day, firing being resumed at 7.43 p.m. with a series of 11 shots. Meanwhile, an investigation was conducted in the area between the firing site and the front line, some 30 kilometres away, to check that no shorts had occurred. None were reported.

The second HDP cannon was ready for action on January 2 but could

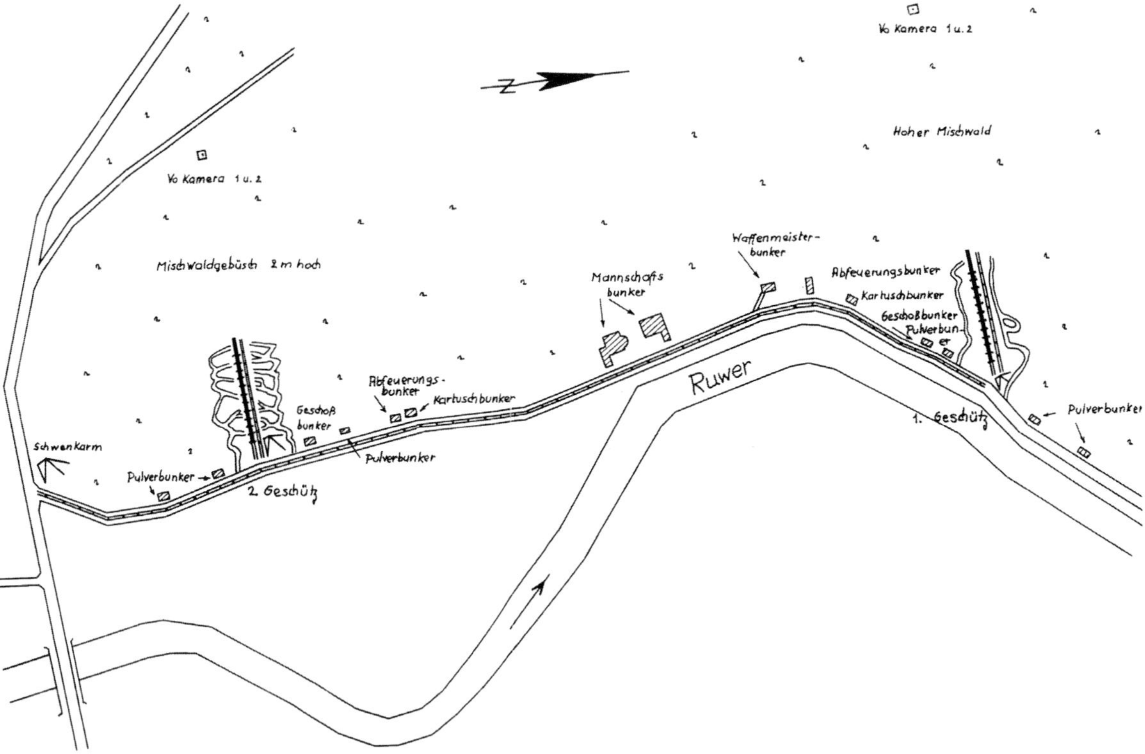

The two HDP cannons of the 1. Batterie of Artillerie-Abteilung 705 were installed near Lampaden, 12 kilometres south of Trier, on the slope on the west side of the Ruwer River. Their objective was Luxembourg, 42.5 kilometres away. The site extended over 300 metres along the bank of the river. At the start of the railway, by the side of the road on the left, a 2-tonne crane (Schwenkarm) was provided to unload the various parts of the guns from trucks to wagons. When the cannon was operational, this same crane was used to move the crates of shells and propellant charges. At the foot of each cannon, another crane bridged the gap from the railway. Running alongside the cannon was a 60cm-gauge railway carrying the mobile crane used to assemble the barrel. At the bottom of the slope, a series of sheds held a total of 50 rounds, 25 for each cannon. There were three sheds for propellant charges (for the side chambers, 18 charges for each shot), one for cartridges (to load the breech, one for each shot) and one for shells. Though this sketch named these constructions 'Bunker', the report called them 'Hütte' and an annex clearly showed what they were: simple wood constructions 3.5 metres long, 1 metre wide and 1.25 metres in height. There was also one firing shed for each gun and two larger sheds for the crews were provided in between them.

not begin firing because of the lack of ammunition. Actually, 20 shells were available but these had been held back as Kammler had ordered that they only be fired when aerial observation was available over Luxembourg to report the fall of shot. The Luftwaffe had detailed Kommando Hecht, a unit equipped with Arado 234 jet aircraft, to fly this mission but the aircraft failed to show up so in the end the last 16 shells were fired blind on the 4th.

When Röchling advised that the third cannon would be ready for delivery on January 5 and the fourth a few days later, on January 3 Kammler ordered that a new firing site be surveyed in the Eifel between Hellenthal and Hollerath. From there, the two new guns could be brought into action against Verviers, a major Allied communication centre in Belgium. For that purpose, a second battery of Artillerie-Abteilung 705 was set up under the command of Oberleutnant Fiedler. However, the military situation was changing by the day and on the 7th Kammler cancelled this plan and instead ordered

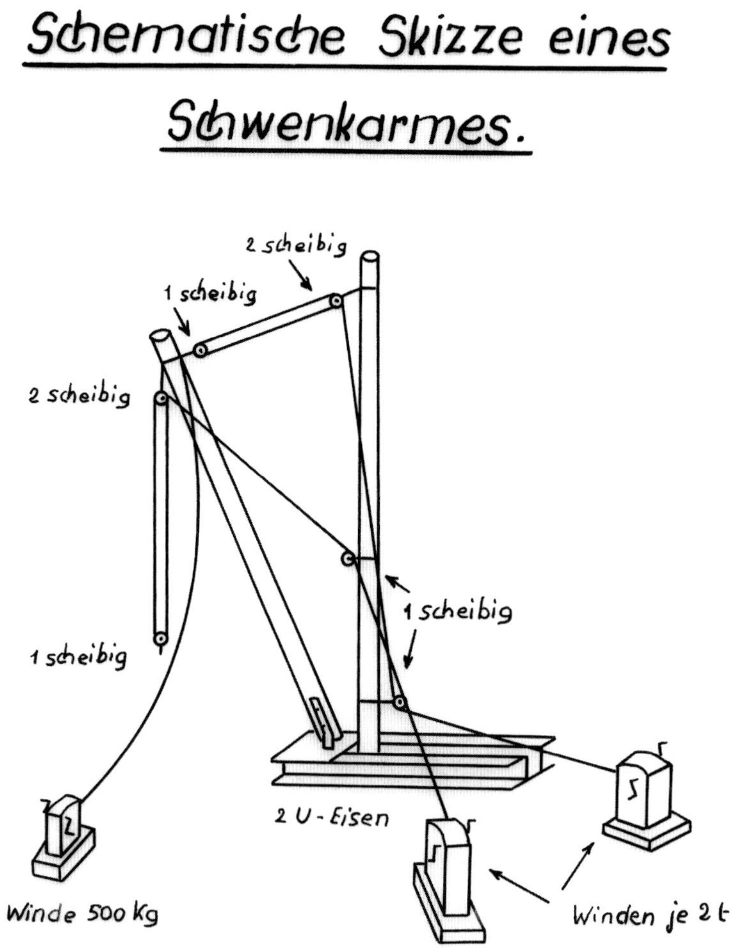

Another genuine plan from 1944 describing how to create a 2-tonne crane (Schwenkarm) at the start of the railway to unload the various parts of the guns from the trucks to the narrow-gauge railway carriages.

Here, by the side of the road between Lampaden (to the left) and Schillingen (right) was the start of the narrow-gauge railway that served the HDP site. The bush on the right is where the crane once stood.

A January 15 report indicates that building an operational ramp – digging the earthworks and building the wooden frame – required 35 men working for eight to 10 days. The actual assembly of the gun took a team of 28 men four days, with ten men needed to bring the gun parts down the ramp and load them onto the mobile crane; 12 men to manoeuvre this crane up and down the slope as no motorised winch was available, and six to erect and assemble the gun.

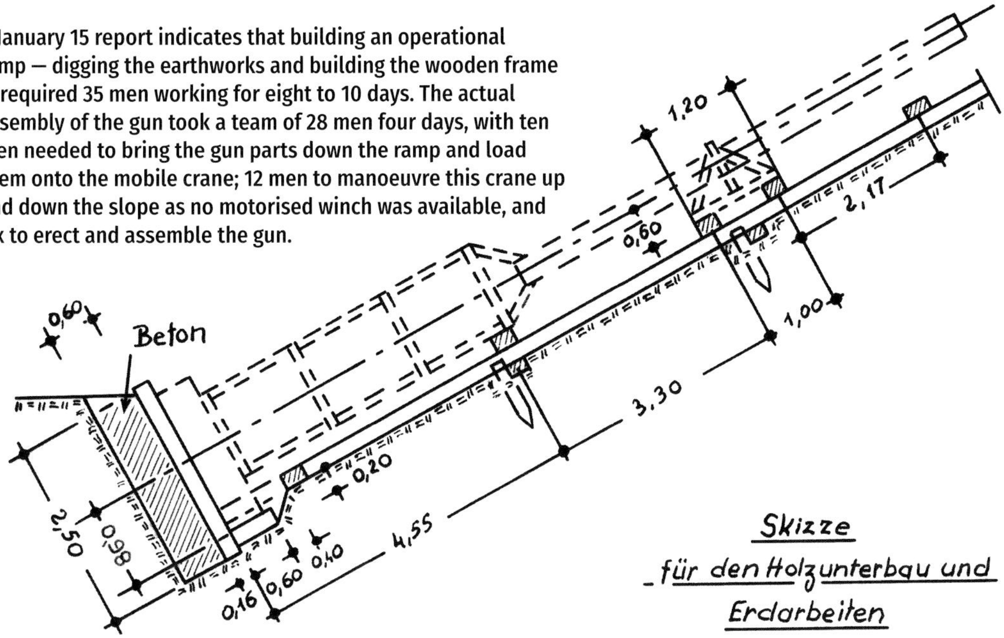

The southern ramp at Lampaden as it appears today. The 1945 report says that engineers from Organisation Todt excavated a total of 250 cubic metres of earth and rocks at Lampaden, all by hands. Explosives had to be used to dig out a large excavation at the top of the ramp where a four-metre clearance had to be provided at the muzzle of the gun. This excavation is still clearly visible at the top of the ramp.

This is the northern ramp as it appears today, one photo taken in the direction of the fire, the other looking down towards the Ruwer River. The HDP guns were installed rigidly on the slope (the 1945 report specified that they had to be adjusted with great precision, plus or minus a tenth of a degree from the theoretical aiming point), their range was adjusted by varying the charges in the side chambers. The first eight pairs of chambers were always loaded with full charges (3.1kg of explosive each) but, depending on the distance to the target, the remaining side chambers would be loaded with either full or half charges (2kg only), or not at all. To hit Luxembourg from Lampaden, the first nine pairs of chambers were loaded with full charges but there were none in the 10th, 11th, and 12th chambers. Together with the charge in the breech, the total propellant was over 60kg and the muzzle velocity was then 884 metres per second.

In a report in 1945, the commander of the 1. Batterie described how difficult it was to hide the site from Allied planes: the gun heated up after firing, which in turn heated up the camouflage placed above the installation, thus melting the snow and the outline of the gun became identifiable. The slopes of the Ruwer River valley at Lampaden were — and still are — covered by bushes and trees but these were not high or thick enough to camouflage the guns from the air. The photo shows where the narrow-gauge railway ended at the bottom of the north ramp.

In the middle of the Lampaden HDP site, between the two cannons, two underground shelters had been built for the gun crews. This is where the plan places these shelters and traces of digging still appear today at the bottom of the slope. The narrow-gauge railway which served the whole length of the HDP site ran on this track, the southern gun being 100 metres or so ahead of the bend in the track and the northern one 100 metres behind the photographer.

This would appear to be the remains of one of the underground shelters provided for personnel.

the immediate construction of a new firing site in the Vosges mountains for operations against Belfort.

On January 5, Heinz Kunze, the director of the Sonderausschuss V-Waffen committee at the Ministry of Armaments and Munitions demanded the production of 5,000 rounds of HDP ammunition. Three days later, another directive specified the production of 1,000 rounds per month from January to March. According to a document dated January 8, and signed by Kammler himself, it was then planned to increase the size of Artillerie-Abteilung 705 to three batteries. Each one, with a strength of 157 men and two officers, was to have two HDP cannons, plus two replacement guns. Together with battery staff and other personnel, the total strength of Artillerie-Abteilung 705 would then be 557 men.

Also in January, plans were made to bring the HDP into action against a new target, Antwerp. From the part of the Netherlands south of Rotterdam which was still held by the Germans, the range to Antwerp was over 60 kilometres. Consequently, the 50 metre-long HDP would have to be used to its maximum range with a total powder charge of 120kg per shot (just over 60kg was necessary to fire at Luxembourg). The muzzle velocity was expected to reach 1050 metres per second. All these plans were illusory and never materialised.

On January 9, another 80 shells were delivered to Lampaden and both cannons opened up again on the 11th. Over three days, 60 shells were fired with the last 20 again held back for the planned aerial shoot. When a further 60 shells were delivered on the 17th, firing resumed on the 18th and the 20th, now with the last 30 shells being retained in case the Luftwaffe showed up.

The shelling of Luxembourg came as a complete surprise to the Allies. As reconnaissance planes failed to detect the two HDP guns, the only measures taken were retaliatory attacks on Trier and, for every HDP projectile

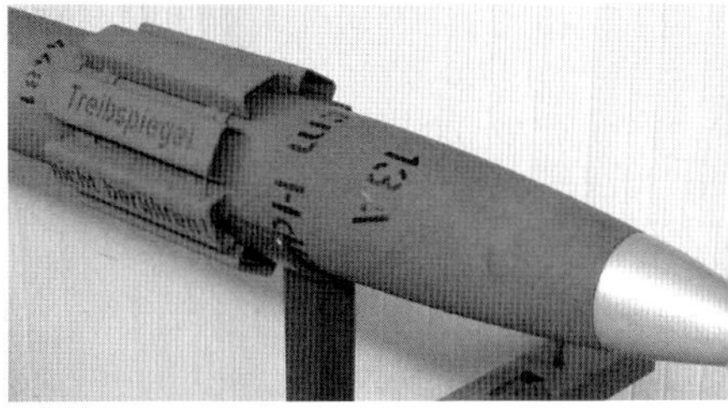

A total of 183 rounds were fired from Lampaden. This HDP shell is now on display at the military museum in Diekirch, 15 kilometres north of Luxembourg. The body is that of a genuine Röchling shell of unknown origin but the nose and tail have been reconstructed by museum staff.

The first gun opened fire from Lampaden on December 30, and the second on January 11. The 150 mm shells were finned projectiles with a discarding sabot, and according to a telex from Kammler of December 18, they weighed 90 kg, including 7 to 9 kg for the explosive charge. We do not know where these two photos were taken but the wooden box appearing in the second photo suggests an operational delivery to Artillerie-Abteilung 705. (USNA)

On January 16, the two HDP guns at Lampaden fired six shots against Luxembourg city. At around 5.18 p.m., a shell hit this spire of the Notre-Dame Cathedral, causing little damage. In 2000, Alain Feltes, the sacristan of the cathedral, took this superb comparison for us from a narrow balcony at the top of the roof.
(G. Mirgain and A. Feltes)

exploding in Luxembourg, eight 155mm shells were fired at Trier by the artillery of the US XII Corps.

Meanwhile, at Buhl in the Vosges, construction work at the second firing site was proceeding apace. By mid-January, the elements of the third cannon were already on their way by rail with those for the fourth following on. However, the military situation in Alsace was deteriorating badly with the position of the 2. Batterie at Buhl becoming more and more untenable and on February 1 Kammler cancelled the installation of the fourth piece. He also ordered the third, the mounting of which had by then been completed, to quickly fire off 20 shells against Belfort before it was dismantled and moved, together with the fourth, back to Hellenthal in the Eifel with Verviers as the target. However, this plan had to be abandoned on the 5th whereupon the 2. Batterie with its two guns was diverted to a new location 30 kilometres south of Trier, at Niederlosheim, to fire at Thionville.

On February 12, Kammler was informed that no further ammunition would be supplied after the delivery of the final lot of 70 shells which were scheduled to arrive by the end of the month. He therefore ordered that the construction of the new firing site at Niederlosheim be abandoned and for the remaining shells to be sent to Lampaden to be fired off against Luxembourg. He also ordered Hauptmann Patzig, the Artillerie-Abteilung 705 commander, to turn his unit into a normal artillery group, detailing him to find his own guns.

While the men of the 2. Batterie started to assemble at Vielbach, near Koblenz, at Lampaden the 1. Batterie was still waiting for the promised aerial observation, However, with the situation at the front worsening, on the 15th, the two guns resumed firing. The same day the order came to start the immediate disassembly of one cannon to move it back to the eastern bank of the Rhine and to fire off the remaining shells with the other. The

WAR DIARY, ARTILLERIE-REGIMENT zV 901

22 November
SS-Gruppenführer Kammler visiting Artillerie-Abteilung 836. Discussion between SS-Gruppenführer and Oberstleutnant Honig regarding construction of emplacements for HDP.

30 November
Artillerie-Abteilung 705 with 7 officers, 33 NCOs and 96 men arrive at Zerf.

16 December
Preparations continuing for installation of HDP at Lampaden. Transportation situation difficult – this resulting in sparse and erratic arrival of equipment.

20 December
Impossible to continue with further construction work for HDP at Lampaden as transports not arriving.

22 December
HDP still able to proceed only to a very limited extent with installation because transports with essential overhead sections are still missing. Work carried out on underground shelters for personnel.

25 December
Steel substructure for HDP cannon No. 1 at Lampaden completed; breechblock and five cross-sections with tubes assembled.

26 December
Hauptmann Patzig, the newly arrived officer commanding Artillerie-Abteilung 705, arrives at Gruppe and reports that the assembly of HDP cannon No. 1 at Lampaden should be completed by December 28. He is presently unable to say when the assembly of cannon No. 2 will be completed as this depends on recovery of parts from the bombed railway sidings at Trier. Gruppe promises him two cranes for this recovery operation.

28 December
HDP cannon No. 1 at Lampaden ready for firing, albeit without munitions at this stage.

29 December
Arrival of first munitions (44 projectiles) for HDP. Substructure for cannon No. 2 being assembled. Arrival of crane for recovery of parts from bombed railway sidings at Trier. The division commander demands that cannon No. 2 be made ready for firing by December 30.

30 December
In the presence of the division commander and the commander of Artillerie-Abteilung 836, HDP opens fire with five projectiles against Luxembourg.

31 December
HDP fires 23 projectiles against Luxembourg. Following the recovery of parts, assembly has commenced of superstructure for HDP cannon No. 2 at Lampaden.

1 January
No HDP firing because on orders from Division zV a munitions stock of some 20 projectiles is to be retained at all times for firing at targets in conjunction with spotter planes. Luftwaffenkommando West has authorised observation flights by the Hecht detachment. Construction of cannon No. 2 at Lampaden completed. Ready for firing following adjustments to cannon.

2 January
No HDP firing.

3 January
No HDP firing. Two more HDP installations have been completed at the factory. Oberstleutnant Honig receives order from division commander to reconnoitre positions in the Eifel area from which to attack Verviers.

4 January
HDP fires 16 projectiles from cannon No. 1 against Luxembourg. Provisional results of Oberstleutnant Honig's reconnaissance are as follows: HDP cannons for use against Verviers should be set up around Hellental-Hollerath, 45km to the west of Ahrweiler.

5 January
No HDP firing due to lack of munitions. Fresh heavy snowfalls making transportation even more difficult. Troops continually having to clear snow to keep roads passable.

6 January
No HDP firing due to lack of munitions. Further heavy snowfalls making transportation considerably more difficult – especially for the specialist heavy vehicles.

7 January
No HDP firing due to lack of munitions. On orders from Division, Oberstleutnant Honig's reconnaissance for HDP positions in the Eifel area for use against Verviers to cease forthwith. An immediate reconnaissance for positions for use against Belfort to commence in the Vosges area around Colmar-Munster-Guebwiller. Division orders cannons No. 3 and No. 4 to be positioned there.

9 January
Eighty projectiles delivered by lorry for HDP. Cartridges for these also on the way by lorry. Heavy snowfalls continuing.

WAR DIARY, ARTILLERIE-REGIMENT zV 901

11 January
HDP fires 20 projectiles from cannon No. 1 against Luxembourg.

12 January
Eighteen projectiles fired by cannons No. 1 and No. 2 against Luxembourg.

13 January
HDP fires 22 projectiles from cannons No. 1 and No. 2 against Luxembourg. Oberstleutnant Honig reports reconnaissance of suitable positions 3km to the north-west of Guebwiller as emplacements for HDP cannons No. 3 and No. 4.

14 January
No HDP firing. Following orders from the Reichsführer-SS, an SS cameraman filmed installations and firing at HDP.

15 January
No firing as munitions all expended apart from 20 projectiles held in reserve on orders from Division. Order issued for transfer of 2./705 to the sector Guebwiller-Schweighouse in the Vosges.

16 January
HDP fires six projectiles from cannons No. 1 and No. 2 against Luxembourg.

17 January
Sixty projectiles for HDP transported overland from Feucht.

18 January
HDP fires 19 projectiles from cannons No. 1 and No. 2 against Luxembourg.

20 January
HDP fires 24 projectiles from cannons No. 1 and No. 2 against Luxembourg.

21 January
No HDP firing.

23 January
As during preceding days, no HDP firing since only 30 projectiles remain (these to be held back for firing in conjunction with spotter aircraft).

24 January
No HDP firing whatsoever as munitions situation remains unchanged.

25 January
Planned firing in conjunction with spotter aircraft has to be abandoned, as the Hecht Luftwaffe detachment does not take off.

26 January
No HDP firing.

27 January
Construction proceeding of cannons No. 3 and No. 4 in the Vosges. Preparatory earth-moving works almost complete. Cannon No. 3 is on the way by rail transport. Cannon No. 4 to be moved up. Production of munitions for HDP most seriously jeopardised by events in the east.

28 January
Munitions situation at HDP remains unchanged – no firing.

29 January
No HDP firing in Lampaden area; assembly of cannon No. 3 commenced in the Vosges area. Heavy enemy pressure on the Alsace bridgehead making situation highly critical for 2./705.

30 January
Munitions situation at HDP remains unchanged – no firing.

1 February
Due to events on the Eastern Front, there is no prospect of an early supply of munitions to HDP. The next batch of 70 projectiles cannot be delivered for four weeks. At the same time, the situation in the Alsace bridgehead is becoming very critical. According to information from the army group in that sector, it is therefore not possible to count on long-term engagement by 2./705 against Belfort from the Guebwiller area. It is therefore decided that cannon No. 4 will not be transferred to the left bank of the Rhine, but instead stay entrained on the right bank. Assembly of cannon No. 3 is complete. Twenty projectiles are to be taken from the munitions stock of 1./705 (30 projectiles) and transferred to 2./705. After the firing of these 20 projectiles, cannon No. 3 is to be rapidly dismantled and moved over to the right bank of the Rhine so as to be transferred with cannon No. 4 over to the area of Hellenthal in the Eifel region. There both cannons are to be set up in the previously reconnoitred position for action against Verviers.

5 February
Orders received from division commander to the effect that 2./705 is not to be committed against Verviers, but rather against Thionville from the Trier area. Oberstleutnant Honig instructed to carry out fresh reconnaissance for the setting up of two cannons. The unfavourable development of the situation necessitates the rapid dismantling of the cannon of 2./705 at its present location at Guebwiller without any projectiles having been fired. The munitions which had been transferred overland (20 missiles) are to be returned to 1./705.

WAR DIARY, ARTILLERIE-REGIMENT zV 901

6 February
Still no further firing by 1./705 as munitions situation is unchanged and what little munitions remain still to be held back for firing in co-operation with spotter aircraft of the Hecht detachment.

7 February
Situation at HDP remains unchanged. Under the prudent leadership of the officer commanding Artillerie-Abteilung 705, Hauptmann Patzig, the entire operation to dismantle and reposition 2./705 to the right bank of the Rhine has been carried out under heavy enemy fire without loss to men or materiel.

9 February
Situation at HDP unchanged.

10 February
No HDP firing as munitions are still being conserved for firing in conjunction with spotter aircraft. Oberstleutnant Honig's reconnaissance of positions for cannons No. 3 and 4 (2./705) against Thionville is complete. The cannons are to be positioned near Niederlosheim.

11 February
Munitions situation at HDP remains unchanged – no firing.

12 February
SS-Gruppenführer Kammler advised by BzbV Heer that the manufacture of munitions for HDP is to end. Apart from the 70 projectiles expected at the end of the month, there will be no further supplies. At the suggestion of Gruppe Süd, SS-Gruppenführer Kammler orders that there is now no longer question of a new emplacement for 2./705 for firing against Thionville. He issues a verbal order to the officer commanding Artillerie-Abteilung 705 that the battalion is to convert to a conventional artillery unit.

13 February
No HDP firing as it is still envisaged there will be firing in conjunction with spotter aircraft.

14 February
Munitions situation at HDP remains unchanged – no firing.

15 February
Despite on-going discussions, the Hecht detail has failed to take off for days; accordingly 20 projectiles fired by 1./705 against Luxembourg from cannon No. 1 without target spotting from the air. Due to the tense situation in the Trier area, 1./705 (upon its own suggestion) is ordered to dismantle forthwith one of the two cannons at Lampaden and withdraw it by rail to the right bank of the Rhine and fire the remaining projectiles from one cannon. In order to assist in the event of any breakdown during the firing of the 80 projectiles which are expected to be available, some barrel sections of the dismantled cannon are to be held back in reserve.

16 February
HDP fires four projectiles against Luxembourg.

17 February
No firing by 1./705 as an attempt will be made to fire at least the last six projectiles currently available with the co-operation of target spotting aircraft.

19 February
No HDP firing.

22 February
The last six projectiles fired by 1./705 against Luxembourg as the situation to the west of Lampaden has become so tense that Division has ordered the immediate dismantling of the last cannon still in position and its removal to safety on the right bank of the Rhine. It is not possible to wait for the opportunity for firing with spotter aircraft due to the urgency of the situation.

23 February
Dismantling and withdrawal of the last HDP cannon commences. Supply of the final batch of 70 projectiles has been halted as permission has been refused for the setting up of another installation.

25 February
HDP must expedite the dismantling of the last cannon and carry out a phased withdrawal of the cannon as the leading enemy tanks have advanced to within 3km of the emplacement.

26 February
1./705 continuing withdrawal of cannon.

27 February
1./705 has without loss withdrawn the entire special installation together with all personnel and miscellaneous equipment and is now proceeding to the sector of the Gruppe where the battery is to undergo artillery training in Herschbach. The entire special equipment of Artillerie-Abteilung 705 is being transported by rail to the Röchling works at Wetzlar.

At Buhl, this is the upstream ramp of the HDP as it appears today. The villagers told the author that the site had been completely cordoned off in January 1945 and none of the villagers saw or knew what was happening, only that the Germans were working day and night at the foot of the hill. Even the toilet windows in a factory that faced the site from across the Lauch River were bricked up so that no one could see in that direction. Three Flak guns were set up and guards patrolled the woods around the site, turning away any children who wandered into the area.

This is the downstream ramp as it appears today, pictured in the direction of the fire. After the liberation of Buhl, curiosity led villagers to explore the place where the Germans had worked so secretively but all they found were two ramps on the slope, with some pieces of wood and an excavation at the bottom. German prisoners were soon tasked with cleaning up the site, removing all the wooden supports and filling in the pit at the bottom of the ramp.

last six shells were fired on February 22 and the disassembly of the last cannon began immediately. The German gunners completed their withdrawal just in time as the US 10th Armored Division reached Zerf, five kilometres to the south, on the 26th.

Symptomatic of the military uselessness of the HDP bombings on Luxembourg, the only military damage that we have been able to trace is that suffered by an American mobile laundry hit on January 12: 'An enemy rocket projectile of an unidentified type landed in the area of the semi-mobile laundry located with the 104th Evacuation Hospital in the city of Luxemburg, injuring seven men, three of them seriously, and causing damage to two vans and one tractor.'

On February 27, all the 'special equipment' of the two companies of Artillerie-Abteilung 705 – the four HDP cannons – was on its way back to the Röchling works at Wetzlar. Meanwhile, Hauptmann Patzig had obtained 12 105mm guns (schwere 10cm Kanone), and he re-organised Artillerie-Abteilung 705 with two batteries of six guns each at Herschbach, near Koblenz.

While the Artillerie-Abteilung 705 was equipped with 12 conventional artillery guns, the four HDP guns were taken back to the Röchling works at Wetzlar. The Americans found them lying dismantled there and they shipped them to the United States. The gun concept was evaluated at the Aberdeen Proving Ground, Maryland, and the gun tubes were finally scrapped there in 1948.

RHEINBOTE, 4-STAGE-ROCKET

IN NOVEMBER 1944, KAMMLER became involved in another rocket development, that of the Rheinbote solid-fuel rocket developed by Rheinmetall-Borsig AG. On the 15th, in company with Dornberger and experts from the Heereswaffenamt and the Waffen-SS, he was shown the launch of four Rheinbote rockets at the Luftwaffe firing range at Leba on the Pomeranian coast. He was favourably impressed, and on the 29th he ordered that allocation of powder to the program be increased.

From the mid-1930s, while the Heereswaffenamt held the monopoly in the field of liquid-fuel rockets, Rheinmetall-Borsig AG developed small solid-fuel rockets and began test-firing them in 1936. In 1940, following a request from the Reichsluftfahrtministerium (RLM – Reich Air Ministry), the company started developing assisted take-off (ATO) rockets for cargo gliders and in

In November 1943, engineers from Rheinmetall-Borsig AG conferred with the Luftwaffe at Leba. In the centre, Generaloberst Hubert Weise and Dr.Ing. Heinrich Klein. This shot was taken during firing trials of the Rheintochter anti-aircraft missile that was produced, like the Rheinbote, by Rheinmetall-Borsig. (Heinrich Klein)

The first Rheinbote trial rockets were launched from the firing range developed by the Luftwaffe in the sand dunes six kilometres west of Leba. This device measured the speed of the missiles that were launched. Today in Poland, Leba has retained its name but the nearby town of Rumbke is now called Rabka.

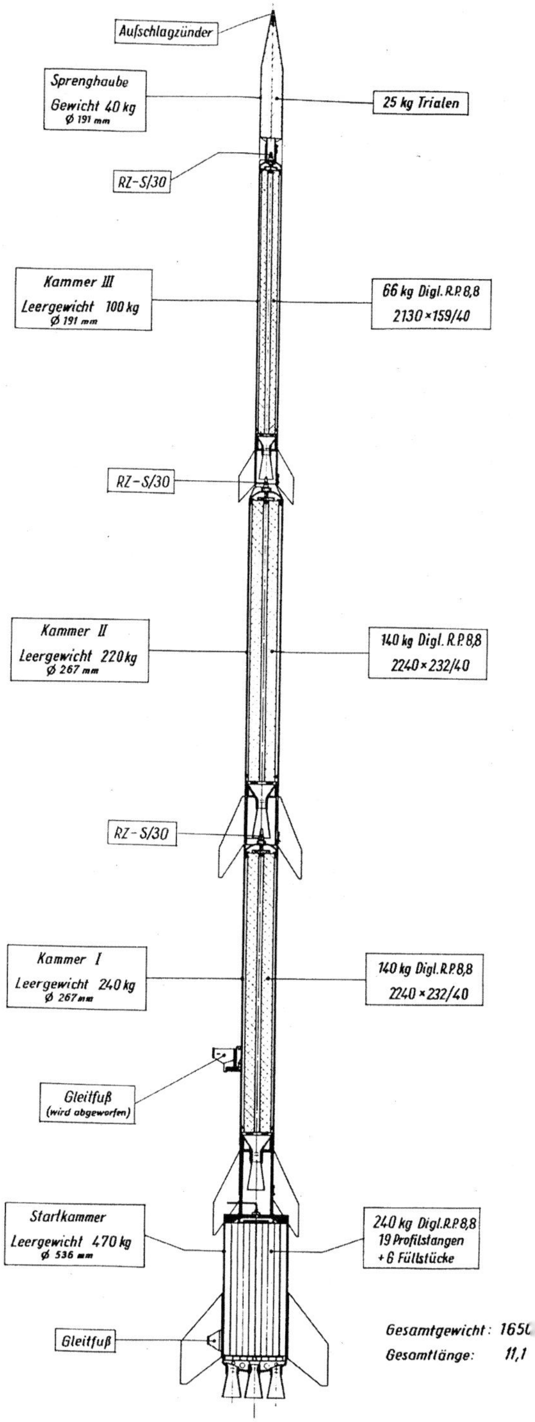

The Rh-Z-61/9 — the operational version of the Rheinbote — was 11.1 metres in length and had a weight of 1650kg. To obtain maximum power the solid propellant in the take-off stage was cast in separate pieces to give as large a burning area as possible. The exhaust discharged through one central and six peripheral nozzles giving a thrust of about 9800kg (21,000lbs). In the next three stages, the propellant was shaped in the form of a tube so that burning occurred on the inner and outer surfaces with the exhaust discharging through one central nozzle. The second and third stages each gave a thrust of 5600kg (12,300lbs) for five seconds, the fourth stage a thrust of 2400kg (5,280lb) for 3.5 seconds. For the launch, two sliding clamps (Gleitfuss), one on the take-off stage (Startkammer) and another on the second stage (Kammer I), allowed guidance on the slide-bar of the ramp, the latter clamp falling free when the rocket cleared the ramp. Ignition was by means of an electrical igniter for the first stage, thereafter each of the other three stages were fired by means of a time fuze (RZ-S/30) primed by the acceleration of the take-off. Staging was achieved by inserting a cylindrical guide attached to the rear of one stage into another guide attached to the top of the stage behind it. Together with the fourth stage (Kammer III) attached to it, the warhead (Sprenghaube) weighed about 140kg, of which 25kg was Trialen explosive. Detonation of the warhead was initiated by a percussion fuze (Aufschlagzünder). As this 1944 drawing shows, the German engineers did not identify the take-off stage of the rocket as the first stage, hence they named the second stage Kammer I, the third Kammer II and so on. For clarity, we have numbered the four stages of the rocket consecutively.

Transported by train to Leba, the components of the Rheinbote were prepared in an assembly workshop and then transported by truck to the launch ramp specially built for the firing tests. Note that the first take-off stage and the second stage have already been assembled at the workshop.

1941, upon receiving a new request from the RLM, the rocket research team directed by Dr Heinrich Klein started to work on an ATO unit with a thrust of 50 tonnes.

From these beginnings, plans were set in motion to develop a long-range solid-fuel rocket and in April 1941 Dr Klcin approached the Heereswaffenamt with the proposal. He was referred to Generalleutnant Dornberger, then the head of WaPrüf 11 which was the office responsible for the development of rockets. From the beginning, Dornberger had strongly supported the development of the A4 liquid-fuel rocket, consequently he was not ready to see his prodigy endangered by competition. Arguing about the shortage

Clearly, the support equipment available at Leba was makeshift, if not rudimentary. The technical team seen at work in these pictures included military personnel from Versuchskommando Tröller and civilian engineers from Rheinmetall-Borsig.

The warhead was already attached to the fourth stage when it was installed, which could suggest that it was not a live warhead. Here, technicians mount the nose cone on top of the percussion fuze.

of propellant powder, he refused to approve the development of the Rheinmetall-Borsig rocket but Dr Klein soon got support from the inspector of heavy artillery, Oberst Gerhard Hüther, who was in the process of asking for heavy artillery rockets. With the A4 still far from being operational, General Leeb, the chief of the Heereswaffenamt, supported Hüther's demand and in June approved the development of long-range rockets by Rheinmetall-Borsig.

Following this decision, the inspectorate for heavy artillery laid down a specification for the rockets in that they were to carry warheads in the range of 200 to 1000kg over distances of 100 to 120 kilometres. Rheinmetall-Borsig started working on a variety of plans for four-stage rockets but these grandiose schemes were soon discarded due to the shortage of propellant powder. Development therefore concentrated on a smaller project, a rocket weighing about 1.7 tonnes, of which the company said it could increase the range to up to 200 kilometres if the warhead was reduced to 40kg.

By the end of 1941, Rheinmetall-Borsig started to test its first designs and, as it was engaged on numerous developments for the Luftwaffe, it was allowed to share the use of the air force firing range at Leba. There, 30 kilometres north of Lauenburg (now Lebork in Poland), the Luftwaffe had developed an experimentation centre, with proving stands for engines and a complete set of ranging measurements, to such a degree that the place was dubbed Klein Peenemünde – little Peenemünde. From there, the trial rockets could be fired on a north-westerly course across the Baltic in the direction of Bornholm, a Danish island occupied by Germany which provided a grandstand view for observation and ranging. The distance from Leba to Bornholm was about 170 kilometres.

FIRING TRIALS AT LEBA AND WALDHEIM

In the meantime, the multi-stage rocket had been given the name Raketensprenggranate 4831 with the code-name 'Rheinbote'. Rheinmetall-Borsig had designed projectile Rh-Z-61, Rh standing for Rheinmetall-Borsig, Z for long-range rocket, while 61 hinted at the planned range (160 kilometres) with inverted number.

The first series of tests at Leba spread over a year and saw the successive launch of ten test rockets. The first was a single-stage rocket, followed by a two-stage and then three-stage before the Rh-Z-V25 – the four-stage prototype – was finally tested. Rheinmetall-Borsig then finalised the design and in April 1943, the Rh-Z-61/2 – the four-stage rocket in its final form – was demonstrated to Generalleutnant Schneider, the chief of the Development Branch of the Heereswaffenamt. Three rockets were launched over the Baltic and one was sighted coming down off Bornholm.

The Rheinmetall-Borsig design having proved sound, the Heereswaffenamt agreed to further development although Speer's ministry would not give any priority to the project. To be allocated the required material to

With the rocket ready for launch, the ramp was cranked up to the appropriate elevation of 64 degrees which had been calculated as giving the maximum range. With the rocket ready for launch, the ramp was cranked up to the appropriate elevation of 64 degrees which had been calculated as giving the maximum range.

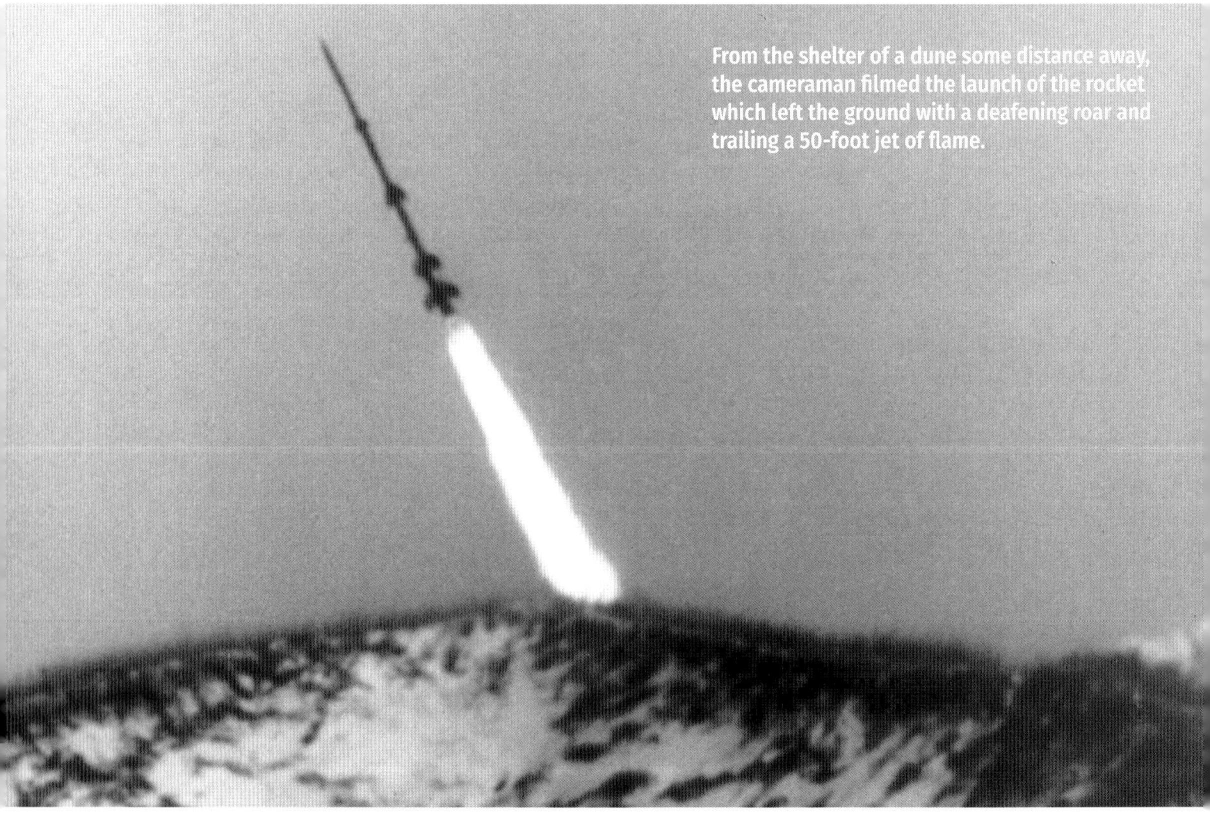

From the shelter of a dune some distance away, the cameraman filmed the launch of the rocket which left the ground with a deafening roar and trailing a 50-foot jet of flame.

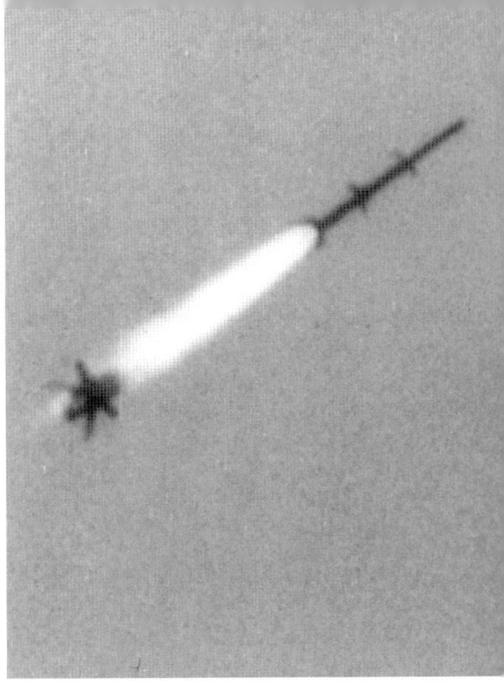

These images are stills taken from German motion pictures made during the summer of 1944, when 20 Rheinbote test rockets were fired from Leba.

produce 30 rockets, Oberstleutnant Alfred Tröller in charge of the project disguised them under a cover name in the overall V-weapons programme. Nevertheless, it still took more than ten months to get the first batch of the combustion chambers delivered from the Rheinmetall-Borsig factory at Berlin-Marienfelde. By early 1944 Speer's priority rules were applied even more strictly so in April Tröller invoked a further subterfuge. Taking advantage of the competition between the army and the SS, he told his chief, Generalmajor Hüther (promoted to that rank in March), that the SS ordnance department was interested in the Rheinmetall-Borsig solid-fuel

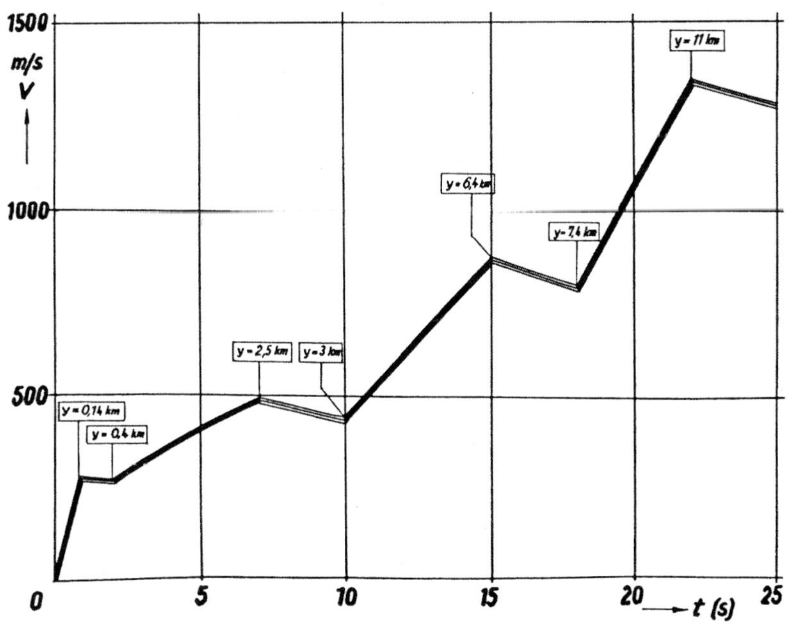

The powered phase of a Rheinbote flight as monitored during the test launches at Leba. The first stage burned for one second, bringing the speed of the rocket up to 275 metres per second (900 feet per second); igniting one second after the extinction of the first stage, the second stage increased the speed of the rocket to 500 metres per second (1,640 ft/sec); the third stage ignited three seconds after the second went out and increased the speed to 850 metres per second (2,788 ft/sec); igniting three seconds after the extinction of the third, the fourth stage increased the rocket's speed to 1,330 metres per second (4,360 ft/sec).

The propelled part of a Rheinbote rocket's flight: the first stage cuts off at 0.9 seconds; the second stage ignites at 2 seconds and cuts off at 7; the third stage ignites at 10 seconds and cuts off at 15; the fourth stage ignites at 18 seconds and cuts off at 22. The burnt-out stages detach successively, the first falling a few hundred metres from the launch pad, the second about 3.5 kilometres down range, and the third and the fourth 9 and 20 kilometres down range respectively.

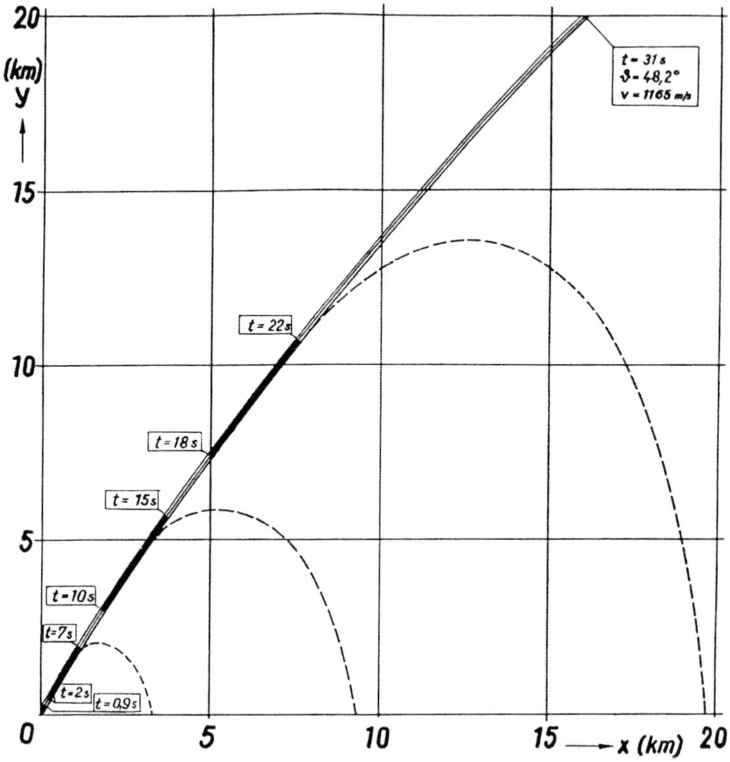

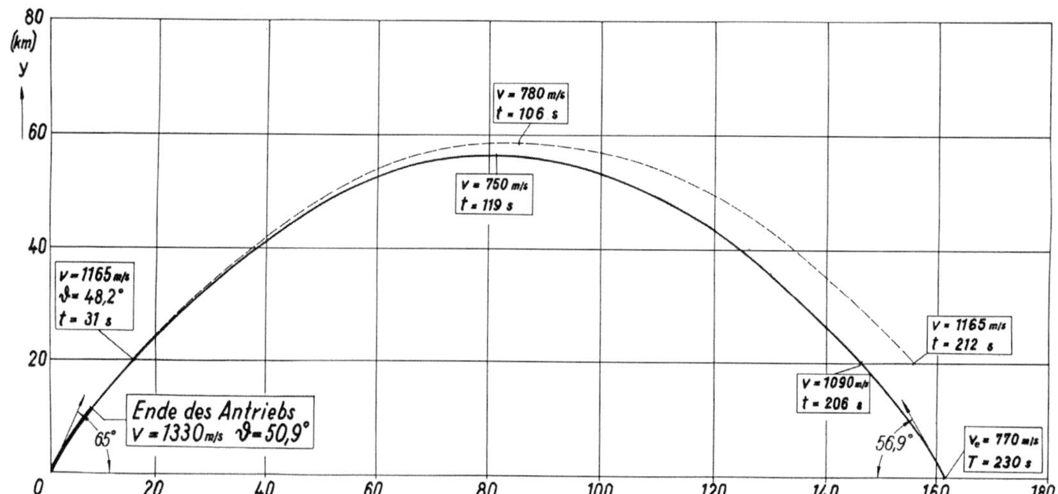

rockets. Hüther immediately turned to General Olbricht, the head of the General Army Office at OKH, and to Generaloberst Fromm, the chief of Army Equipment, both well-known for their opposition to the SS's push for power. They immediately gave their support and 200 Rheinbote rockets were ordered for military deployment. To this end, the programme was allocated 150 tons of powder, 250 tons of steel and 30 tonnes of non-ferrous metal. A Versuchskommando Tröller (Test Command Tröller) was also set up to supervise development and production.

Unlike the V1 and the V2, internal guidance and control was not part of the Rheinbote design and the rocket reached its target simply on a ballistic trajectory like an artillery shell. Its accuracy therefore depended solely on how its trajectory was initially adjusted, so the launch ramp had to be oriented precisely in height and direction. Initially, it was intended to use the stable and finely adjustable mount of an 88mm Flak gun as the base for the Rheinbote launching ramp. However, when it proved impossible to lose the production of even one gun, the Meiller trailer (Meillerwagen or Fahrzeug 102), used to bring the V2 rockets to their launch site and raise them to the vertical, was chosen instead. It was hoped that it could be quickly adapted into an effective launching ramp for the Rheinbote, but it turned out that the chassis and the lever arm were not stable enough to withstand the stresses of the rocket launch. Vibration occurred, which led to considerable inaccuracy and, at its maximum range, the rocket lateral deviation amounted to some 20 kilometres.

The Rheinbote launching slide bar was mounted on the hydraulically adjustable lever arm of the Meiller trailer in such a way that it could be moved 14 degrees on either side. So the rocket could be adjusted for height (by raising the lever arm to a given angle) and direction (by angling the slide bar on the arm). The first two operational FR-Wagen (FR standing for Fernrakete, long-range rocket) were tested at Waldheim at the beginning of December.

There were still some problems with unexplained airbursts of the rocket, faulty powder burning in the fourth stage, and stabilising fins breaking off when the rocket broke the sound barrier, so experts from the Luftfahrtforschungsanstalt (LFA – Air Research Institute) in Braunschweig were called in. With the help of wind-tunnel experiments and 20 test launches from Leba in the summer, the causes of the troubles were progressively identified and by August 1944 most of Rheinbote's teething troubles had been solved.

The first rockets of the pilot production batch, the type Rh-Z-61/9, left the Berlin-Marienfelde factory in October and one of them fired from Leba reached a distance of 157 kilometres at the end of the month.

On the morning of November 15, four Rheinbote rockets were demonstrated to Kammler and Dornberger and experts from the Heereswaffenamt and the Waffen-SS. The first three rockets behaved perfectly and Bornholm signalled that the ranges achieved were 153, 155 and 157 kilometres, respectively. However, when the fourth was launched, there was a problem with the clamps guiding the rocket on the launching rail which broke one of the stabilising fins. As the rocket rose vertically into the air, Dornberger said, 'we ducked involuntarily in our narrow trench. The different stages

Twelve Rheinbote rockets were launched in a series of tests carried out in Waldheim during the first two weeks of December. The rockets proved far from reliable, with the time fuzes designed to ignite the various stages at the right time being erratic. Nine rockets failed to function properly and of the three that flew as expected, one reached a distance of 194 kilometres. It has been said that Rheinbote trials were conducted from the German town of Waldheim, 30 kilometres north of Chemnitz, but the author traced in 1999 a document dated November 23, 1944, which indicates that Waldheim was located '6 km ostwärts Alt-Burgund (Szubin)': the correct Waldheim is therefore Drogoslaw in Poland, about 20 kilometres south of Bydgoszcz (then Bromberg). From there, the Rheinbote were fired towards the Tucheler Heide (now Tuchola) test range.

were bound to fall on top of us. After the first three stages had dropped among the pines without doing any damage, we waited for the fourth and last. It contained a live warhead. Splinter effect might be dangerous. In a few minutes we heard the whistle of the falling charge and shortly afterwards its impact on the left flank of the battery. The detonation did not seem very loud. Nothing serious had happened. When we reached the point of impact, we looked at each other in astonishment and some embarrassment. A small, shallow crater 1,2 metres wide had been made in the loose sand. Little or no splinter effect could be traced. Such was the insignificant result of burning 580kg of powder and hurling one ton of steel!'

Kammler and Hüther overruled Dornberger's realistic assessment and the military deployment of the Rheinbote rockets was agreed. On November 29 Kammler ordered that allocation of powder to the Rheinbote programme be increased.

RF ⚡⚡, Sb 2

Geheime Kommandosache

Rheinbote.

2051/44

~~5. Ausfertigungen~~
2. Ausfertigung

MASZSTAB 1:100.

KALIBER ETWA 19,1 cm
SCHUSZWEITE: 160 Km
STREUUNG: NICHT BEKANNT
GESCHOSSGEWICHT: 1650 Kg,
davon 40-50 Kg Sprengstoff
Vo = 1330 m/sec (nach 10 Km)
TREIBSTOFF: 585 Kg/Schuss
STARTBAHN AUF MEILLERWAGEN
LEISTUNG: 1 Schuß je Stunde
WIRKUNG: 15-21 cm Mörser
20 cm Granate
BAUFIRMA: RHEINMETALL-BORSIG
ENTWICKLUNGSFACHMANN: Oberstlt Troeller AHA-JN IV.
EINSATZ: ZUNÄCHST 8 LAFFETTEN, dazu 300 Schuß
AUFBAU FÜR ZIELWECHSEL: 15 Min.

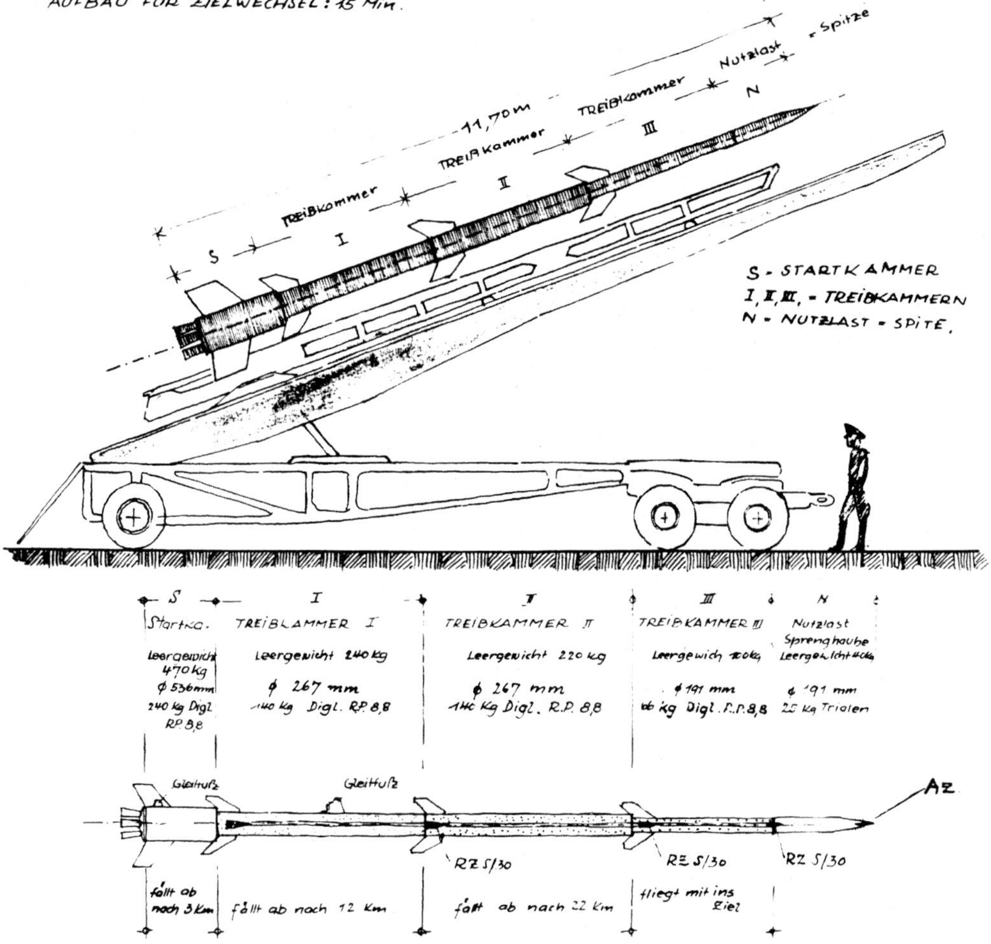

GESAMTGEWICHT 1650 Kg
GESAMTLÄNGE 11,7 m

BERLIN, DEN 26. NOVEMBER 1944

⚡⚡-GRUPPENFÜHRER UND
GENERALLT. D. WAFFEN-⚡⚡

On November 26, Kammler signed this sheet summarising the Rheinbote's data. It notes that eight FR-Wagen were ready for action, and that 300 rockets were available. The rate of fire is given at one shot per hour.

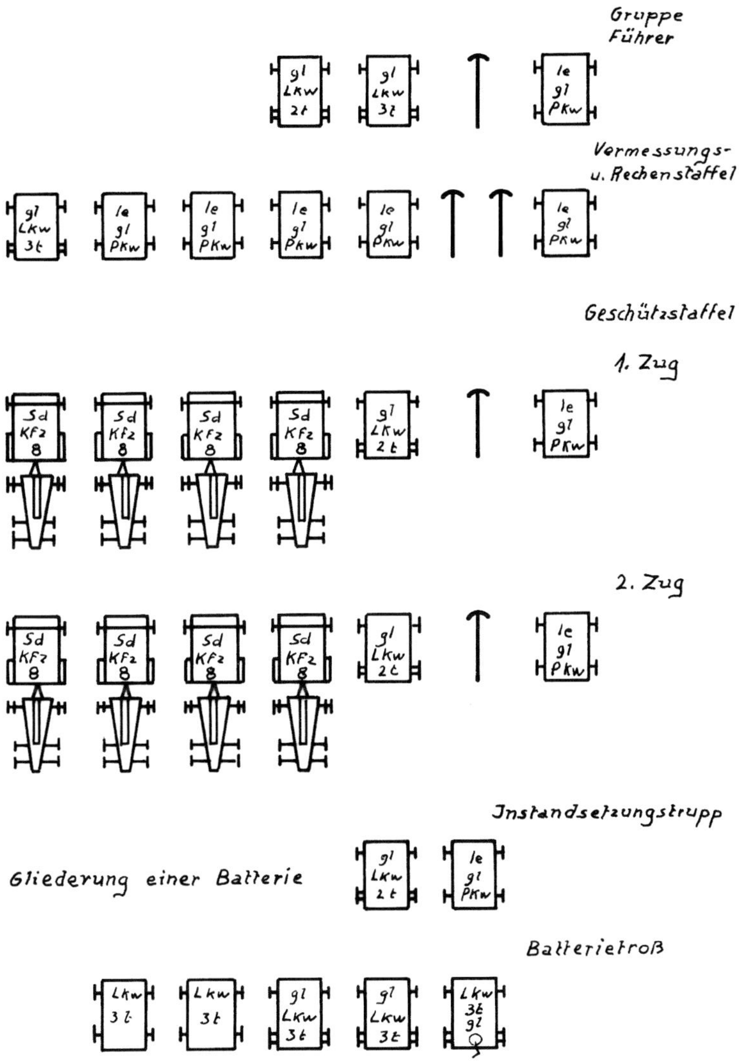

For field operations, the Kommando was constituted as Artillerie-Abteilung 709, with only one battery, and on December 12 the unit was moved by rail to its operational area in the West. The battery consisted of a headquarters with a communications section, a survey platoon, two weapons platoons, each with four FR-Wagen, a maintenance section and a combat train. The battery included 28 vehicles and five motorcycles (the arrow symbols). The vehicles included 11 lorries (Lkw), nine personnel carriers (Pkw) and eight SdKfz 8 half-tracks to tow the FR-Wagen.

With the support of the experts of Versuchskommando Tröller, the engineers of Rheinmetall-Borsig worked hard to perfect the rocket and in December more trial firings were carried out at Leba and Waldheim (now Drogoslaw in Poland, six kilometres east of Szubin). Waldheim was an annex to the new rocket test range established on the Tucheler Heide (Tuchel Heath), 15 kilometres east of Tuchel (now Tuchola in Poland), in the summer of 1944 for further development of the V2 after the Russian offensive had put an end to development work at the test site at Blizna, further to the east. From Tucheler Heide, the V2 rockets were being fired in a southerly direction, the target area being seemingly a training range in the Warthe valley. That distance was too far for the Rheinbote so to shorten the range the firing point was moved to Waldheim, nearly 100 kilometres to the south of Tucheler Heide. On December 13, after the launch of 36 test rockets, engineers from Rheinmetall-Borsig reported: 'Failures amounting to 50 per cent still have to be expected. The intended range of 160 kilometres will surely be achieved.'

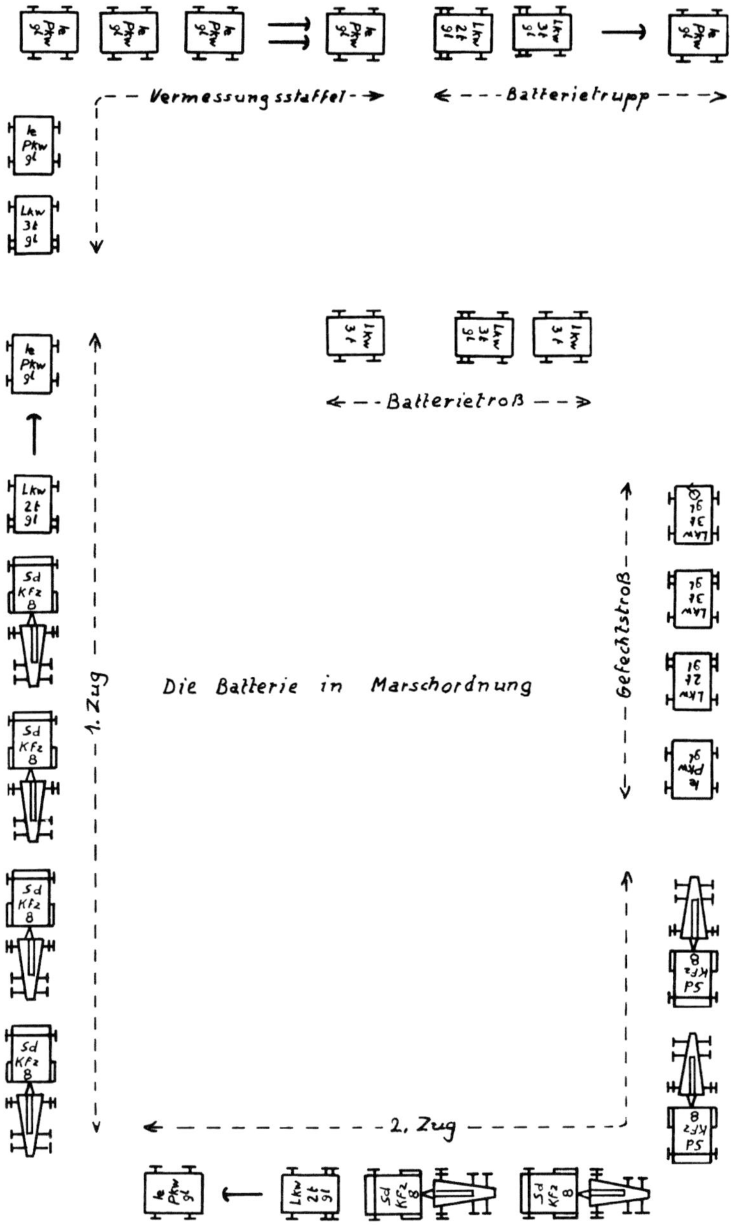

A set of instructions was prepared for the crew of Artillerie-Abteilung 709, including this sketch for the marching order: first the battery staff, then the survey platoon, the first weapon platoons, then the second, each with four FR-Wagen, then the maintenance section and finally the combat train.

As far as the destructive power of the warhead was concerned, one rocket launched from Waldheim which crashed into a farmyard gave a more reassuring picture after the disappointing experience of November 15 at Leba. The crater was reported as being 3.5 metres in diameter and 1.2 metres deep and the surrounding buildings showed heavy damage to the walls. The roof of the stables, 15 metres from the point of impact, had been completely blown off; the roof of a barn 50 metres away had partially been ripped off and that of the farmhouse, 350 metres away, heavily damaged. All the poultry and the farm dog had been killed and two cows injured.

However, the Rheinbote was still not 100 per cent reliable, and the time fuzes which had to ignite the various stages at the proper time were

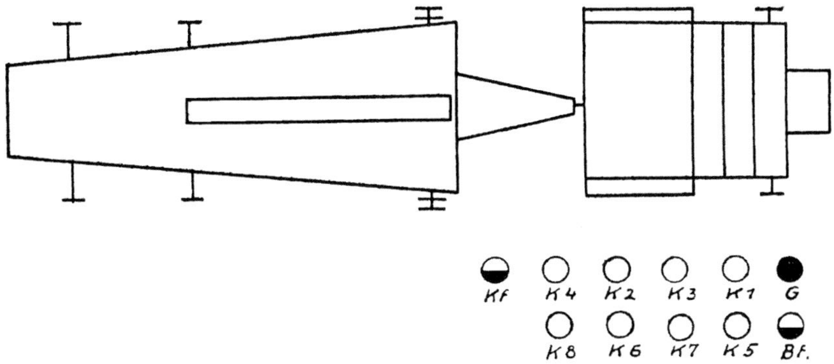

The 'gun' crew consisted of the crew chief (Geschützführer G) and eight gunners (Kanoniere K1 to K8); in addition, the crew of the SdKfz 8 half-track comprised one driver (Zgkw. Fahrer, Kf) and one co-driver (Beifahrer, Bf).

particularly troublesome. In a series of tests at Waldheim between December 1-17, 12 rockets were launched of which only four ignited properly; five failed and the whereabouts of three had not been traced when the report was written. The greatest range achieved was 194.2 kilometres, with a lateral deviation of 20.9 kilometres; the shortest 45 kilometres, with a deviation of 7.5 kilometres.

Following Kammler's order of late November for the first batch of 300 rockets, 115 units had been produced by December 12. In addition, another 222 rockets were scheduled to be delivered by the end of January.

Powerful prime-movers were needed to manoeuvre the heavy Meiller trailers (nearly 12 tonnes when a rocket was transported). Here, an FR-Wagen is being towed into position by an SdKfz 7 half-track at Waldheim during the operational training of Artillerie-Abteilung 709.

From the experience gained at Leba and Waldheim, a 125-page document detailed every aspect of the employment of a Rheinbote battery, from the assembly of the various stages on the ramp, to the orientation of the ramp in direction and height and the firing. To detail the role and duties of each of the eight gunners, the instructions named them K1 to K8. As to the mounting and assembly of the various stages of the rocket, the document gave the following details: Having unpacked the second stage from its crate, K5 and K6 fastened a strap to it. Meanwhile, from behind the ramp, K4 put a wood trestle on the slide bar. K1 winched down the hoist, K5 hooked the strap and K1 winched the second stage up. He set it just behind the ramp with the sliding clamp in line with the slide bar. Under the command of K4, K2 and K3 inserted the clamp into the slide bar and pushed the stage up along the bar until it rested onto the wood trestle. K1 unhooked the hoist and K3 turned the crane arm aside. K4 inserted a shaft into the slide bar until it hit the sliding clamp. While K4 pushed the clamp with the shaft, K2 and K3 had the stage slid up the bar for about 60 centimetres. Having unpacked the take-off [first] stage from its crate, K7 and K8 fastened a strap to it. K1 winched down the hoist, K8 hooked the strap, K1 winched the stage up and moved it behind the slide bar, in line with it. Under the command of K4, K1 lowered the stage and K3 and K4 inserted the sliding clamp into the slide bar. The take-off stage was then pushed up along the bar until the clamp reached the proper position. K2, K3 and K4 then slowly pushed the second stage backwards until its rear cylindrical guide inserted into the one in front of the take-off stage. 'The two lugs in the latter must fit into the two grooves in the second-stage rear cylindrical guide.' The second stage was then pushed into the take-off stage cylindrical guide until the two spring bolts caught in.

This done, K5 and K6 unpacked the third stage and fastened a strap to it. K1 winched down the hoist, K5 secured the strap and K1 winched it up. It was moved and set so that K3 and K4 could insert its rear cylindrical guide into the one in front of the second stage. 'The markings on the two stages must fit. K3 and K4 have the two spring bolts catch in.' The fourth stage is mounted in the same way. 'The fitting of the warhead must be done with the greatest care. Beforehand, it must be checked that the safety pin is still set into the fuze. K6 and K7 take the warhead on the munitions truck and cautiously bring it to the gun.' K5, who had climbed on the ramp, then carried the warhead on his shoulder and K6 and K7 adjusted it onto the fourth stage. The elevation of the ramp was trained by K3. Having first set the given elevation on the gunner's quadrant, K3 put the quadrant on the launching rail. 'With hand signals, K3 indicates to K5 whether the ramp should be raised or lowered. K5 raises or lowers the ramp by actuating the hydraulic hand pump, this until the clinometer of the quadrant is level.' To aim the gun in the proper direction, the crew needed precise setting and to the command: 'Richtkreis rückwärts des Geschützes!' (Bring the direction of fire back to the gun) K5 then went to the survey and computing team. He wrote the number given to him on a slip of paper and brought it back to K1. K1 set this number on the laying device and balanced the cross level. Turning the traversing handwheel, he then oriented the launching rail until the vertical cross-wire matched with the red mark of the aiming post. 'The matching of the cross-wire with the aiming post must be done three times at least for the laying device moves when the rail is adjusted.' When the rail was precisely trained, it was fixed in position and K1 reported to the gun chief: 'Geschütz eingerichtet!' (Gun aimed). When the gun was trained, the gun chief shouted: 'Räumt Feuerstellung!' (Evacuate the firing position) K2, K3 and K4 moved away about 50 metres to the left, K5, K6, K7 and K8 did the same on the right. Together with K1, the gun chief checked that all parts of the laying equipment had been removed and that nobody remained near the ramp. He then ordered: 'Zündleitung anschliessene' (Connect the firing cable) K1 connected the firing cable to the wires reaching out of the take-off stage. This done, he shouted: 'Geschütz feuerbereit!' (Gun ready to fire) Both went to the foxhole in which the firing apparatus had been set. Having checked the electrical continuity, K1 connected the firing cable to the exploder. 'Before that, he must check that the safety key is not inserted into the exploder. He must always carry this key on him and it is just before the fire that he inserts it into the exploder.' To the order of the gun chief, 'Geschütz Feuer!' (Fire the gun), K1 turned the exploder key and fired the rocket.

INTO ACTION: FIRING AT ANTWERP

In the meantime, Tröller had shaped his Versuchskommando into an operational unit, the officers being trained with the rockets at Leba and Waldheim and the men being instructed at the Rheinmetall-Borsig production plant at Marienfelde. For operations in the field, the Kommando was formed into Artillerie-Abteilung 709, with only one battery, and on December 12, it was moved by rail to its operational area in the West.

Assigned to Kammler's Division z.V., Artillerie-Abteilung 709 received the order to bombard Antwerp and it set up its launching site in a wooded area

By mid-December, Artillerie-Abteilung 709 had set up its launch ramps in a wood near Nunspeet in the Netherlands. The target was Antwerp, 165 kilometres away.

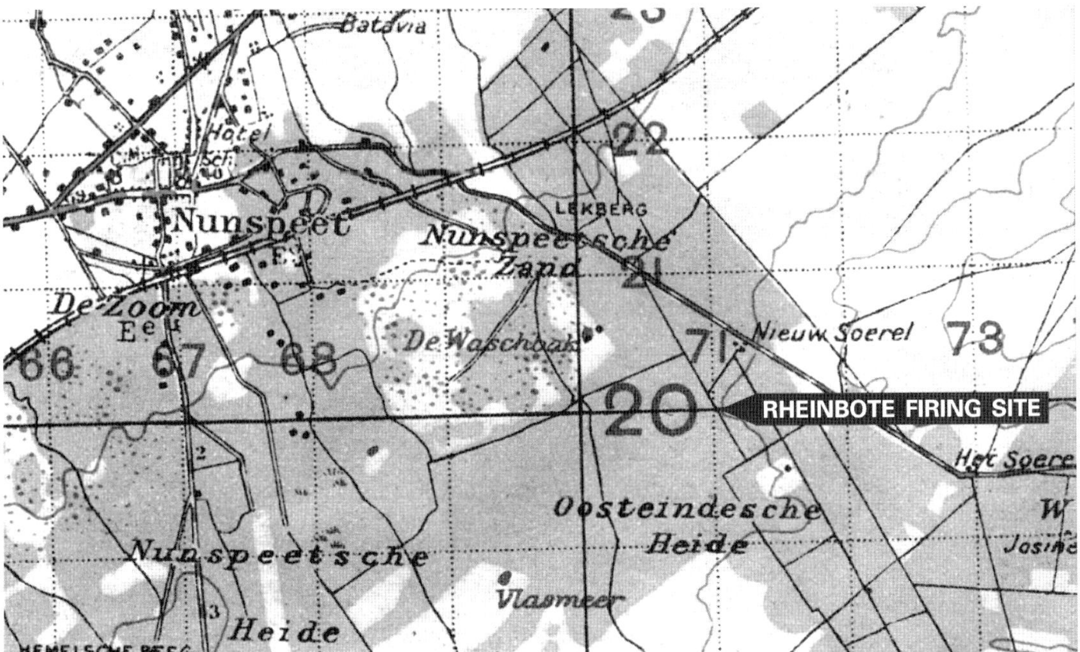

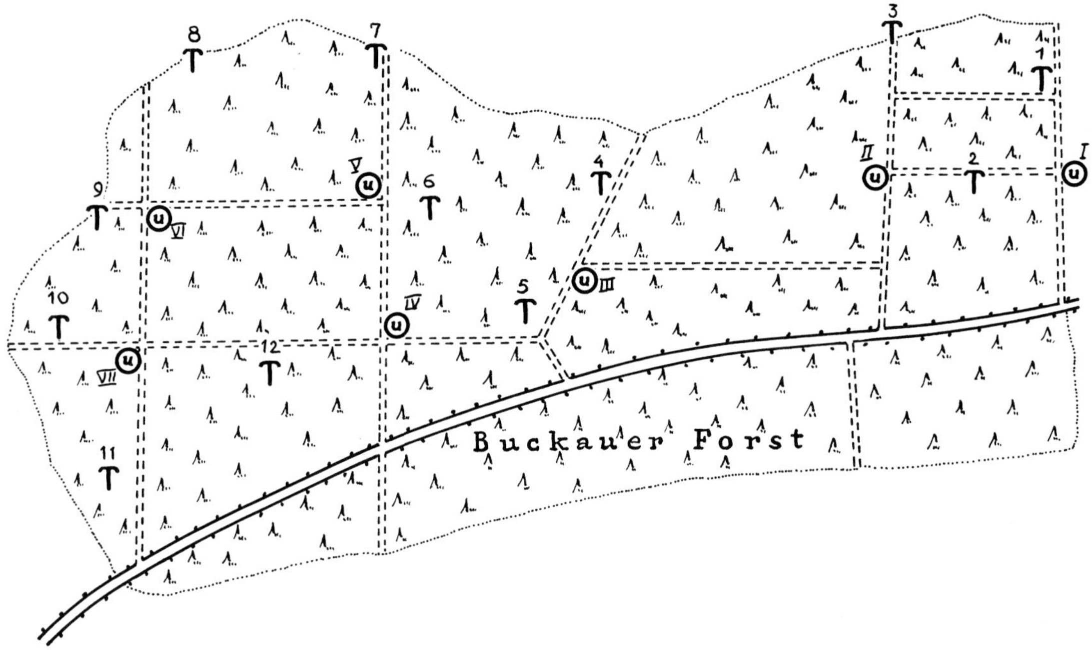

In this sketch reproduced from the set of instructions prepared after trials at Leba and Waldheim, one battery equipped with three weapon platoons — hence a total of 12 FR-Wagen (numbered from 1 to 12) — was in a hidden position in a forest area. This drawing also indicates seven widely separated unloading spots (U for Umladestellen, numbered from I through VII) where the rocket parts were delivered in crates. When Artillerie-Abteilung 709 went in operation at Nunspeet, it had only one weapons platoon, that was only four FR-Wagen.

at Nunspeet, some 25 kilometres west of Zwolle, in the Netherlands, some 165 kilometres from the target. According to a report dated December 13, there were then only four Startbahngeschütze (launching ramp vehicles) to hand although none were serviceable as some vital components were still missing.

These were finally delivered and Artillerie-Abteilung 709 opened fire on December 24. Oberstleutnant Tröller reported: 'The firing sites, carefully camouflaged against view from the air and spread out widely, were located in the approaches to the V2 division. Nearby, 24 rockets were stored in the open, also spread out, in readiness. Each launching site was assigned to an officer. They could hardly believe their ears when they were informed that action was becoming serious. Excitement with the officers and crews was only small. They knew that nothing could go wrong, as they were very familiar with the rocket. The distance between Nunspeet and Antwerp amounted to 165 kilometres. According to provisional firing procedures, the raising for this range was 64 degrees. The Startbahnen headed towards the port of Antwerp. At 12 a.m. precisely, the first salvo of four rockets started off without trouble. Within one hour, all 24 available rockets had been launched towards Antwerp. I have ordered the officer in charge of each site to test the rockets which were launched from his site as to the perfect function of the units. In other words, to note the typical three sounds which should be heard after 2, 10 and 22 seconds. The reports from each firing site indicated no failures.'

Tröller and his men had launched an additional 20 Rheinbote rockets by the middle of January. (Some sources give higher numbers, up to a total

These photos taken during the training course for the crews of Artillerie-Abteilung 709 in Waldheim perfectly illustrate what Mr Karsten saw in Nunspeet in January 1945. At a time when V1s and V2s were regularly hitting Antwerp and its suburbs, and errant V1s were crashing all over the countryside, it seems that the impacts of the small Rheinbote warheads went unnoticed. The archives of the Belgian gendarmerie noted 14 impacts of V-weapons in the Antwerp region on the afternoon of December 24, but these archives did not make out the difference between V1s and V2s, and let alone identify the smaller V4 missile.

of 200 rockets, but these figures seem implausible). When all the available rockets had been fired, Artillerie-Abteilung 709 was withdrawn back to Tucheler Heide.

There, Tröller met the team from Rheinmetall-Borsig, which had in the meantime carried out additional trial launches from Waldheim for the setting up of a firing table, who told him of a surprising increase in range. According to the new data, when fired at an elevation of 64 degrees the Rheinbote rockets averaged a range of 230 kilometres. However, no one at Rheinmetall-Borsig had known where Artillerie-Abteilung 709 was operating so this vital information could not be passed on to Tröller. When the Rheinbote rockets at Nunspeet were fired at Antwerp at an elevation of 64 degrees they may have

In 1986, *After the Battle* managed to trace Gerrit Karsten who had observed the men of Artillerie-Abteilung 709 as they operated the Rheinbote rocket against Antwerp in the winter 1944-45. At that time, Mr Karsten lived on the Nieuw Soerel farm, a few kilometres east of Nunspeet. 'Early in November 1944, the Germans ordered us to evacuate our home and property within two days. It was immediately occupied by Wehrmacht troops who started preparations for launching rockets. The whole area became out of bounds and German troops started preparations at four sites, two pairs about 70 to 80 metres apart. The missiles were delivered on long trailers and went along gravel roads and dirt tracks past the farmhouse into the woodlands behind it. To facilitate negotiating several sharp bends, trees were cut down and many more were felled to create openings for the mobile launchers to move into and out of position.

'Although nobody was allowed anywhere near the place, I managed in January 1945 to get permission to go into the vicinity with horse and cart to collect a load of firewood. Accompanied by an armed guard, I succeeded in getting quite near the launching site and through the trees I saw one of the rockets on its ramp. When the guard noticed my interest, I was told not to look in that direction again and to hurry loading the timber and leave'.

The Nieuw Soerel farm was demolished in the mid-1960s, new trees were planted, so the exact location of the launch pads could only be pinpointed with Mr Karsten's help.

The diary of G. Rooker held in the collection of the NIOD (Netherlands Institute of War Documentation) provides further testimony to the launch of the Rheinbote rockets from Nunspeet. 'Sunday, December 24. Today brought nice clear weather, and a sensation. At 11 a.m. two V1s were launched one after the other from the east, probably from the area of Soerel-Oldebroek. First you hear a rumbling in the east that increases in height quickly until it is right above you. Then a white stripe appears which shoots forward at great speed until it ends. Then a soft rumbling and the V1 has disappeared. Sometimes the top end of the stripe is blackish and brown. Grey clouds [of smoke] hang over the launching area.' What Mr Rooker had heard and seen was not the launch of V1s but Rheinbote rockets fired at Antwerp by Artillerie-Abteilung 709. The place he named, Soerel-Oldebroek, corresponds perfectly with Mr. Karsten's testimony.

overshot their target by over 50 kilometres, possibly impacting somewhere between Ghent and Aalst.

The first production of 1,000 rockets was planned to begin in December, in two monthly production runs of 500 each. This would permit 450 rockets to be available per month to be launched in operations while the remaining 50 were to be set aside for further development and testing but because of a lack of materials and powder, these plans proved illusory. On January 15 the scheduled monthly production for February had to be reduced to 150, of which 60 were to be reserved for development, leaving only 90 rockets for deployment. The production for March was set at 150, 30 rockets being earmarked for development.

However, the Rheinbote was still far from being reliable enough for operational deployment as reported by Major Axster of B.z.b.V. Heer on January 14: 'Further investigations have revealed that failures at the last trial firings were caused by problems with the time fuzes. B.z.b.V. Heer and WaPrüf 11 have already taken the necessary measures to ensure that, starting with the next test firings, only new faultless fuzes will be used.'

Yet it was now too late to perfect a weapon of doubtful effectiveness and on February 6 Kammler ordered all work on the Rheinbote cancelled.

END OF THE THIRD REICH

LIBERATION AT NORDHAUSEN

In January 1945, to cope with the growing number of inmates in the Mittelbau area, the SS took over the Boelcke-Kaserne, a former Luftwaffe barracks located on the southern outskirts of Nordhausen. At that time, the possibility of transporting the dead and dying to other camps for execution and cremation no longer existed and the SS used the Boelcke barracks as a

Reaching Niedersachswerfen on the morning of April 11, the leaders of the CCB, 3rd Armored Division, found rows of V2 parts stored in front of the Kohnstein underground complex. These V2 tailplanes still packed in transport chassis were stored just outside Tunnel A, the camouflaged entrance of which is visible on the right. (USNA)

The original caption for this photo reads 'a liberated French slave worker, in striped suit, shows an American soldier the rows of camouflaged fuel tanks for V2 rockets'. In the centre, the entrance to Tunnel A. (USHMM)

The GIs discovered the underground factory, with its power and ventilation systems still operating, as if the work crews had gone out to lunch and would soon return. Here the production line of Tunnel B where the half-shells padded with glass wool were mounted around the tanks to form the central part of the rocket. (Raphaël Algoet)

American leaders also discovered that 10,000 people had taken refuge in the underground complex, including German locals and evacuees as well as inmates from the 'Dora' concentration camp. (USHMM)

place to house sick inmates until they died. In April, around 3,500 inmates were housed in Boelcke-Kaserne.

On the night of April 3/4, and again the following night, Bomber Command attacked Nordhausen with 250 bombers in each of the two raids, destroying three-quarters of the town. More than 8,800 people were killed, German locals and refugees, as well as slave workers. The Boelcke barracks were hit hard and hundreds of inmates were killed in the two attacks.

With the Americans approaching from the west and the Russians from the east, the SS evacuated 40,000 prisoners from the Mittelbau district between April 4 and 7. Between 25,000 and 30,000 of them were evacuated by train to the concentration camps at Bergen-Belsen, Sachsenhausen and Ravensbruck, while inmates of smaller subcamps were forced to march away. The SS guards shot all those too weak to keep up and the roads were littered with dead bodies. At Gardelegen, a group of 1,000 inmates who could no longer be moved due to damaged railway tracks were all murdered by their guards.

In the south, another CCB task force discovered horrific scenes at the Boelcke barracks where some 1,300 inmates lay dead. Signal Corps photographer Harold M. Roberts took this photo of 'dead workers lying in uneven rows on floors of barracks. (LC)

Leading the VII Corps on the left wing of the US First Army, Combat Command B of the 3rd Armored Division entered Niedersachswerfen on the morning of April 11. In the Kohnstein underground complex, they found parts and sub-assemblies of V1s and V2s throughout the galleries and tunnels, and more than 10,000 local people and slave workers who had taken refuge there. They reached the 'Dora' camp on the southern side of the mountain and discovered the emaciated survivors lying among the bodies of the dead.

Another Combat Command B task force reached Nordhausen and discovered the horror at Boelcke barracks. As the history of the 3rd Armored Division describes: 'No written word can properly convey the atmosphere of such a charnel house, the unbearable stench of decomposing bodies, the sight of live human beings, starved to pallid skeletons, lying cheek by jowl with the ten-day dead.'

Among the corpses, the Americans found 400 emaciated survivors and immediately provided them with medical treatment. Two photos of Roberts: a 'starved Frenchman sitting among the dead', and a Belgian inmate, whose prison number, 113284, allows him to be identified as Georges Decroix, then aged 26. (LC)

A French survivor, Michel Depierre, later recalled: 'They distributed some food. It was so good, since we were dying of hunger for the last nine months. Only skin was left on our bones. On April 19, we had gained a little more strength so they walked us to the airfield of Nordhausen. There Dakotas brought supplies to the front. American military set up tents. There were some beautiful white breads on the tables, but nobody to care for us. Maybe to avoid diseases? But also because of the war, they did not have time for us.' (USHMM)

Roberts took photos of a 'a starved, almost dead Polish worker being carried to ambulance by American medics'. (LC)

The 104th Infantry Division took control of the sector on April 12 while the 3rd Armored Division continued east. The division's chief surgeon, Lieutenant Colonel Hugh W. Jones, had 100 male citizens of Nordhausen collect corpses from the bombed buildings of the Boelcke barracks and arrange them in long rows in the street. German civilians denied knowing about the conditions in the camps, but the Americans did not really believe them. (USHMM)

Many Signal Corps photographers were sent to Nordhausen to bear witness to the Nazi horror. There were seven of them taking photos of a row of dead detainees in this photo taken by Tech/4 James E. Myers of the 165th Signal Photo Company. Among the identified photographers present at Nordhausen, in addition to Myers, were Charles Sellers, Harold M. Roberts, John R. Driza, Richard W. Elliot, Wesley B. Carolan, and Richard Crampton. In *Nordhausen Then and Now*, Karel Margry notes that the fact that many of the dead found at Boelcke barracks died during the Bomber Command raids of early April was 'left unsaid in the contemporary accounts'. (LC)

The dead from the Boelcke barracks were buried in a mass grave dug into the side of a hill overlooking Nordhausen. On April 14, Signal Corps photographer John R. Driza photographed German civilians digging the burial pits and laying out the corpses. The process lasted until April 16. (USHMM)

'DORA' TRIAL

Of approximately 60,000 inmates who passed through the Mittelbau-Dora complex between August 1943 and March 1945, an estimated 13,000 to 18,000 died there, nearly a third of them.

Only a very small number of the 2,400-strong staff of the Mittelbau-Dora complex could be found and indicted, and the 'Dora' trial took place in 1947 in the former Dachau concentration camp. The defendants included George Rickhey, the general manager of the Mittelwerk, 14 SS men and four Kapos. All were accused of neglecting, torturing, or killing prisoners, with some accused of specific offenses committed during the evacuations and forced marches. Neither von Braun, who by his own admission visited the Mittelwerk '10 or 15 times', including an extended stay during the terrible construction period at the end of 1943, nor other important representatives of the Mittelwerk GmbH were indicted or required to appear in court to testify.

On September 19, Tadeusz Patzer showed the court the location of offices in the 'Dora' concentration camp. Seated in front is Captain William F. McGarry, assistant prosecutor, and standing is Major Leon B. Poullada, defence attorney. Patzer was a Polish political prisoner in Germany since October 1941, first at Auschwitz, then at Buchenwald, before being transferred to the 'Dora' concentration camp in September 1943. (USNA)

60

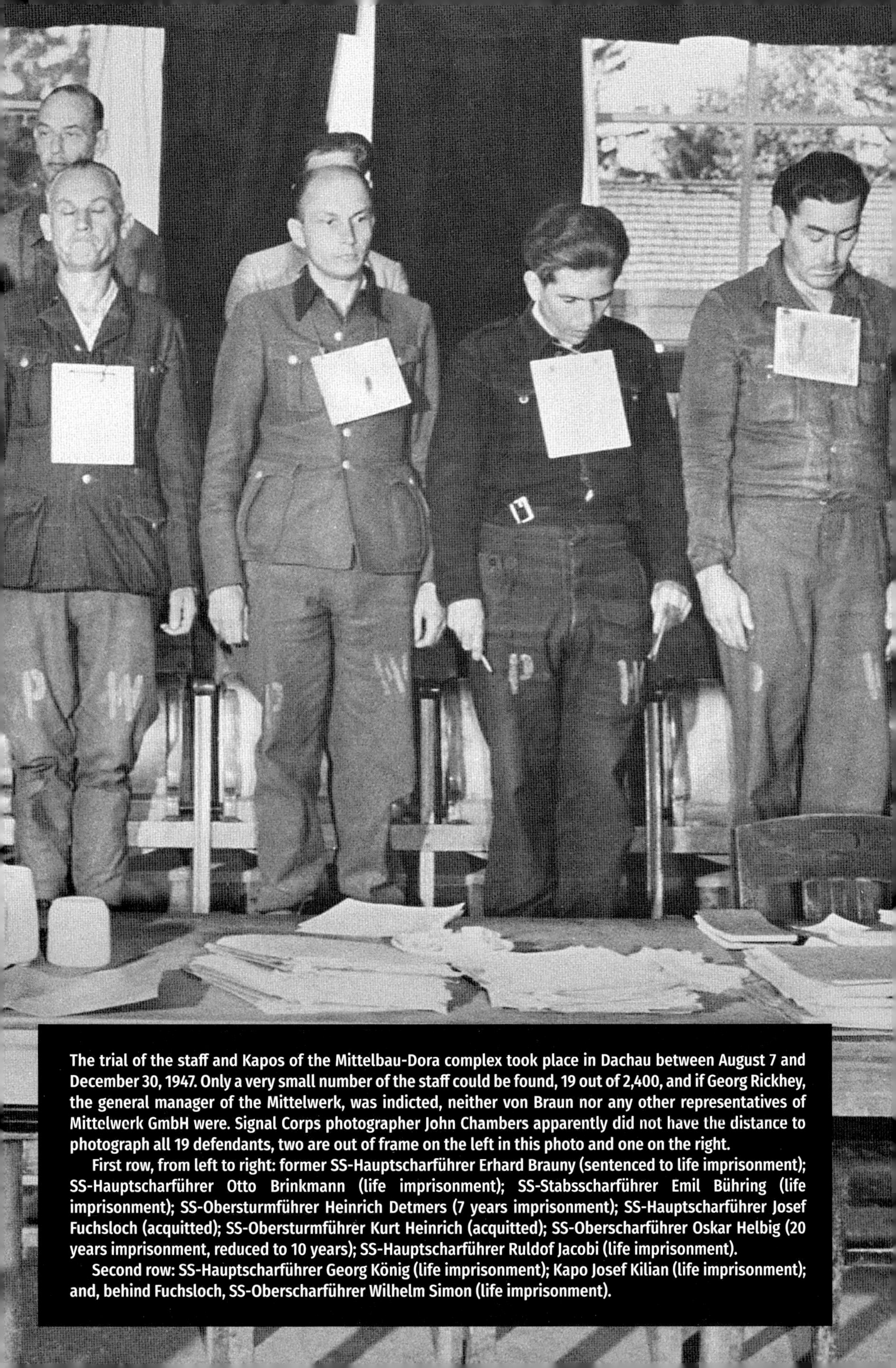

The trial of the staff and Kapos of the Mittelbau-Dora complex took place in Dachau between August 7 and December 30, 1947. Only a very small number of the staff could be found, 19 out of 2,400, and if Georg Rickhey, the general manager of the Mittelwerk, was indicted, neither von Braun nor any other representatives of Mittelwerk GmbH were. Signal Corps photographer John Chambers apparently did not have the distance to photograph all 19 defendants, two are out of frame on the left in this photo and one on the right.

First row, from left to right: former SS-Hauptscharführer Erhard Brauny (sentenced to life imprisonment); SS-Hauptscharführer Otto Brinkmann (life imprisonment); SS-Stabsscharführer Emil Bühring (life imprisonment); SS-Obersturmführer Heinrich Detmers (7 years imprisonment); SS-Hauptscharführer Josef Fuchsloch (acquitted); SS-Obersturmführer Kurt Heinrich (acquitted); SS-Oberscharführer Oskar Helbig (20 years imprisonment, reduced to 10 years); SS-Hauptscharführer Ruldof Jacobi (life imprisonment).

Second row: SS-Hauptscharführer Georg König (life imprisonment); Kapo Josef Kilian (life imprisonment); and, behind Fuchsloch, SS-Oberscharführer Wilhelm Simon (life imprisonment).

SS-Obersturmführer Hans Möser was sentenced to death, seven defendants were sentenced to life imprisonment and seven to prison terms ranging from 5 to 25 years. Four of the defendants, including Rickhey, were acquitted. The verdicts appear lenient compared to those of the Dachau, Mauthausen or Flossenbürg camp trials.

DIVISION z.V. INTO CAPTIVITY

Since February, Kammler had been considering converting the rocket units into infantry regiments, but most of the officers of Division z.V. knew it made no sense. They also knew that Kammler could not be reasoned with, and that any suggestion of surrender would result in a death sentence. To render his plans ineffective, Oberst Georg Thom, the division's Chief-of-Staff, issued orders delaying the reorganisation of the troops. Kammler left division headquarters at the end of March and never returned, but Oberst Thom was soon dismissed, perhaps because word had gotten to Berlin of his capitulation plan.

In mid-April, XXXXI. Armeekorps to which the Division z.V. was attached, made plans to engage the rocket units as infantry against the Russians and ordered the division to cross to the east bank of the Elbe and assemble in the Lenzen area.

At the end of April, Oberst Gerlach von Gaudecker arrived as the new division commander. Major G. Matheis, the divisional quartermaster, and SS-Obersturmbannführer Wetzling, the divisional judge officer, wasted no time and met with him on the 29th to discuss the surrender plan. They stressed that they must not let the V2 experts fall into the hands of the Soviets, but must surrender to the Americans. Von Gaudecker agreed to send Matheis and Wetzling as emissaries to the Americans and signed two documents, one in German and one in English, as well as a fictitious order for service in the Lenzen area in case they were arrested by German security patrols. The two men left during the night, accompanied by a signals officer.

The next afternoon, near Wootz, a few kilometres downstream from Lenzen, they saw Americans on the other side of the Elbe but despite the large white flag they were waving, they were greeted by mortar fire. They eventually attracted the attention of the Americans, and they were taken across the river and brought to the local headquarters. They eventually spoke with officers of the 29th Infantry Division and explained to them that the Division z.V. was ready to surrender, provided they had assurances that they would not be handed over to the Russians. The Americans agreed to transport the division across the Elbe and directed it to move to this same point near Wootz, with every ten vehicles carrying a white flag. Boats will be ready to transport the division on the morning of May 1.

The two emissaries returned to division headquarters, arriving late on the morning of April 30. The situation was chaotic and Oberst von Gaudecker was about to give the order to engage his units against the approaching Russians. Wetzling and other officers convinced him not to do so and instead order the division to disengage immediately and move to the Lenzen area.

Von Gaudecker then went to XXXXI. Armeekorps headquarters to inform them of his decision, and he was arrested. Major Karl Schütze, Chief-of-Staff of Division z.V., then took command.

On the morning of May 2, the first elements of the division arrived at the agreed crossing point where American posts disarmed them all. Storm boats from the 121st Engineer Battalion then transported the men across the river, while a ferry at Gorleben transported the vehicles to the west bank. The operation was completed around noon on May 3, with a total of 10,367 officers and men from Division z.V. going into captivity.

CAPTURE OF VON BRAUN

On January 31, 1945, Kammler ordered the evacuation of the Heeresversuchsanstalt Peenemünde and its relocation to central Germany. On February 3, at the last meeting held in Peenemünde regarding the move,

Von Braun and his six companions arrived in Reutte at nightfall on May 2, and the next morning several army photographers were on hand to photograph the German scientists. Among them was Signal Corps photographer T/5 Louis Weintraub who took this photo. (USNA)

The German scientists posed with members of the 44th Infantry Division. From left to right: CIC officer Charles Stewart, Dr. Herbert Axster, Dieter Huzel, Wernher von Braun, Magnus von Braun, and Hans Lindenberg. (NASA)

the Heeresversuchsanstalt consisted of around 3,800 people, 2,000 people involved in the development of the A4, 1,500 in the development of the anti-aircraft rockets Wasserfall and Taifun, and 300 of the administration and logistics. The first train left Peenemünde on February 17 with more than 500 people, and the evacuation was completed in mid-March.

On March 15, von Braun was traveling to Berlin when his driver fell asleep and the car crashed off the road. The wrecked vehicle was spotted a few hours later by two Peenemünde associates who were also traveling to Berlin. Von Braun suffered a broken arm and shoulder, and although he was in no condition to move, he insisted that his arm be placed in a cast so he could leave the hospital.

On April 6, as Allied forces advanced deeper into Germany, Kammler ordered that the Peenemünde's engineering team, consisting of around 450 specialists, be moved from their temporary headquarters at Bleicherode to Oberammergau in the Bavarian Alps, where it was rumoured that a 'redoubt' was to be established for the last stand. His badly damaged arm and shoulder preventing him from leaving immediately, von Braun did not finally leave until April 9.

Albin Sawatzki, the technical director of Mittelwerk, did not carry out the SS order to destroy the Kohnstein tunnel complex and decided instead to stay behind to hand it over to the Americans. Interrogated by the Americans on April 14, Sawatzki died under unknown circumstances on May 1 in Warburg, north of Kassel.

These photos illustrate both sides of the A4/V2 rocket program: a monumental technological feat forever stained by the suffering and death inflicted on the slave workers who produced them. Von Braun undoubtedly knew of the criminal conditions of rocket production at the Mittelwerk, but he was quietly confident in his future, boasting to his captors at Reutte that his invention was 'sure to shape the course of the next war'. (USNA)

In Oberammergau, the Peenemünde scientists were held in a small internment camp surrounded by SS guards. Despite the barbed wire, it was a very comfortable camp, with good food and drinks. Realising that they were in fact being held hostage, von Braun decided it was wise to distance himself from Kammler's men. He pointed out to SS-Sturmbannführer Kummer, Kammler's local deputy, that the camp was at high risk of being bombed by Allied planes and that the scientists were all at risk of being killed. He thus convinced Kummer to order the dispersal of the scientists to neighbouring villages.

Von Braun and a small group then moved west and eventually settled at Haus Ingeborg, at Oberjoch in the Allgäu mountains. On May 1, they heard on the radio the fall of Berlin and the news of Hitler's death. They decided that Magnus von Braun, Werner's brother, who spoke broken English, would go out and contact the Americans.

On the morning of May 2, Magnus cycled east to Austria where he soon established contact with elements of the 44th Infantry Division. He received safe conduct passes and returned to Oberjoch in the afternoon. In his book Peenemünde to Canaveral published in 1962, Dieter Huzel describes the group's surrender in a gloomy and rainy afternoon. The seven men – Magnus and Wernher von Braun, Walter Dornberger, Herbert Axster, Huzel, Hans Lindenberg and Bernhard Tessman – packed their belongings into three vans and travelled east along the route Magnus followed in the morning until they suddenly met an American soldier who signalled them to stop. Magnus showed the passes and half an hour later two jeeps arrived to escort the group to Reutte where they arrived at nightfall.

The rocket scientists were soon transferred to a prison compound in Garmisch-Partenkirchen, where various Allied interrogators began questioning them.

KAMMLER'S DISAPPEARANCE

The end of the V-weapons campaign in March did not halt Kammler's rise and on March 27 he was appointed Generalbevollmächtigten des Oberbefehlshabers der Luftwaffe für Strahlflugzeuge (Plenipotentiary of the Commander-in-Chief of the Luftwaffe for jet aircraft) and promoted to SS-Obergruppenführer. On April 3, he spoke with Hitler and the next day Goebbels noted in his diary that Kammler 'who now bears much of the responsibility for the reform of the Luftwaffe on his shoulders' was 'doing well, and great hopes rest on him'.

In the following days, Kammler's intentions and movements became difficult to follow. On April 22, he arrived in Oberammergau in a road convoy with a group of around 600 men. The local authorities did not like seeing him and his large team in the town, and he argued with them for a few days. He finally left on the night of April 28 as American forces approached. In early May he is believed to have been in Ebensee, just east of Salzburg, and on May 5, around 4 a.m., he left for Prague.

He allegedly committed suicide by cyanide poisoning on May 9. His driver, SS-Oberscharführer Kurt Preuk, later stated that he had personally seen the corpse and attended the burial that day near Jílové u Prahy (Eule in German), 20 kilometres south of Prague.

Another version of Kammler's death is that he died in Prague on May 9, while he and around twenty SS men were defending a bunker against an attack by Czech resistance fighters. One of his collaborators then shot him to prevent his capture. This version was attributed to Dornberger, who would have heard it from eyewitnesses. Another version, reported by SS-Obergruppenführer Gottlob Berger, head of the SS Central Office, was that Kammler had defected to the Russians.

In July 1945, Kammler's wife requested that he be declared dead and, reviewing the available information and statement, including Preuk's, the Berlin-Charlottenburg District Court ruled in September 1948 that Hans Kammler was officially dead on May 9, 1945.

Authors have recently proposed that he did not commit suicide in 1945 and was instead captured by the Americans. They found two documents which they believe prove that Kammler was detained by the Americans in May 1945. A document, written by Colonel Loyd K. Pepple, at the headquarters of the US Strategic Air Force in Europe, and dated of May 30, lists 'key German Air Force non-technical personnel presently being held for interrogation'. Topping this list of 34 names are Göring and Speer, and the 18th name is SS-Obergruppenführer Kammler, 'Inspector of All Jet Fighter Units of the Luftwaffe'. The second document brought forward is a letter from Brigadier General George Clement McDonald, director of intelligence for the US Army Air Force in Europe, who instructed Major Ernst Englander 'to make the necessary arrangements to personally interrogate Speer, Kammler and Saur' and report his findings as soon as possible.

While these documents prove that the US Army Air Force was willing to interrogate Kammler, they do not appear to constitute evidence that Kammler was in American custody. Confusion was high in May 1945 and the information that Kammler was in custody may have been a misunderstanding. The fact that these two documents come from a single agency, the US Army Air Force in Europe, lends more weight to this observation.

The claim of Donald W. Richardson, a former agent of the Office of Strategic Services, has also been put forward. Richardson reportedly told his sons shortly before his death in the late 1990s that he took Kammler to the United States and that he was then interned in maximum security conditions until he hanged himself in his cell in 1947. However, there was not a single piece of evidence supporting this story of Kammler's stay and subsequent suicide in the United States.

What particular value would Kammler have had for the Americans? He was a civil engineer, not a scientist, and while he ruthlessly managed the production of V-weapons, he was not part of the technical teams that developed the rockets and jet planes. The Americans had captured prototypes of most of them and had recruited, under Operation 'Paperclip', hundreds of the scientists who had developed them.

SS-Obergruppenführer Kammler (third from left in this photo from earlier years), key figures in the production and operational deployment of V-weapons, disappeared under unclear circumstances in May 1945. At the end of April he was in Oberammergau, then in Ebensee, and on May 5 he is said to have left for Prague. He allegedly committed suicide there on May 9. Another version is that he died in a fight against Czech resistance fighters and yet another version is that he defected to the Russians. A recent version, without any supporting evidence, is that he was secretly held in the United States under maximum security until he hanged himself in 1947.

V-WEAPONS, VICTIMS AND DAMAGE

BETWEEN JUNE 1944 AND MARCH 1945, the V1s killed 6,184 people in England and injured 17,981, of which the figures for London are 5,566 and 16,182.

For the period between September 1944 and March 1945, the V2s killed 2,754 people, and injured 6,523, of which most were in the greater London area, 2,511 and 5,869 respectively.

The worst V1 bombing occurred in East Barnet on August 23 when 211 people lost their lives. Other dramatic incidents occurred at the Air Ministry on the Strand on June 28, a flying bomb killing 198 people, and in Chelsea on July 2, when 124 people lost their lives.

The most serious V2 incidents occurred at Deptford when a rocket hit a crowded shop on November 25, killing 168 people, and at Stepney when a rocket crashed on an apartment block on March 27, killing 134.

The last V2 to strike London hit on March 27, about 5 p.m., killing one person in Orpington.

The last German action of any kind on British soil was on March 29 when a V1 exploded in a field at Woolmer Green, Hertfordshire, at 9.00 a.m. The second-to-last V1 to hit British soil, albeit in pieces, was shot down by AA gunners near Iwade in Kent at 9.59 a.m. and the very final V1 to approach Britain was destroyed by AA fire off Orford Ness, Suffolk, at 12.43 p.m.

The damage caused in England by V-weapons cannot be subdivided into that caused by V1s and that caused by V2s: it amounted to 31,600 houses destroyed and 1,420,000 damaged, mainly in the London area.

The respective losses to V1 or V2 impacts in Belgium for the period between September 1944 and March 1945 is not precisely known: 6,448 peoples were killed by V-weapons, and 22,524 wounded. Of those killed, 4,429 were in the Antwerp area, 1,649 in Liège and suburbs, and 508 in Brussels and its suburbs. Of the wounded, 6,993 were in the Antwerp area, 2,558 in Liège and suburbs, and 3,134 in Brussels and suburbs.

The worst incident in Belgium occurred on December 16 when a V2 rocket hit the Rex cinema in Antwerp, killing 567 people and injuring a further 291. Of those killed, 296 were allied soldiers. Another painful V2 bombing was on November 27 when a rocket crashed on Teniers Plaats, the busiest intersection in town, killing 126 people, including 26 Allied soldiers, and leaving another 309 injured. (Another source that included the wounded who died in hospital in the days that followed the attack, puts the death toll at 157, including 29 Allied soldiers.)

The damage caused by V-weapons cannot be subdivided into that caused by V1s and that caused by V2s: total damage in Belgium amounted to 5,682 houses destroyed, and 167,675 damaged, of which the figures as for Antwerp were 3,118 houses destroyed and 95,275 damaged.

A third V-Waffe, the HDP gun, fired against Luxembourg but the effect of its bombardment was insignificant. In his book *Bombenangriffe auf Luxemburg in zwei Weltkriegen* E. T. Melchers indicates that 10 people were killed and 35 injured.

The deployment of the Rheinbote rocket was another insignificant failure, not a single Rheinbote impact was ever identified in Antwerp that was then hit day after day by much more powerful V1s and V2s. On December 24 afternoon, when Artillerie-Abteilung 709 launched 24 Rheinbote rockets at Antwerp, 14 incidents were reported in the Antwerp area between midday and 8 p.m., including a 'barrage' of 11 missiles between 5 p.m. and 6.30 p.m. As only one V2 was launched during this period, and probably a few V1s, we can guess that at least a few of the Rheinbote rockets hit their target.

For the period June 1944 to March 1945, the V1s killed 6,184 people in England and injured 17,981, of which 5,566 and 16,182 respectively in London. On October 31, 1944, a V1 crashed on the St Marie Hotel in Purley, in the borough of Croydon, killing 17 and injuring 31.

OPERATION 'BACKFIRE'

THE IDEA OF A V2 ROCKET firing demonstration was proposed on May 1, 1945, by Junior Commander Joan C.C. Bernard, Army Territorial Service, aide to Major General Alexander Cameron, head of the Air Defence Division, SHAEF. He found the idea appealing and so he called a staff meeting the next day and a report to this effect was sent to the deputy Chief-of-Staff of SHAEF.

The Americans were already collecting V2 rockets and equipment for the Pentagon Ordnance Department had asked Colonel Holger N. Toftoy, chief of the US Army's Ordnance Technical Intelligence teams assigned to Europe, to acquire and ship 100 operational V2 rockets to the United States. When leaders of the 3rd Armored Division reported the discovery of the underground factory in Nordhausen on April 11, Toftoy immediately sent a team to investigate.

When the 3rd Armored Division reported having found V2 rockets stacked near the entrance to an underground factory in Nordhausen, Colonel Toftoy immediately sent a team to investigate. This photo of three war correspondents standing in one V2 tail was taken on April 16. (USNA)

Two GIs posed in front of a half-section of the rocket body, probably in Gallery 23 where the half-sections were stored. Half-sections were produced at the Mittelwerk, but a significant portion of those used on the assembly line, about half of the total, were produced by Zeppelin at Saulgau, just north of Lake Constance, and were transported by train to the Mittelwerk. (USHMM)

Arriving at Nordhausen, the 'Special Mission V2' found around fifty complete rockets in the marshalling yard, but all were damaged during the Bomber Command raids which had hit the site in early April. The team began collecting what they found, including partially completed rockets and various components, and loading them into rail cars.

Understanding that V2 rocket equipment that was available was going to be salvaged and evacuated haphazardly, on May 4, SHAEF issued an order that no V2 rocket equipment would be removed from the theatre of operations pending further instructions. Nevertheless, the 'Special Mission V2' teams in Nordhausen continued to collect equipment and materials and the first train was dispatched on May 22. By the end of the month, the team had shipped 341 rail cars to Erfurt, from where the US Army's Military Rail System transported them to Antwerp. From there, the equipment was shipped to New Orleans and then to White Sands Proving Grounds, a new testing facility being developed in the southern New Mexico desert.

The British complained to SHAEF, but by the time action could be taken,

The chalking on the fuselage of this rocket photographed in Tunnel B indicates that it was assembled by the CCR, 5th Armored Division. By leaving the rocket with only the lower half of its body and tail, this operation was intended to show the internal parts. This particular rocket was later photographed, in May or June, in the centre of Ellrich, a town ten kilometres west of the Mittelwerk factory. The 5th Armored Division took over the Nordhausen area in late April and remained there until it was handed over to Soviet administration. (USNA)

On May 1, the US Congressional Commission investigating Nazi atrocities visited Camp 'Dora' and the underground Mittelwerk factory. In Tunnel B, Missouri Congressman Dewey Short and Massachusetts Senator Leverett Saltonstall viewed details of a V2 rocket's combustion unit. Saltonstall points to the air storage cylinders that powered the steam unit and the alcohol and oxygen valves. (USHMM)

Major James P. Hamill, head of 'Special Mission V2' sent to Nordhausen, later recounted how 'the written orders I received indicated that Nordhausen was to be in the Russian zone and that all plans and equipment were to be left for the Soviets. Unofficially and off the record, I was told to remove as much material as I could, without making it obvious that we had looted the place.' We do not know whether these men photographed in front of the southern entrance to Tunnel A belonged to one of the teams of 'Special Mission V2'.

everything the 'Special Mission V2' teams had brought to Antwerp was already en route to the United States.

On June 22, General Eisenhower gave instructions for an operation whose 'main object is to verify the German technique of launching long-range rockets and prove it with an actual launch.' The Allies would thus learn of

In mid-1944, a workshop was established at Kleinbodungen, 20 kilometres west of Nordhausen, to salvage components that were in good order from the damaged rockets returned to the Mittelwerk. A sub-camp of 'Dora' called 'Emmi' was established at Kleinbodungen, and one inmate who worked at the salvage workshop later stated that this Kommando operated until the very end in April 1945. Some of these trains photographed in May at the marshalling yard brought damaged rockets to the workshop while others were loaded with recovered components to deliver them to the Mittelwerk. (USHMM)

In May or June 1945, Captain George Phillips, officer of the 5th Armored Division, took this photo of a train in Niedersachswerfen station. In the foreground were two wagons ready to deliver V1s to front depots. The missiles were transported two by two side by side in a wagon, with the wings and equipment attached above the pulsejet. In the background, a wagon with a V2. (Georges Phillips)

the 'preparation of the rocket, the ancillary equipment, and the handling of fuel.'

The Supreme Commander delegated responsibility for the organisation and conduct of the operation to General Cameron. As it was necessary to fire over the North Sea, the decision was made to carry out the operation in the British zone. To simplify administration, it was planned to have a primarily British organisation, with

This was one of the trains delivering V2 rockets to launch batteries. We see in this photo two wagons on a section of three: the wagon on the left transported a V2 without its warhead, while another wagon, hidden in the tunnel, transported a second rocket. The middle wagon, seen here, carried the two warheads, with the noses of the two rockets overhanging it. Note that members of the 'Special Mission V2', or curious GIs, had removed the access panel to control compartment 4. (USHMM)

'Special Mission V2' teams worked around the clock, loading wagons with partially completed rockets, tail sections, various subassemblies and components, and a large collection of blueprints and manuals. Before the end of May, more than 300 wagons were shipped from Nordhausen to Antwerp.

Another photo by Captain Phillips, of wagons parked at the south entrance to Tunnel A. On the left, one loaded with the tail section of a V2. (Georges Phillips)

the detachment of a small American team to monitor American interests and help procure the necessary personnel and equipment. The project was named Operation 'Backfire'.

When SHAEF ended in July, the British component of the Air Defence Division became the Special Projectile Operations Group, SPOG. Under the command of General Cameron with Colonel W. S. J. Carter as second in command and Colonel G. W. Raby as chief technical superintendent, SPOG was tasked with carrying out the proposed launches of the V2.

A British team arrived in Nordhausen in early June, after the Americans had already looted the place. They loaded several more trains with various subassemblies and components and left on the 19th.

American photographer James Baker took this photo of V2 rockets being crated at Antwerp shipping docks for transshipment to the United States. A train loaded with V2 tail fins can be seen in the background. (USHMM)

With the Americans having evacuated most of the V2 rockets and equipment found at the Mittelwerk factory, and all of this already on its way to the United States, finding complete V2s was a challenge. On June 10, a search team reported finding 18 incomplete rockets in Jerxheim, east of Hanover, and another 12 rockets were found near Leese. (Charles Black)

FINDING ROCKETS AND EXPERTS

With the Americans having already taken away most of the rockets and associated equipment they had salvaged from the Mittelwerk factory, finding complete V2s was a challenge. British teams had the opportunity to tour the Mittelwerk once the Americans were done with it and they collected parts and equipment before the Russians took over. Fortunately, 18 incomplete rockets were found in an abandoned train in the British occupation zone and a further twelve near Leese, including one almost complete.

However, many key components were still missing, as well as support vehicles and equipment: fuel tankers, firing tables, transport and assembly

At the end of May, interrogations of the Germans made it possible to establish a list of those items of ground equipment required. Operation 'Backfire' report: 'The amount of equipment to be recovered was formidable, including, as it did, control cars, oxygen, alcohol, and hydrogen-peroxide tankers, firing platforms, transport and erection vehicles, testing vehicles, generators, cranes, ladders, air compressors and other ancillary equipment such as cables, connecting plugs, hoses and igniters.' (Charles Black)

vehicles, control vehicles, generators, cranes, ladders, and other auxiliary equipment, such as cables, connecting plugs, hoses, and igniters.

A search of former operational launch sites in the Netherlands and Germany yielded no results, as the German rocket troops had withdrawn with all their equipment in the face of the Allied advance. Finally, most of the missing items were found in and around the areas of Leese, Celle and Fallingbostel, where rocket troops from The Hague and Burgsteinfurt sectors had withdrawn.

Major difficulties remained, however, for example with the batteries of the guidance gyroscopes, the specimens of which found had all been damaged by exposure. The control amplifiers (Mischgerät, the equipment which transmitted the signal received from the gyroscopes to the servomotors) of which only a few could be found in working order posed another problem. Ultimately, with only enough of these vital devices available to make eight rockets suitable for firing, the decision was made to assemble only eight rockets.

In total, 400 wagons and 70 Lancaster flights were needed to transport the 250,000 pieces and 60 specialised vehicles to the chosen launch site in the British occupation zone, the former German artillery range at Altenwalde, near Cuxhaven.

Vehicles and support equipment were found in the area south and southeast of Bremen, where rocket troops had withdrawn. Here a damaged Vidalwagen found at Steyerberg.

In Altenwalde, the month of June was dedicated to cleaning the site and building the necessary additional facilities, such as the Vertical Test Chamber designed to service a rocket in a vertical position. It was 56 feet high and equipped with a 5-ton overhead crane. (Charles Black)

With the proximity of the North Sea and good radar tracking points downrange, Altenwalde was a perfect location for long-range test launches. When the advance of the Red Army forced the evacuation of Zempin, some test flights of V1s took place there in late 1944 and early 1945.

After reaching the west bank of the Elbe in early May, the officers and men of the V2 units were gradually moved further west by trucks. From May 4, they were gathered at a sports stadium in Herford, about 80 kilometres west of Hanover. The place was overcrowded, there was little to eat or drink, and US military police routinely used beatings and violence to maintain control. Officers of the Division z.V. asked the Americans about the future of the rocket troops and in exchange they were asked to locate a hundred V2 specialists in the masses of prisoners. This was done and on May 7, the selected officers and men were transferred from the sports stadium to a nearby public swimming pool.

According to the Operation 'Backfire' report, this first group included 107 officers and men selected 'from amongst those with the longest practical experience and the most knowledge of improvements and simplifications in launching methods'.

On May 9, they were all loaded onto trucks and the convoy headed west toward Belgium. 'They were segregated in a camp near Brussels and interrogated intensively, not only with a view to finding out what further personnel would be required, but also with a view to locating rocket equipment abandoned by the Division. By the beginning of July, the party had

The main assembly shop, in which four rockets could be assembled simultaneously, was a Marston shelter 200 feet long and 45 feet wide. The effective height from the ground to the hook of the 10-ton overhead gantry was 17 feet. (Charles Black)

The central part of a rocket in the main assembly shop, with the alcohol tank in front and the liquid oxygen tank behind. The alcohol tank was tapered slightly forward to fit the shape of the missile, there was a refueling pipe on top (foreground in this photo) and the pipe leading to the turbopump passed through the liquid oxygen tank. (Frank Micklethwaite)

been increased to 137 in all, and was removed to Altenwalde near Cuxhaven'.

As soon as it was clear that 'the building of rockets was going to be a complicated and tricky business', it was decided to complete the first team with 79 technicians from among those the Americans had concentrated in Garmisch-Partenkirchen, and they arrived in Cuxhaven at the end of July.

The German experts were organised into two groups. The main group was 'Camp A', responsible for producing the rockets, handling them at the launch site, and finally launching them. 'Camp A' was organised as a military unit under the command of the senior German officer, Oberstleutnant Wolfgang Weber, who had commanded Lehr- und Versuchsbatterie 444. They adopted the old operational jargon and called themselves AVKO or Altenwalde Versuchskommando.

The second group, 'Camp C', included 15 to 20 civilian experts held at a separate camp a few kilometres away in the village of Brockeswalde for interrogation purposes only. Operation 'Backfire' Report: 'It was hoped by this means to ensure that information provided by one party could be checked against information provided by the other party.'

Dr. Kurt Debus, who had led the Test Stand Group at Peenemünde, acted as technical and diplomatic liaison between the two camps and between the Germans and the Allies. (In 1962, Debus became director of NASA's Launch Operations Center, soon renamed the Kennedy Space Center, and under his leadership NASA conducted 150 military missile and space rocket launches, including 13 Saturn V rocket launches of the Apollo lunar program.)

The steam unit and the frame assembly. (Frank Micklethwaite)

Major General Alexander Cameron, the head of Operation 'Backfire', with Brigadier Leslie Lockhart, commander of the 307th Infantry Brigade, and Colonel W. S. J. Carter, in charge of field operations, at the Altenwalde launch site.

The Germans gathered at Altenwalde for Operation 'Backfire' called themselves AVKO or Altenwalde Versuchskommando. Oberstleutnant Weber and four of his aides discussed the details of the work with a British officer.
(Frank Micklethwaite)

General Dornberger had been brought to Cuxhaven, but it was feared that his influence would be embarrassing and he was kept apart from both parties. Surprisingly, von Braun was not there, not because the Americans would have kept him for themselves, but because the British were not interested in having him participate in the operation. After the war, Colonel Carter explained the reason: 'we always regarded von Braun as more of a visionary and front man than a scientist and technician'.

Operation 'Backfire' Report: 'It was realised from the beginning that the handling of the Germans would be a delicate matter. If the difficulties of building rockets were to be overcome, and the launching procedure learnt, active co-operation rather than passive obedience was essential.'

At first, some of the Germans were prisoners of war, others were disarmed enemy personnel, and still others were civilians. To eliminate potential problems with these different statuses, all prisoners of war were converted to disarmed enemy personnel and all civilians were transformed into German army officials.

The fact that they were well fed, well housed and generally well treated naturally contributed to the good mood that reigned in the German camp. Furthermore, the V2 specialists were all happy to work with their rockets again and the fact that the operation was a demonstration of their work added to their satisfaction.

A total of 200 German rocket experts were employed by Operation 'Backfire', of whom some 130 were men from the operational rocket units and 70 were civilian technicians from the experimental establishments. In addition, 400 Germans were employed, soldiers and civilians, who had no previous connection with the V2.

An additional 2,500 British Army men supplemented the operation's personnel, including operators for the radar tracking stations and ATS crews for operating the theodolites.

This caricature taken from the report published by AVKO illustrates the particular situation in which the Germans found themselves in Altenwalde: they were prisoners of war, but at the same time they were the experts listened to by the Allies.

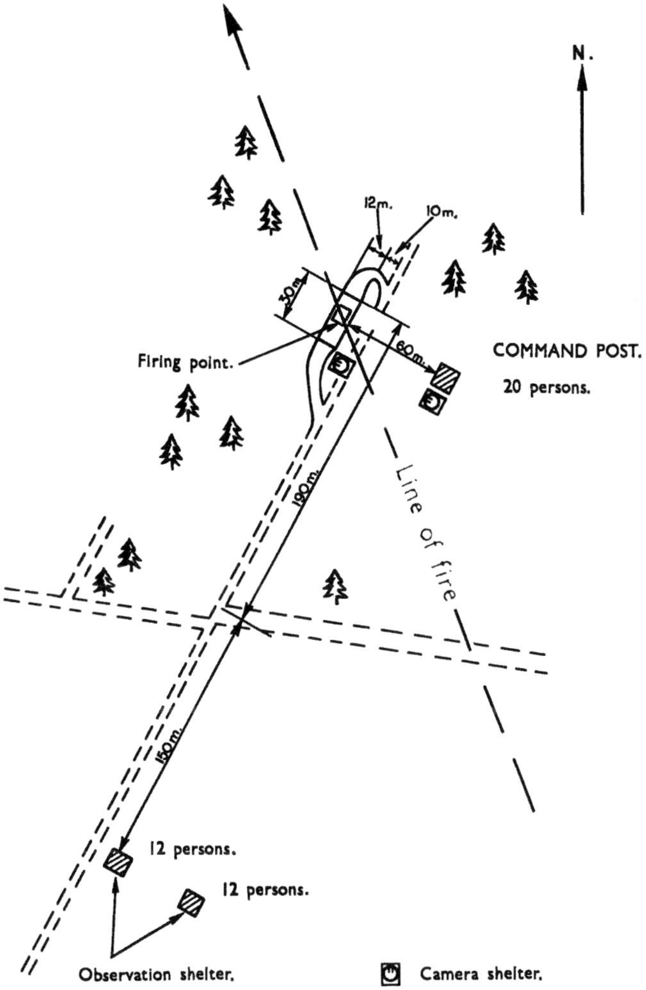

The layout of the launch site from a plan from the Operation 'Backfire' report. It consisted of a 60 metre by 30 metre concrete platform and a concrete command post. So that visual observation would not be disturbed by dirt and dust thrown up by the rocket jet, strips of coconut mats held in place by heavy mesh were laid on the uneven terrain between the launch pad, the command post and the camera shelter. The line-of-sight bearing was 336° 51' true, including a correction of -34' for the rotation of the earth. To allow more officers to study the launch procedure, launch control was not exercised from a Feuerleitpanzer but from the much larger concrete command post. Additionally, two concrete observation shelters were installed, each accommodating 12 people, 350 metres south of the launch site. To record the missile's flight, four theodolite stations were deployed in Altenwalde and nine radar stations along the German and Danish coasts.

THREE LAUNCHES

A facility 60 metres long and 14 metres wide was erected at Altenwalde as the main workshop for the simultaneous assembly of four rockets; it was equipped with a 10-ton overhead crane to handle rockets and heavy assemblies. The hangars and other facilities at the former German firing range were used for logistics. A 17 metre high Vertical Testing Chamber was constructed from sections of Bailey bridge to service the rockets in an upright position, and a large concrete firing platform was created at the launch site, with a concrete command post and two concrete observation shelters.

By mid-September, the eight operational rockets had been produced. To facilitate tracking during their first ten seconds of flight, they were painted with a black and white checkerboard pattern, similar to early Peenemünde rocket designs.

Five rail tankers containing 70 tons of ethanol were discovered near Nordhausen and shipped to Cuxhaven, along with hydrogen peroxide found in Kiel. To produce the necessary liquid oxygen, the plant in Fassburg, 200 kilometres from Altenwalde, was brought back into operation. Sending the

The cable mast has been adjusted so that the cables were directly aligned with the Stotz plugs. The Meillerwagen's lifting frame was lowered and the Meillerwagen was towed away. (Frank Micklethwaite)

rockets to their maximum range would have caused them to fall far from the Danish coast and observation would have been difficult, so it was decided to limit the range to 250 kilometres.

The first launch attempt took place on October 1. A few days earlier, the rocket had been put into firing position and placed in a storage tent under the protection of British special guards.

Difficulties were encountered in getting the steam unit valves to function and, after necessary repairs, a launch attempt was made at 3.50 p.m. The igniter worked satisfactorily but the Hauptstufe (full thrust) did not turn on because the Stotz plugs (ground connector plugs) did not come off. No defects could be found and the Germans explained that failure of the plugs to detach had occurred in one in ten rockets. A new igniter was inserted and another attempt made. The igniter ignited but was ejected before it had time to ignite the fuel. It was too late to make another attempt that day and the rocket was drained and returned to the Vertical Test Chamber for overhaul.

A new rocket was positioned to be fired on October 2. The weather was perfect, with little wind and clear skies. The rocket was successfully launched on the first attempt at 2.43 p.m. The take-off was steady, the turn-over from vertical occurred at the right time and the engine cut-off occurred after 65 seconds as planned. Flight time was four minutes 50 seconds. The

The weather was perfect for the first launch on October 2 and the chronological sequence of events for that day was as follows. 10.55 a.m.: theodolite sites occupied; 10.55 a.m.: tests completed; 12.00: fuel column arrived at launch site; 12.45 p.m.: start of the refuelling procedure; 1.44 p.m.: 'Everything is clear!'; 2.06 p.m.: unnecessary personnel directed to leave the launch site; 2.08 p.m.: tanking completed; 2.15 p.m.: igniter inserted; 2.25 p.m.: minus 15 warning to recording sites; 2.30 p.m.: departure of the Meillerwagen; 2.37 p.m.: tests completed, launch troops took cover, H minus 3 warning; 2.41 p.m.: launch. (Charles Black)

line error was 1.2 kilometres left, and the distance error was 1.9 kilometres short. A perfect flight. Words of congratulations and thanks were exchanged from both sides.

Having been checked over, the rocket that had failed to fire on October 1 was set up at the launch site on October 4. Weather conditions were again ideal. The rocket was launched at 2.15 p.m. but engine cut-off occurred after only 35 seconds of burning and the rocket fell 25 kilometres from the point of launch. Flight time was only two minutes 16 seconds. No satisfactory explanation for the early engine shutdown could be found but the report pointed that no physical break-up of the rocket occurred, neither did it burst into flames.

The third and final rocket was launched on October 15, as a demonstration to representatives of the United States, Russia, France, Dominion and Whitehall officials, and the press. Weather conditions were poor this day, with low cloud cover and winds but as the main objective of the launch was to demonstrate to visitors, it was carried out despite the unfavourable conditions.

Soviet representatives were invited to attend the demonstration and permission to enter the test area was issued to a delegation of three people. However, on the day of the launch, six Soviet officers showed up. Cameron remained firm and only the three accredited visitors – General Andrei Sokolov, Colonel Yuri Pobedonostsev, and Colonel Valentin Glushko – and their interpreter were allowed entry into the facility. The uninvited guests had to witness the launch through the barbed wire fence surrounding the facility. Among them was Lieutenant Colonel Sergei Korolev.

The launch took place exactly on time at 3.06 p.m., the rocket performed perfectly and landed about 19 kilometres short and five kilometres to the right of the aiming point. Flight time was four minutes 37 seconds.

In the decade to come, Korolev and Glushko would become the Soviet Union's leading rockets and rocket engines designers, and Korolev would launch the first artificial satellite of Earth, Sputnik, and the first man in space, Yuri Gagarin.

The rocket rose into the blue sky, the British and Germans watching it travel all the way through to engine cut-off. Words of congratulations and acknowledgments were spoken from both sides. This caricature from the report by the German AVKO illustrates this remarkable situation.

FROM 'PAPERCLIP' TO THE MOON

IN EARLY APRIL, FEARING that their invaluable rockets engineering documentation would be destroyed by the SS, and knowing that these documents could be used as bargaining chips in negotiating with the Allies, von Braun had 14 tons of the most important plans and documents discreetly

Engineers at Wright Field reverse-engineered the V1 from remains of crashed missiles brought from England. The original caption for this photo of V1 parts pointed to 'the armed guard in the upper left and the Secret stamp in the upper right'. The first working example of the US-built Argus As 014 jet engine was fired in July, and in September Republic Aviation delivered a first batch of 13 JB-2s. (US Air Force)

concealed by Dieter Huzel and Bernhard Tessmann in an abandoned mine at Dörnten, 80 kilometres west of Magdeburg. The entrance to the gallery was blown, so that a pile of stone and rubble sealed off access.

From late April, Major Robert Staver, from the Research and Development branch of the US Ordnance Office, was in the Nordhausen area to search for rocket specialists. On May 20 he obtained from one of them, Karl Otto Fleischer, information as to the location of the hidden documents. There was a great deal of urgency as in less than a week, the Dörnten area was to be

The Air Force's JB-2 and a navalised version designated KGW-1 were put into production for use in the invasion of Japan, but Japan's surrender in August 1945 made their use unnecessary. The JB-2/KGW-1 later played an important role in the development of more advanced surface-to-surface missile systems, and, by launching a KGW-1 in 1947, USS *Cusk* became the first submarine to launch a guided missile.

handed over to the British and a team was immediately sent to the site.

Valuable time was lost when a British intelligence team claiming to be looking for weapons the Germans might have hidden in the mine arrived and began a meticulous search. The Americans posed as geologists pretending to search for iron ore samples, which were graded and convincingly packed by a team of local miners until the British left. A frantic scramble then ensued to clear the heap of rubble obstructing the gallery, crate the documents and bring them back to Nordhausen. This was finally completed on the morning

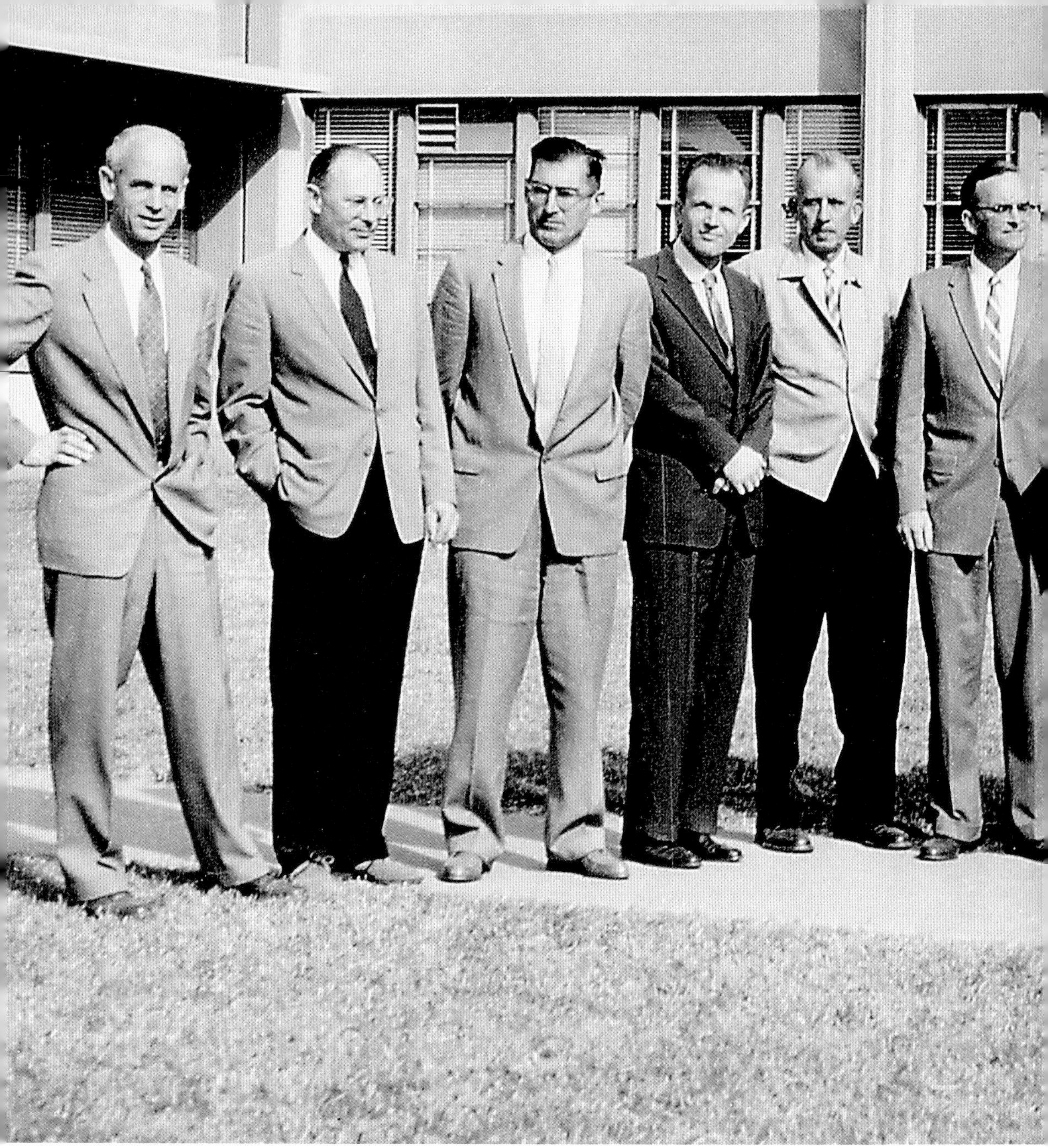

Operation 'Paperclip' brought an initial group of some 130 German rocket scientists to the United States. The group was subdivided into two sections: the larger one at Fort Bliss, Texas, for research, and a smaller one at White Sands, New Mexico, for test launches of rockets. In 1950, von Braun and his team were transferred to the Redstone Arsenal in Huntsville, Alabama. Pictured here (from left to right) in front of building 4488, the Peenemünde team was the core of the new agency: Dr. Ernst Stuhlinger, Director, Research Projects Office; Dr. Helmut Hölzer, Director, Computation Laboratory; Karl L. Heimburg, Director, Test Laboratory; Dr. Ernst Geissler, Director, Aeroballistics Laboratory; Erich W. Neubert, Director, Systems Analysis Reliability Laboratory; Dr. Walter Häussermann, Director, Guidance and Control Laboratory; Dr. Wernher von Braun, Director Development Operations Division; William A. Mrazek, Director, Structures and Mechanics Laboratory; Hans Hüter, Director, System Support Equipment Laboratory; Eberhard Rees, Deputy Director, Development Operations Division; Dr. Kurt Debus, Director Missile Firing Laboratory; Hans H. Maus, Director, Fabrication and Assembly Engineering Laboratory. (NASA)

of May 27, and the crates were quickly dispatched to Paris, then to the United States.

Meanwhile, Major Staver was hurrying to identify rocket specialists before the scheduled handover of the region to the Russians in July. To help decide which of the thousands of German technicians in the area should be offered evacuation to the American zone, he had some senior German engineers sent back to Nordhausen at the beginning of June. On June 20, some 1,000 rocket personnel and their families were finally put in a train, which took them to Witzenhausen, 70 kilometres to the south-west, inside the American zone.

The original caption for this photo taken at White Sands in the late 1940s stated that 'these German scientists, whose talents were once the property of the Nazi Luftwaffe, are now aiding US Army Ordnance in research on rocket projectiles'. Martin Schilling, on top of the engine, von Braun and Ernst Steinhoff examined for the photographer the rocket engine used to train crews at the White Sands Proving Grounds. (NASA)

In July, the US Joint Chiefs of Staff established a secret recruitment program, code named Operation 'Overcast', the aim of which was to recruit German scientists 'to assist in shortening the Japanese war and to aid our post-war military research'. Despite the attempt to keep it secret, the press interviewed several of these scientists later that year. The code name was leaked when the scientists' quarters at Landshut became locally known as 'Camp Overcast', and the program was renamed Operation 'Paperclip' in November 1945. The name 'Paperclip' is believed to have come from Ordnance Corps officers who attached a paperclip to the files of German experts they wanted to employ in the United States.

In August, one-year contracts were offered to the German scientists, and 127 of them accepted. In September, the first group of seven rocket scientists, including von Braun and six aeronautical engineers, were flown to the United States. After briefings, the rocket experts were sent to Fort Bliss, Texas, and the aircraft experts to Wright Field, Ohio.

Japan's defeat did not change American policy, especially since the British, French, and Soviets were known to actively recruit German experts, and many more Peenemünde scientists were recruited in the following months.

The first launch of a V2 at White Sands took place on April 16, 1946, in front of the media. The black and yellow paint was supposed to make the rocket more visible when taking off but the combination proved ineffective (the yellow colour appears very dark in this black and white photo) and for later launches the rockets were painted Peenemünde style black and white patterns. German equipment, such as the Meillerwagen and the liquid oxygen trailer seen here, were still used in the first launches. A steering vane broke at 6 seconds into this first flight, then a fin was lost and the engine shutdown was directed at 19 seconds. A second launch, on May 10, was a success, the rocket reaching an altitude of 112 kilometres. (NASA)

Immediately after its launch on November 7, rocket No. 14 began to rotate violently, then stabilised at an altitude of 300 metres. After 31 seconds of flight, the operators sent the emergency cut-off signal and the missile crashed within the confines of the Proving Grounds. The cause of the failure could not be clearly identified

The plan to launch a two-stage combination of a V2 as the first stage with a WAC Corporal rocket as the upper stage was conceived in 1946 by Colonel Toftoy, then director of the Army guided missile program. German engineers worked on the initial studies regarding the mating of the V2 and the WAC Corporal, but they were not directly involved in the Bumper project. After six launches at White Sands, with Bumper 5 reaching an altitude of 400 kilometres, the final two launches of the Bumper program took place at the newly established Long Range Proving Ground at Cape Canaveral, Florida. In July 1950, the WAC Corporal (on a trailer in the left foreground) was being prepared for attachment to the nose of the V2. (NASA)

In a secret directive issued on September 3, 1946, President Truman officially approved Operation 'Paperclip' and expanded it to include 1,000 German scientists.

When news of the project broke, prominent public figures protested in the United States, including Albert Einstein and Eleanor Roosevelt. However, as the Cold War developed, there was no difficulty in issuing visas to those recruited by Operation 'Paperclip'.

Operation 'Paperclip' lasted less than two years, but similar programs continued until 1962. Eventually, more than 1,500 German scientists and technicians, along with their families, were transferred to the United States, the most of them later became American citizens. The US military withheld information about the Nazi backgrounds of the 'Paperclip' scientists and engineers they employed. The fact that most joined the Nazi Party was explained by the fact that this membership was a necessary condition for

On July 24, 1950, Bumper 8 became the inaugural launch at Cape Canaveral which was soon to become the famous American spaceport, still in use today. (NASA)

obtaining a good job within the Third Reich. The fact that some, like von Braun himself, had been in the SS was carefully concealed.

As for the Germans, they claimed that they were unaware of the concentration camp system and the extent of forced labour in Nazi Germany. As for von Braun himself, he was involved in decision-making about the use of slave labour, and he visited the Mittelwerk factory around 15 times between late 1943 and February 1945. He said he was aware of the treatment of prisoners, but felt powerless to change the situation. He said it became clear to him in 1944 that deaths had occurred but claimed he never personally witnessed any deaths or beatings. He denied ever visiting the Mittelbau-Dora concentration camp itself.

The extent of what each of the 'Paperclip' men knew and their participation in the crimes committed around them, is difficult to measure objectively but their knowledge they had of the concentration camp system and forced labour is indisputable.

Only one 'Paperclip' scientist, Georg Rickhey, who worked for the US Air Force at Wright-Field, was tried for war crimes. He was managing director of

Mittelwerk GmbH from May 1944 until the end and oversaw the production of the V1 and V2 there. He was indicted in the Dora Trial in 1947, but was acquitted due to lack of evidence. He returned to the United States after the trial ended but did not return to his work on Operation 'Paperclip'.

In 1979, the Department of Justice opened the Office of Special Investigations whose mission was to find and bring to justice all Nazi war criminals living in the United States. OSI did not bring any 'Paperclip' scientists or engineers to justice, but an investigation led to a settlement with Arthur Rudolph, who retired from NASA in 1969 after serving as project manager of the Saturn V program. A veteran of Kummersdorf and Peenemünde, one of the first groups of rocket scientists to arrive in the United States in 1946, Rudolph had been director of V2 production at Mittelwerk and thus had used forced labour from the 'Dora' concentration

German scientists and their families quickly obtained American citizenship due to the rapidly developing Cold war. Pictured on April 14, 1955, are Dr. Schilling, Dr. Stuhlinger, and Dr. von Braun signing certificates of US citizenship. (NASA)

camp. Under the terms of the agreement, Rudolph would not be prosecuted but would leave the United States and renounce his American citizenship. He left for West Germany in 1984.

Germany requested documents from OSI to determine whether Rudolph should be prosecuted and the Hamburg public prosecutor investigated the case. The investigation concluded in 1987 that there was no basis for prosecution and Rudolph was granted West German citizenship.

USSR, FRANCE, AND GREAT BRITAIN WAR BOOTY

With many research facilities and personnel having been evacuated to Saxony and Thuringia during the final months of the war, the Russians had many German scientists on hand in these two states which became part of their zone of occupation in July 1945. They first hired some of them to rebuild the V2 production facilities at Nordhausen, an operation which was completed at the end of 1945.

On October 22, 1946, the Soviets launched Operation 'Osoaviakhim', the massive kidnapping of German scientists and technicians: in one night, more than 2,200 German specialists, or more than 6,000 people when including their families, were forcibly and unexpectedly transferred to Russia. The rocket experts, 170 men, including Helmut Gröttrup, were sent to the island of Gorodomlya, on Lake Seliger, 300 kilometres north-west of Moscow, and the team became Branch 1 of the research bureau NII-88.

Unlike Western weapons development policy, which integrated German rocket experts into their own teams, the Soviets were careful not to involve the Germans in new development work, leaving them aside while the

In May 1946, the Soviet government established a missile testing range at Kasputin Yar, about 100 kilometres east of Stalingrad, from where the first V2 rocket was launched on October 18, 1947. This photo: a R-1 rocket, the Soviet copy of the V2, is transported to the launch site on a Vidalwagen. On October 4, 1957, the Soviet Union stunned the world by launching Sputnik 1, Earth's first artificial satellite.

Russian teams appropriated their know-how and technologies. By 1955, most of German scientists had been sent back to East Germany.

In 1946, France created the LRBA (Laboratoire de Recherches Balistiques et Aerodynamiques) in Vernon, about fifty kilometres north-west of Paris, with the aim of developing rocket, propulsion, and guidance technologies. A total of 150 German engineers and technicians came with their families to Vernon, including rocket engine expert Karl-Heinz Bringer, guidance expert Otto Müller, and electronics expert Helmut Habermann. To avoid friction with the local population, hostile to all Germans after years of painful occupation, German families lived in an isolated hamlet.

The initial program to design a 'Super V2' was quickly abandoned and work was transferred to the successful development a sounding rocket, the Véronique, that was regularly launched from Hammaguir in the Sahara from 1952. From 1958, the LRBA developed a family of rockets, finally producing the Diamant which launched the first French satellite in November 1965, the first satellite not launched by the United States or the USSR.

Most German rocket scientists returned to Germany after years of work in France but some, like Karl-Heinz Bringer, applied for French citizenship and remained in France.

Walter Riedel and a group of rocket experts who had worked at Peenemünde were recruited and transferred to the United Kingdom in 1946. However, there was not much funding in Britain for rocket development in the post-war years, not even a strategy. The German experts worked first at the Royal Aircraft establishment at Farnborough, then from 1948 at the Rocket Propulsion establishment in Westcott. In 1957, Riedel became a British citizen.

The German experts were involved in the development of the Blue Streak ballistic missile, which was cancelled in 1960, with Britain purchasing the Polaris system from the Americans instead. The German team also participated in the development of the Black Arrow rocket, which launched Prospero, Britain's first satellite, in 1971.

SPACE CONQUEST

Five V2s were launched from White Sands, New Mexico, between May and July 1946, reaching altitudes of over 100 kilometres. Von Braun and his team then participated in the development of the Bumper, a two-stage sounding rocket, which reached an altitude of 400 kilometres in February 1949. In 1950, the German team was moved to Huntsville, Alabama, where it became part of the Redstone Arsenal. By 1955, some 760 German rocket experts were working in Huntsville.

Between 1952 and 1956, von Braun led the Army's rocket development team, designing the Redstone and Jupiter ballistic missiles, as well as the launchers derived from them. It was a Jupiter C that put the first American satellite, Explorer I, into orbit on February 1, 1958, and a Redstone that took

In December, the United States rushed the launch of a Vanguard satellite billed as 'America's answer to Sputnik', but it was a humiliating failure. The Army Ballistic Missile Agency was then called on a crash program and Explorer 1 was successfully launched on February 1, 1958, GMT (or January 31, Eastern Time). The creators of Explorer 1 triumphantly displayed a model of it shortly after the satellite's launch. From left to right: Jet Propulsion Laboratory Director Dr. William H. Pickering, Dr. James van Allen of the State University of Iowa, and Army Ballistic Missile Agency Technical Director Dr. von Braun. The Jet Propulsion Laboratory packed and tested the payload, a radiation detection experiment designed by Dr. van Allen, and von Braun's rocket team developed the launch rocket. (NASA)

Alan Shepard on a ballistic trajectory into space on May 5, 1961, the first American to travel into space.

In 1959, President Eisenhower approved the transfer of all space activities from the military to the newly created NASA and on July 1, 1960, the George C. Marshall Space Flight Center, MSFC, officially opened at Redstone Arsenal. Von Braun was its director and Eberhard Rees his deputy for research and development. All but one of the MSFC's 16 technical divisions were led by German experts who came to the United States as part of Operation 'Paperclip'.

Under von Braun's leadership, the Marshall Space Flight Center developed the Saturn V rocket, which placed the first men, Neil Armstrong and Edwin Aldrin, on the Moon on July 21, 1969.

From 1960, von Braun was the director of the George C. Marshall Space Flight Center, MSFC. In early 1962, NASA finalised its plans to launch a crewed spacecraft to the Moon with the Saturn V, the rocket designed by von Braun's MSFC. May 1964, this photo shows a dispirited von Braun facing the endless difficulties plaguing the launch of the SA-6 rocket at Cape Canaveral. The sixth flight of the Saturn I, the SA-6 will finally bring the first prototype (boilerplate) of the Apollo spacecraft into orbit on May 28. (NASA)

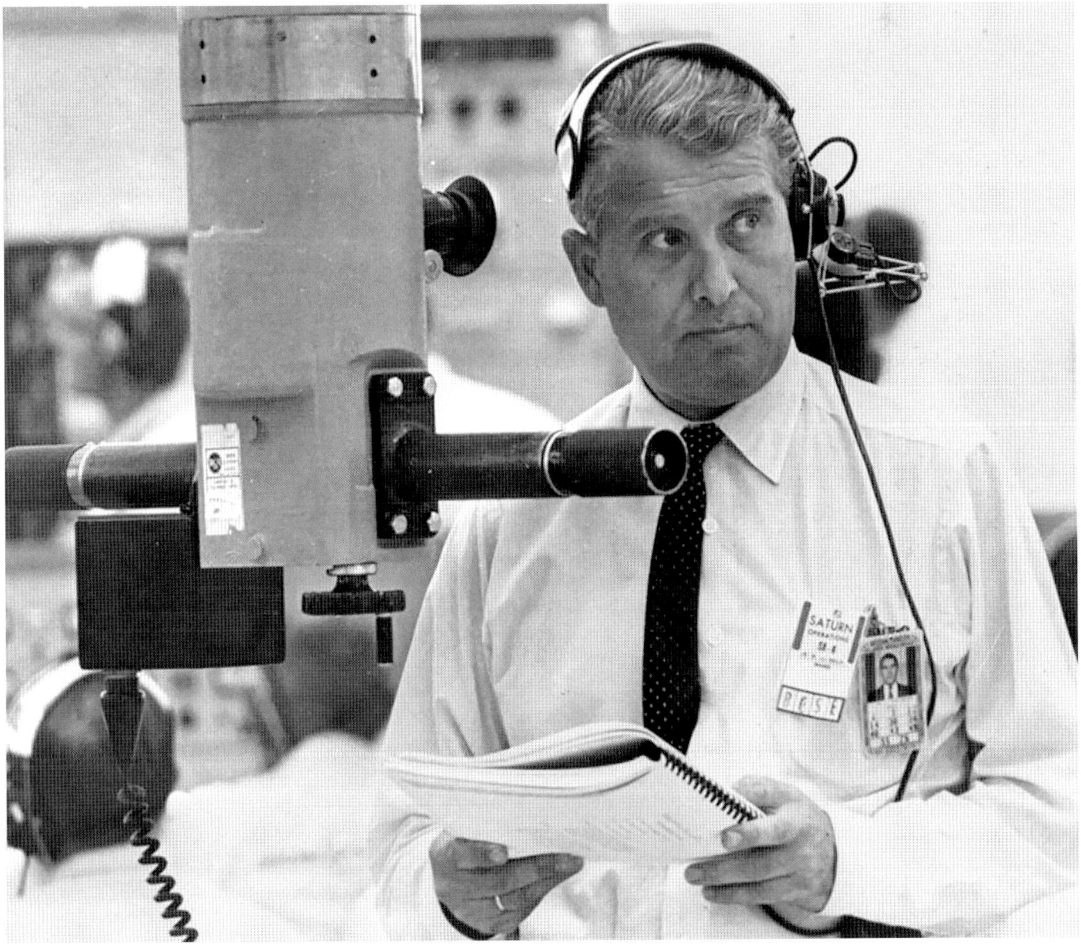

From Peenemünde to the Moon. Two veterans of Peenemünde attended the rollout of AS-500F from the Vehicle Assembly Building at the Kennedy Space Center in May 1966. By then von Braun had become Director of the MSFC and Kurt Debus was the Director of the Kennedy Space Center. This inert rocket was designed to test the mating of the Saturn V's stages, the fit of the service platforms, the launcher-transporter operation, the propellant loading system, and the connections to the launch tower. Thirteen Saturn V rockets were launched from Kennedy Space Center, sending a total of 24 astronauts into Space, from Apollo 8 in December 1968 to Apollo 17 in December 1972, 12 of whom would walk on the Moon. (NASA)

PEENEMÜNDE HISTORICAL TECHNICAL MUSEUM

By the end of the war, most of the Peenemünde Army Research Centre was in ruins and the Soviets cleared them in the early 1950s. In 1956 the headquarters of the 1. Flottille of the East German Navy was established at Peenemünde harbour that the Soviets had just turned over to East Germany, and in 1961 the former Luftwaffe airfield at Peenemünde West became home of the East German Jagdfliegergeschwader 9. This is the water-filled pit at former Prüfstand VII as it appeared to *After the Battle* in 1991.

The liquid oxygen plant was unaffected by the bombings of 1943 and 1944 and it also survived attempts to destroy it by the Russians and then by the East Germans. It remains the most impressive exhibit of wartime Peenemünde. (Gunnar Klack, Wikimedia Commons)

The Historical Technical Museum opened its doors in 1992 in the former power station of the Heeresversuchsanstalt Peenemünde. Among the pieces on display outdoors is a life-size replica of the A4 rocket.

A replica of a Fi 103 flying bomb is also on display at the power station site, as well as a genuine catapult ramp acquired in 2006 in the Netherlands. (Derzno, WC and Chmee2, Wikimedia Commons)

Starting from the Historical Technical Museum, the 'landscape of monuments' is a 25-kilometre-long circular route, with 20 stations distributed throughout the Peenemünde peninsula. Station 22 is at Zempin, to the south-east of the peninsula, where the Lehr- und Versuchskommando Wachtel has installed launch ramps to train troops in the live firing of flying bombs. The remains of the site are visible by the side of the cycle path between Zinnowitz and Zempin. (GB27, Wikimedia Commons)

At Station 16 are the remains of storage bunkers built to store the rockets produced by the Production Works until their delivery to the Army. However, the Production Works never produced rockets as initially planned, and the bunkers were eventually used for short-term storage of rockets sent from the Mittelwerk to Peenemünde for quality testing. After the war, these bunkers were all demolished. (Tnemtsoni, Wikimedia Commons)

MITTELBAU-DORA MEMORIAL

In mid-1944, the Ministry of Armaments and War Production commissioned a photographer, Walter Frentz, to report on the production of the V2 at the Mittelwerk. Having worked as a cameraman on Leni Riefenstahl's famous film Olympia about the 1936 Berlin Olympics, Frentz served as a Luftwaffe photographer throughout the war and photographed and filmed the leaders of Nazi Germany. Due to poor lighting in the galleries and tunnels, additional lighting devices were specially delivered for this photo session at the Mittelwerk. (Walter Frentz)

These two prisoners were working on a welding machine to make the outer sheets of the rocket body, probably in Galleries 24 or 30, while two others, probably in Gallery 28, were assembling the main electrical distribution box that was to be installed in the Control Compartment II. In addition to providing additional lighting fixtures, the Mittelwerk had prepared workers and workshops for the session: the inmates were all clean-shaven, with clean striped uniforms and caps, and shoes or clogs. (Walter Frentz)

These propaganda photos focus on showing normal places and working conditions, never showing any sign of the real conditions in which the slave workers lived and worked. On the far right, looking at the photographer, is Frenchman Léon Navaro, prison number 40629. According to his recollection, this photo was taken in Gallery 28, a workshop staffed mainly by Belgian, Dutch, and French inmates. (Walter Frentz)

Many additional lighting devices had to be installed to illuminate the 14-metre-tall missile for this photo of Gallery 41 where the rockets were raised upright for a final test. (Walter Frentz)

The southern entrance to Tunnel B as it appeared in May or June 1945 when the Mittelwerk was still occupied by the Americans. All entrances were destroyed by the Soviets in the summer of 1948 and, to make the underground galleries accessible to visitors, a new tunnel was dug in the early 1990s next to the southern entrance to Tunnel B.

After the liberation, the Americans directed the male citizens of Nordhausen to collect the corpses in the 'Dora' camp and the Boelcke barracks, and bury them. From April 12, German civilians dug a mass grave on the side of a hill overlooking the town (this photo) to bury the dead inmates of Boelcke Barracks.

The 'Dora' camp was dismantled in the post-war years, and all the huts and fences were cleared, except for the crematorium which became the centre of the memorial established by the East German authorities. This bronze sculpture depicting five slave workers by Jürgen von Woisky was dedicated in 1964. (KZ-Gedenkstätte Mittelbau-Dora)

After German reunification in the early 1990s, large parts of the 'Dora' camp, which East German authorities had allowed to disappear under bushes and trees, were cleared to expose the foundations of huts and buildings. One of the original huts was rebuilt and a new exhibition opened on April 11, 1995, the 50th anniversary of the liberation of the camp. (JesterWr, Wikimedia Commons)

Thanks to the new 180-metre-long tunnel dug next to the southern entrance to Tunnel B, visitors can access a 100-metre section of Tunnel A, but only as part of guided tours led by the Memorial staff. (Vincent van Zeijst, Wikimedia Commons)

Zeppelin produced half-sections that composed the central part of the rocket body in Bad Saulgau, west of Munich. The work was carried out by civilian employees and inmates from an associated concentration subcamp and the half-sections produced were transported by train to the Mittelwerk. It is estimated that around half of the V2 rockets produced at the Mittelwerk used half-sections produced at Saulgau. (Stadtmuseum Bad Saulgau

BLIZNA HISTORICAL PARK

After the major air attack on Peenemünde in August 1943, the A4 rocket test and troop training launches were transferred to Blizna in south-eastern Poland. Test launches started in November and a total of 215 rockets were launched before the evacuation of the site at the end of June 1944. Here, the Technical Troop checked the 20 securing studs holding the warhead. (W. Frentz)

The Blizna Historical Park now sits on the site of the German launch base, with a replica of a V2 rocket standing in the centre. Taking a walk in the forests surrounding the park, one can see remains of rocket assembly hall and launch pads. (Marek-Kosniowski, Wikimedia Commons)

A dozen kilometres to the south, in Pustków, the site of the SS-Truppenübungsplatz Heidelager is today a place of remembrance. (Marek-Kosniowski, Wikimedia Commons)

V-WEAPONS BUNKERS, THEN AND NOW

Most of the V1 launch sites built in northern France were cleared after the war but many remain to be seen, such as the Bois Carré site, 10 kilometres north-east of Abbeville, well known for having given its name to the ski site design. The site is now well overgrown but most of the buildings remain visible, such as the protective walls of the launch ramp and the non-magnetic building where the compass of the flying bombs was collimated. (Chriusha, Wikimedia Commons)

At Siracourt, the huge Wasserwerk where V1 flying bombs were to be assembled, stored, and launched against London still exists today. At the south end of the building, this is the entrance of the railway line into the bunker as it appears today, filled in almost to the top. (Chriusha, Wikimedia Commons)

North of Saint-Omer, the KNW bunker, now called Blockhaus d'Éperlecques, is open to the public as a private museum that presents the history of the site and the German V-weapons program. The area around the bunker is still heavily scarred by bomb craters, although all reforested, and various WW2 military equipment is on display along the paths, including a V1 on a launch pad and a replica of a V2. (Nilfanion, Wikimedia Commons)

When the project to establish a museum on the SNW site of Wizernes was born in 1986, the tunnels of the V2 launch bunker were blocked but the abandoned quarry remained almost as it was in 1944, with sections of railway track still in place on the quarry floor. To publicise the project, an open weekend was organised in June 1987, it was a huge success attended by more than 20,000 people. At this occasion, the dome's designer Werner Flos, former Chief Engineer of Organisation Todt in Berlin, met Reginald Jones, former member of the Crossbow Committee. Here Werner Flos looks at the 5-metre-thick concrete slab protecting the planned launch site.

La Coupole Museum opened in 1997. Visitors enter and exit through the railway tunnel, and war artifacts are on display in the short side tunnels leading off on either side. Another tunnel leads to an elevator that takes visitors up to the space under the dome, where the main exhibition area is located. Though the site is known since the war as being at Wizernes, it is in reality at Helfaut.

The museum houses many original exhibits, including a V1 and a V2. Presenting audio-visual displays in English, French, Dutch and German, the tour focussed on the story of the V-weapons, the suffering of the forced labour used by the Germans to build the site, and the conquest of space after the war. (Zairon, Wikimedia Commons)

August 16, 1944. Flight Lieutenant John Malloy flying a Tempest of the 274 Squadron tipped over a V1 and the flying bomb dived to the ground and crashed at 4.47 p.m. under the railway bridge at Oak Lane, Rainham. A passenger train was just approaching and though the driver slammed the emergency brake, the engine crashed down into the gap. 'The Train that Jumped the Gap' then headed The East Kent Gazette. Eight people were killed, and 16 seriously injured, in the incident.

The wreckage was quickly cleared and a new bridge was constructed in November 1944. It still exists today. Though the comparisons that appear in publications generally show the bridge as seen from its southern side, this is the right comparison, seen from the north. The train was going from Victoria Station to Ramsgate, so steaming eastwards, and the east was on the left in the photo. (Google)

On September 8, just after 11 a.m., a A4 rocket hit Maisons Alfort, south-east of Paris. Several houses were destroyed, many others damaged. Six persons were killed, and 36 injured. It was the first ballistic missile attack in history. (AMAH)

A sign now stands in the Bois de Beuleu a few ten metres from the spot that François Catin pointed to me in 1989 and where he saw, only a few hours after the departure of the German launch team, the roadway melted and blackened by the jet of flames from the rocket. (Dirk Gezel)

A V1 scored a hit on No. 32 Old Jewry on October 6, 1944. At the northern end of the street, in front of Estate House, the wounded were moved away on Gresham Street. Gresham Street Then and Now, looking westwards. (SSETO and Eileen Green)

Gresham Street Then and Now, looking eastwards. (SSETO and Eileen Green)

We described on pages 65 and 66 how a V1 crashed on the St Marie Hotel in Purley on October 31, killing 17 and injuring 31. New houses now stand where the hotel was but, as seen from Olden Lane, these three houses on Dale Road make a perfect link with the tragic past. (Google)

November 25, 1944. At 11.16 a.m., a V2 launched from Loosduinen by the Lehr- und Versuchsbatterie 444 hit Warwick Court, a small alleyway off Holborn. Five residents were killed and 40 injured in the attack. Rescue workers search through the rubble and wreckage. (Google)

November 27. Four minutes after midday, a V2 rocket launched from Reinsfeld, near Hermeskeil, by the first battery of Artillerie-Abteilung 836 hit the intersection of Frankrijklei and De Keyserlei and Teniersplaats in Antwerp. A British convoy moving from the docks was caught in the blast, several of the vehicles caught on fire. (Google)

The rocket had exploded above ground, possibly after hitting the tram's overhead lines, and no crater was ever discovered. A water main was broken and the entire place was soon filled with water. The explosion killed 126 people, including 26 Allied soldiers, and injured over three hundred. (Including the wounded who died in hospital in the days following the attack, other sources put the death toll at 157, including 29 allied soldiers.) (Google)

December 16, 1944. About 3.20 p.m., a V2 rocket launched from Eelerberg, near Hellendoorn, by SS-Werfer-Batterie 500 hit the crowded Rex cinema in Antwerp, killing 567 people, including 296 Allied soldiers. This was the single highest death total from one V2 rocket attack. The rubble and debris were up to five metres high in the cinema and it took six days for the rescue teams to dig out all the dead. A cinema is still an attraction at 15 De Keyserlei, and the buildings on each side of the reconstructed cinema remain remarkably recognisable.

January 5, 1945. A V1 flying bomb hit about 1 p.m. at the junction of Carnot Straat with Koningind Astridplein (left) in Antwerp. US Signal Corps photographer T/3 Ingledew was soon on the spot to picture rescue squads working amidst damage.
(USNA and Google)

On January 5, at 10.45 p.m., a V1 reportedly launched from a Heinkel He 111 crashed at Fairfield Road in Beckenham, south of London. The explosion destroyed 20 houses and severely damaged 35 more as well as Christ Church. Thirteen residents perished in the blast at No. 24 Fairfield Road, No. 40-42, and No. 151 Burnhill Road and No. 1-5 Lea Road. Thirty-two were injured. Signs of repairs are still visible today on the church. Much of the site has remained undeveloped and it used as a car park. (SSETO and Daniel Taylor)

On February 11, 1945, about 3 p.m. a V2 rocket launched by the 3. Batterie of Artillerie-Abteilung 485 impacted in the Walthamstow marshes, a few ten metres from the Stanstead Mill Stream, one person was injured. One of London's last areas of floodplain grassland and home to many rare plants and insects, Walthamstow Marshes was designated a nature reserve in 1985. Remarkably, the crater dug by the V2 explosion still remains, today it is a pond where toads come to reproduce in the spring and lay their strings of eggs. (Google and Eileen Green)

On March 27, 1945, about 7.15 p.m. a V2 rocket launched by the 3. Batterie of Artillerie-Abteilung 485 from the Haagse Bos, The Hague, impacted Hughes Mansions in Stepney. Two blocks were flattened, 134 people were killed, and 49 seriously injured. This was the penultimate V2 to strike London. The final V2 to fall on London hit Orpington, Kent, a few minutes before 5 p.m. that same day, killing one person, and seriously injuring 23. (SSETO and Eileen Green)

SURVIVING V-WEAPONS

Many surviving V1s are on display in museums around the world. Most of them are authentic, but some are replicas. We can also see four Fieseler Fi 103R Reichenbergs, the piloted version of the V1, some Loons, the American copy of the V1, and CT 10s, the French copy. This V1 flying bomb now on display at the Imperial War Museum in London, serial number 477663, retains its original wartime paintwork. (Peter Trimming, Wikimedia Commons)

A V1 is displayed on a partial ramp section at the Imperial War Museum Duxford in Cambridgeshire. To the right of the missile is the launch device that carried electrical connections to the missile. Bottom left is the starter trolley, which produced the steam for the catapult. (Desmoh, Wikimedia Commons)

The Duxford Museum also has a partially recreated launch ramp with a mock-up V1 displayed in the north-west corner of the site. (Clemens Vasters and David P. Howard, Wikimedia Commons)

Serial number 114635, the V1 now displayed at La Coupole Museum, at Wizenes/Helfaut, is remarkable for it was launched in action in June 1944. After flying a few kilometres, the missile landed without exploding in a marsh just east of Eu. The Germans attempted to detonate it there but they failed and the missile sank slowly in the mud in the post war years. It was only in 1975 that it was recovered, and the wings and pulsejet engine that had been torn off during the crash were unearthed a few metres from the main body. The missile was remarkably restored and was displayed from 2000 at the Tosny Museum. The museum sadly closed and from 2022, this V1 is on display at La Coupole Museum.

The Evergreen Aviation & Space Museum is best known as the home of the iconic huge Hughes Hercules flying boat. In addition, over 50 military and civilian aircraft are on display, and rockets and spacecraft, and this JB-2 Loon, the American copy of the V1 flying bomb.

A V1 is on display at the RAF Museum Cosford, Shropshire. In the background, the museum A-4/V2 rocket on a Meillerwagen, one of only three that survive today. This rocket has been prepared for Operation 'Backfire' but was not launched. In between, painted red and orange, an Enzian, a German WW2 anti-aircraft missile. The museum also has in storage the world's only known Vidalwagen trailer, a firing table, and a Strabo gantry crane. (Rept0n1x, Wikimedia Commons)

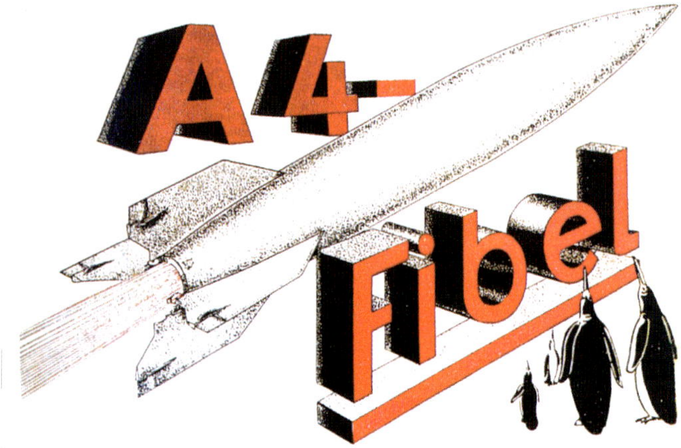

In 1943, to capture the attention of the young crews of the new Panther and Tiger tanks, simple and engaging training manuals were produced: the Panther-Fibel and Tiger-Fibel were light manuals, with puns and burlesque illustrations, including scantily clad girls, and the instructions have been kept to a minimum. In 1944, faced with the challenge of training soldiers to operate the extremely complex A4 rocket, officers at the Fernraketen-Schule decided to use the same approach and designed the A4-Fibel.

The document insistently recalls the strict secrecy measures which were the rule, and this sketch appears twice, on page 3 and on the back cover. On the latter, the sketch is accompanied by a poem, which translates as follows (we did not try to keep the rhymes): 'We wanted to overcome the difficulties with funny texts and lots of images, but you must always keep in mind that this light form does not give you the right to look at the whole thing with humour! Above all, content serves serious purposes and must be hidden from friend and enemy alike. Do not say a word about it, even if you become exuberant, you will be caught up as soon as the other person speaks! Remember, every hour, whoever asks you: Shut your mouth!'

Since 1976, this V2 rocket has been on display in the Space Hall in the Smithsonian National Air and Space Museum, in Washington. It was painted in the black and white scheme of the V-4 prototype launched at Peenemünde on October 3, 1942, which was the first successful test flight of the A4 rocket. (NASM)

As part of a major transformation project of the exhibit, the rocket was dismantled in April 2022 for a major renovation. The renovated rocket will return in a plain grey-green livery, the German standard at the end of the war, when the hall reopens as Living in the Space Age. (NASM)

The museum's restoration team also refurbished the launch table, reportedly one of only four remaining in the world. It was painted black and the team stripped it in the hope of finding traces of the original paint, but they found none. Images of 1944 show launch table painted in dark sand-yellow, the late-war Wehrmacht vehicle painting, and it was painted in that colour. (NASM)

Surviving V2s are many on display in museums all over the world, as well as components of them, propulsion unit, turbo-pump, or venturi for example. This V2 and Meillerwagen are on display at the National Museum of the US Air Force. In Dayton, Ohio, the museum is reportedly the world's largest military aviation museum with over 350 airplanes and missiles on display, including 'Bockscar', the B-29 that dropped the atomic bomb on Nagasaki on August 9, 1945. (Goshimini, Wikimedia Commons)

After the end of Operation 'Backfire', Australia acquired two V2 rockets, along with a Meillerwagen, a Vidalwagen, and an oxygen tanker trailer. This V2 is now on display at the Treloar Centre of the Australian War Memorial, in Canberra. This rocket has reportedly the most complete set of guidance components of all surviving V2s, and the Meillerwagen is the most complete of the three examples known to exist. (Bidgee, Wikimedia Commons)

At Zalesie, the three ramps of the HDP test site still stand on the hillside. This is the centre ramp, with concrete steps on the ground in the lower part and large concrete supports in the upper part. Built at a 50-degree angle, it was the steeper of the three test ramps. (Gunnar Klack, Wikimedia Commons)

The north ramp is only visible today as an earthwork but pieces of metal from the base of the cannon have been unearthed at the bottom. Just to the north, a museum is set up in the small bunker of the former HDP test site. (Chriusha, Wikimedia Commons)

In spite of the Royal Engineers efforts to destroy the huge HDP bunker at Mimoyecques in 1945, most of the underground tunnels and galleries have survived and were first used as a mushroom farm from the late 1960s. A museum opened in 1984 and after an update in 2019 the renovated museum now welcomes the public six months a year, from mid-April to mid-October, and closes its doors the rest of the year to let the bats hibernate in peace. (Nils Gerhard, Wikimedia Commons)

Despite the many air attacks that made the whole site to look like a lunar landscape, the five-metre-thick concrete slab and the firing slots remained mostly unscathed and in 1945 the Royal Engineers blew them up. This picture shows a section of the broken firing slot above Shaft No. III.

In a one-hour tour of the galleries at the 30-metre level, the visitors could see tunnel and galleries, and a full-size replica section of an HDP cannon angled skywards in what remains of Shaft No. IV. There are memorials to the forced workers who lost their lives at the site, to the bomber crews killed while attacking the site, and to Lieutenant Joseph Kennedy, brother of the late US President, killed in 1944 during an attempted attack with a B-24 'Aphrodite' plane. (Matthias Alloy)

The Rąbka Rocket Launcher Museum now sits on the site of the former Luftwaffe experimentation centre in the Słowiński National Park, near Łeba. The site was used to test Rheinbote rockets and Rheintochter anti-aircraft rockets in the last year of World War 2. In the forefront in this photo is a replica of a Rheintochter R I two-stage missile, and behind a replica of a Rheintochter R III, a new development with two side-mounted solid-fuel boosters. In the right background, a replica of a Rheinbote ballistic missile can be seen. All these are replicas, as is a replica of a V2 (set at an odd angle when it was launched vertically) but a SAM 2 Guideline, post war Soviet anti-aircraft rocket, appears to be genuine. (Paul Chron, Wikimedia Commons)